Reading to Learn Hebrew

The Progressive Torah

Level Two

שְׁמוֹת

Exodus

טhe Pרogרessive Toרaה is a production of
Minister 2 Others

Second Edition

English Scripture modified
from the 1917 Jewish Publication Society

ISBN 978-1-947751-74-3
Copyright © 2018 Minister 2 Others
Minister2others.com

*May you be blessed by this work,
and may you draw closer to* יהוה
by reading
טhe Pרogרessive Toרaה

Introduction

What you are holding in your hands right now is not just another way to learn Hebrew. The Progressive Torהה: Exodus is a journey through the amazing book of Exodus! There are so many things hidden within the passages of the Hebrew text.

There are various colors used in this text:

> Hebrew names are indicated with a brown font: אַבְרָהָם (*Abraham*)
> Vocabulary words are indicated with a blue font: אֱלֹהִים (*Elohim*)
> Verbs are indicated with a red font: וַיֹּאמֶר (*And he said*)
> Words of יהוה are indicated with a green font: יוֹם (*Day*)
> Miscellaneous words are in black: עֶרֶב (*Evening*)

Also, the numbering of the verses can vary between English versions and Jewish versions so, where the numbering is not the same, both systems have been used. The English version in black, and the Jewish version in light blue. Here is an example of a dual numbered verse: (9) (32:10)

If the reader is not familiar with the Hebrew Alef-Bet, it may be prudent to get a copy of The Progressive Alef~בet produced by Minister 2 Others, and learn the letters and vowels. This is not a necessary step in order to read through this series, it is only advised for those who would like the extra help.

Table of Contents

Chapter 1	1	Chapter 22	168
Chapter 2	4	Chapter 23	181
Chapter 3	8	Chapter 24	194
Chapter 4	21	Chapter 25	197
Chapter 5	33	Chapter 26	212
Chapter 6	37	Chapter 27	230
Chapter 7	47	Chapter 28	240
Chapter 8	55	Chapter 29	260
Chapter 9	64	Chapter 30	280
Chapter 10	74	Chapter 31	295
Chapter 11	82	Chapter 32	301
Chapter 12	86	Chapter 33	309
Chapter 13	103	Chapter 34	316
Chapter 14	107	Chapter 35	328
Chapter 15	114	Chapter 36	336
Chapter 16	119	Chapter 37	340
Chapter 17	128	Chapter 38	343
Chapter 18	132	Chapter 39	347
Chapter 19	136	Chapter 40	352
Chapter 20	144	Index	360
Chapter 21	154	Final Notes	367

Chapter One

The Children Of Israel

(1) Now these are שְׁמוֹת (the names of) בְּנֵי יִשְׂרָאֵל (the children of Israel) who came מִצְרָיְמָה אֵת יַעֲקֹב (to Egypt with * Jacob) אִישׁ (a man) וּבֵיתוֹ (and his house) they came:

(2) רְאוּבֵן שִׁמְעוֹן לֵוִי וִיהוּדָה

(3) יִשָּׂשכָר זְבוּלֻן וּבִנְיָמִן

(4) דָּן וְנַפְתָּלִי גָּד וְאָשֵׁר

(5) And כָּל-נֶפֶשׁ (every soul) that came out the loins of יַעֲקֹב were seventy נֶפֶשׁ (soul) וְיוֹסֵף was בְמִצְרָיִם

(6) And יוֹסֵף died וְכָל-אֶחָיו (and all his brothers) וְכֹל הַדּוֹר הַהוּא (and all that generation).

(7) וּבְנֵי יִשְׂרָאֵל (And the children of Israel) were fruitful, and increased abundantly and multiplied, and waxed exceeding mighty; and הָאָרֶץ (the land) was filled אֹתָם

Israel Is Enslaved

(8) Now there arose a new מֶלֶךְ (king) over מִצְרָיִם who did not know אֶת יוֹסֵף

(9) וַיֹּאמֶר (And he said) אֶל-עַמּוֹ (to his people):

"Behold עַם (the people of) בְּנֵי יִשְׂרָאֵל (the children of Israel) are too many and too mighty for us;

(10)

Come, let us deal wisely לוֹ (to him), lest he multiply, and it shall be, that when there comes a war, he also joins גַּם-הוּא (also he) to

Exodus ~ 1

our enemies, and fight בָּנוּ (in us), and ascend מִן-הָאָרֶץ (from the land)."

(11) Therefore, they set over them taskmasters to afflict them with their burdens. And they built לְפַרְעֹה אֶת פִּתֹם וְאֶת רַעַמְסֵס עָרֵי (cities of) provisions

(12) But the more they afflicted אֹתוֹ the more they multiplied and the more they spread abroad. And they were vexed מִפְּנֵי (from the faces of) בְּנֵי יִשְׂרָאֵל (the children of Israel).

(13) And מִצְרַיִם made אֶת-בְּנֵי יִשְׂרָאֵל (* the children of Israel) to serve with rigor.

(14) And they made אֶת-חַיֵּיהֶם (* their lives) bitter with hard service, in mortar and in brick וּבְכָל-עֲבֹדָה (and in all service) in the field אֵת כָּל עֲבֹדָתָם (* all their service), which they served בָּהֶם (in them) with rigor.

Pharaoh Kills The Babies

(15) וַיֹּאמֶר מֶלֶךְ מִצְרַיִם (And the king of Egypt spoke) לַמְיַלְּדֹת הָעִבְרִיֹּת (to the female Hebrew midwives) of whom שֵׁם (the name of) the one was שִׁפְרָה וְשֵׁם (and the name of) the second פּוּעָה

(16) וַיֹּאמֶר (And he said):

בְּיַלֶּדְכֶן אֶת הָעִבְרִיּוֹת (In your being a midwife to * the female Hebrews) וּרְאִיתֶן (and you look) עַל-הָאָבְנָיִם (on the stones): if בֵּן (a son) is הוּא (he) then you shall kill אֹתוֹ but if בַּת (a daughter) is הִיא (she), then she shall live."

(17) And הַמְיַלְּדֹת (the midwives) feared אֶת הָאֱלֹהִים and did not do as דִּבֶּר אֲלֵיהֶן מֶלֶךְ מִצְרַיִם (the king of Egypt spoke to them) but they saved אֶת הַיְלָדִים (* the boys).

Level Two   שְׁמוֹת ~ א

(18) וַיִּקְרָא מֶלֶךְ־מִצְרַיִם (And the king of Egypt called) לַמְיַלְּדֹת (for the midwives) וַיֹּאמֶר (and he said) לָהֶן (to them):
"Why have you done הַדָּבָר הַזֶּה (this thing) and have saved אֶת־ הַיְלָדִים (* the boys)?"

(19) וַתֹּאמַרְןָ הַמְיַלְּדֹת (And the midwives said) אֶל־פַּרְעֹה (to Pharaoh):
"Because not כַנָּשִׁים (as the women) הַמִּצְרִיֹּת (the female Egyptians) are הָעִבְרִיֹּת (the female Hebrews) for they are lively, וְיָלָדוּ (and they give birth) before הַמְיַלֶּדֶת (the midwife) can come אֲלֵהֶן (to them)."

(20) And אֱלֹהִים did good לַמְיַלְּדֹת (to the midwives); and הָעָם (the people) multiplied, and waxed very mighty.

(21) And it was, because הַמְיַלְּדֹת (the midwives) feared אֶת הָאֱלֹהִים that He made לָהֶם (for them) בָּתִּים (houses).

(22) And פַּרְעֹה charged לְכָל־עַמּוֹ (to all his people) לֵאמֹר (saying):
וְכָל־ כָּל־הַבֵּן (Every son) that is born you shall cast in the river הַבַּת (and every daughter) you shall let live."

Chapter Two

Moses Is Saved

(1) וַיֵּלֶךְ אִישׁ (And a man went) מִבֵּית לֵוִי (from the house of Levi) and he took אֶת בַּת לֵוִי (* a daughter of Levi).

(2) And הָאִשָּׁה (the woman) conceived וַתֵּלֶד בֵּן (and she bore a son) וַתֵּרֶא (and she saw) אֹתוֹ that הוּא (he) was good, she hid him three months.

(3) And when she could no longer hide him she took לוֹ (for him) תֵּבַת (an ark) of bulrushes, and daubed it with slime and with pitch; and she put אֶת-הַיֶּלֶד (the * boy) therein, and laid it in the flags עַל (on) the shore of the river.

(4) And אֲחֹתוֹ (his sister) stood afar off to know what would be done לוֹ (to him).

(5) And בַּת-פַּרְעֹה (the daughter of Pharaoh) came down to bathe in the river וְנַעֲרֹתֶיהָ הֹלְכֹת (and her maidens were walking) עַל-יַד (on hand / near) the river וַתֵּרֶא (and she saw) אֶת-הַתֵּבָה (* the ark) among the flags וַתִּשְׁלַח (and she sent) אֶת אֲמָתָהּ (* her handmaid) to get it.

(6) And she opened it וַתִּרְאֵהוּ (and she saw him) אֶת הַיֶּלֶד (* the boy); and behold נַעַר (a lad) was crying. And she had compassion עָלָיו (on him) וַתֹּאמֶר (and she said):

"This is מִיַּלְדֵי הָעִבְרִים (from the boys of the Hebrews.)"

(7) וַתֹּאמֶר אֲחֹתוֹ (And his sister said) אֶל-בַּת פַּרְעֹה (to the daughter of Pharaoh):

הַאֵלֵךְ (Shall I go) וְקָרָאתִי (and call) לָךְ (for you) אִשָּׁה (a woman) nursing מִן הָעִבְרִיֹּת (from the female Hebrews) that she may nurse לָךְ אֶת-הַיָּלֶד (* the boy for you)?"

(8) וַתֹּאמֶר לָהּ בַּת פַּרְעֹה (And the daughter of Pharaoh said to her):

Level Two ~ שְׁמוֹת ב

לְכִי (*Go*)."

וַתֵּלֶךְ הָעַלְמָה (*And the maiden went*) וַתִּקְרָא (*and she called*) אֶת אֵם הַיָּלֶד (* *the mother of the boy*).

(9) וַתֹּאמֶר לָהּ בַּת פַּרְעֹה (*And the daughter of Pharaoh said to her*):

"Take אֶת-הַיֶּלֶד הַזֶּה (* *this boy*), *and nurse him* לִי (*for me*) וַאֲנִי (*and I*) *shall give* אֶת *your wages.*"

And הָאִשָּׁה (*the woman*) took הַיֶּלֶד (*the boy*), and nursed him.

(10) And הַיֶּלֶד (*the boy*) grew, and she brought him לְבַת פַּרְעֹה (*to the daughter of Pharaoh*), and he was לָהּ (*to her*) לְבֵן (*for a son*) וַתִּקְרָא שְׁמוֹ מֹשֶׁה (*And she called his name Moses*) וַתֹּאמֶר (*and she said*):

"Because I drew him מִן-הַמַּיִם (*from the water*)."

Moses Flees From Pharaoh

(11) And it was in those days, and מֹשֶׁה was grown up, that he went forth אֶל-אֶחָיו (*to his brothers*) וַיַּרְא (*and he looked*) on their burdens וַיַּרְא (*and he saw*) אִישׁ מִצְרִי (*an Egyptian man*) smiting אִישׁ-עִבְרִי (*a Hebrew man*) מֵאֶחָיו (*from his brothers*).

(12) וַיִּפֶן (*And he faced*) this way and that way וַיַּרְא (*and he saw*) that there was no אִישׁ (*man*), he smote אֶת הַמִּצְרִי (* *the Egyptian*) and hid him in the sand.

(13) And he went forth the second day, and, behold, two אֲנָשִׁים עִבְרִים (*Hebrew men*) were striving together וַיֹּאמֶר (*And he said*) to the wicked one:

"Why are you smiting your fellow?"

Exodus ~ 2   The Progressive Torah

(14) וַיֹּאמֶר (And he said):

"Who made you לְאִישׁ (for a man) a ruler and a judge עָלֵינוּ (over us)? To kill me אַתָּה אֹמֵר (* you say) as which you killed אֶת הַמִּצְרִי (* the Egyptian)?"

And מֹשֶׁה feared וַיֹּאמַר (And he said):

"Surely הַדָּבָר (the thing) is known."

(15) וַיִּשְׁמַע פַּרְעֹה (And Pharaoh heard) אֶת-הַדָּבָר הַזֶּה (* this thing) and he sought to slay אֶת-מֹשֶׁה And מֹשֶׁה fled מִפְּנֵי פַרְעֹה (from the face of Pharaoh) and he dwelt בְּאֶרֶץ-מִדְיָן (in the land of Midian) and he sat down עַל (on) a well.

Moses Starts A Family

(16) Now the priest of מִדְיָן had seven בָּנוֹת (daughters) and they came and drew out and filled אֶת the troughs to let the flock of אֲבִיהֶן (their father) drink.

(17) And the shepherds came and drove them away; and מֹשֶׁה stood up and helped them and let אֶת their flock drink.

(18) And they came אֶל-רְעוּאֵל אֲבִיהֶן (to Reuel their father) וַיֹּאמֶר (And he said):

"How is it that you come so soon today?"

(19) וַתֹּאמַרְןָ (And they said):

אִישׁ מִצְרִי (An Egyptian man) delivered us מִיַּד (from the hand of) the shepherds וְגַם (and also) and also he drew out לָנוּ (for us), and let אֶת the flock drink."

Level Two — שְׁמוֹת ~ ב

(20) וַיֹּאמֶר (And he said) אֶל-בְּנֹתָיו (to his daughters):

"And where is he? Why is it that you left אֶת-הָאִישׁ (* the man)? קִרְאֶן לוֹ (Call for him), and he may eat לֶחֶם (bread)."

(21) And מֹשֶׁה was content to dwell with אֶת הָאִישׁ (* the man) and he gave אֶת צִפֹּרָה בִתּוֹ לְמֹשֶׁה (* Zipporah his daughter to Moses).

(22) וַתֵּלֶד בֵּן (and she bore a son) וַיִּקְרָא אֶת שְׁמוֹ (and he called * his name) גֵּרְשֹׁם for אָמַר (he said):

"I have been גֵּר (a sojourner) בְּאֶרֶץ נָכְרִיָּה (in a foreign land)."

Pharaoh Dies

(23) And it was in the course of many days that מֶלֶךְ מִצְרַיִם (the king of Egypt) died and בְּנֵי יִשְׂרָאֵל (the children of Israel) sighed מִן-הָעֲבֹדָה (from the work) and they cried, and their cry came up אֶל-הָאֱלֹהִים (to the Elohim) מִן הָעֲבֹדָה (from the work).

(24) וַיִּזְכֹּר אֱלֹהִים וַיִּשְׁמַע אֱלֹהִים (And Elohim heard) אֶת their groaning (and Elohim remembered) אֶת בְּרִיתוֹ (* His covenant) with אֶת-אַבְרָהָם אֶת יִצְחָק וְאֶת יַעֲקֹב

(25) וַיַּרְא אֱלֹהִים (And Elohim saw) אֶת-בְּנֵי יִשְׂרָאֵל (* the children of Israel) and אֱלֹהִים knew.

Chapter Three

The Burning Bush

(1) וּמֹשֶׁה was shepherding אֶת the flock of יִתְרוֹ his in-law, the priest of מִדְיָן and he led אֶת the flock to the farthest end of הַמִּדְבָּר (*the wilderness*), and he came אֶל הַר הָאֱלֹהִים (*to the mountain of the Elohim*) חֹרֵבָה (*to Horeb*).

(2) וַיֵּרָא מַלְאַךְ יהוה (*And the messenger of YHVH appeared*) אֵלָיו (*to him*) בְּלַבַּת־אֵשׁ (*in a flame of fire*) out of the midst of a bush; וַיַּרְא (*and he looked*), and, behold, the bush burned בָּאֵשׁ (*with fire*) and the bush was not consumed.

(3) וַיֹּאמֶר מֹשֶׁה (*And Moses said*):

"I will turn aside now, וְאֶרְאֶה (*and I will see*) this great אֶת־ הַמַּרְאֶה (** sight*) why the bush is not burnt."

(4) וַיַּרְא יהוה (*And YHVH saw*) that he turned aside לִרְאוֹת (*to see*) וַיִּקְרָא אֵלָיו אֱלֹהִים (*and Elohim called to him*) out of the midst of the bush וַיֹּאמֶר (*And He said*):

מֹשֶׁה מֹשֶׁה

Moses Moses

וַיֹּאמֶר (*And he said*):

"Here am I."

(5) וַיֹּאמֶר (*And He said*):

אַל־תִּקְרַב הֲלֹם

שַׁל־נְעָלֶיךָ

You must not draw near

put off your shoes

Level Two   שְׁמוֹת ~ ג

מֵעַל רַגְלֶיךָ

כִּי הַמָּקוֹם אֲשֶׁר אַתָּה עוֹמֵד עָלָיו

אַדְמַת-קֹדֶשׁ הוּא

from off your feet

for the place whereon * you stand

it is holy ground.

(6) וַיֹּאמֶר (*And He said*):

אָנֹכִי אֱלֹהֵי אָבִיךָ

אֱלֹהֵי אַבְרָהָם

אֱלֹהֵי יִצְחָק

וֵאלֹהֵי יַעֲקֹב

I am the Elohim of your father

the Elohim of Abraham

the Elohim of Isaac

and the Elohim of Jacob.

And מֹשֶׁה hid פָּנָיו (*his face*); for he was afraid to look אֶל הָאֱלֹהִים

(7) וַיֹּאמֶר יהוה (*And YHVH said*):

רָאֹה רָאִיתִי

אֶת-עֳנִי עַמִּי

I have surely seen

* the affliction of My people

אֲשֶׁר בְּמִצְרָיִם

וְאֶת־צַעֲקָתָם שָׁמַעְתִּי

מִפְּנֵי נֹגְשָׂיו

כִּי יָדַעְתִּי אֶת־מַכְאֹבָיו

that are in Egypt

and * their cry I have heard

by reason of their taskmasters

for I know * their pains

(8)

וָאֵרֵד לְהַצִּילוֹ

מִיַּד מִצְרַיִם

וּלְהַעֲלֹתוֹ מִן־הָאָרֶץ הַהִוא

and I am come down to deliver them

from the hand of Egypt

and to bring them up out of that land

אֶל־אֶרֶץ טוֹבָה וּרְחָבָה

אֶל־אֶרֶץ זָבַת

חָלָב וּדְבָשׁ

to a good land and a large

to a land flowing with

milk and honey

Level Two שְׁמוֹת ~ ג

אֶל־מְקוֹם הַכְּנַעֲנִי
וְהַחִתִּי וְהָאֱמֹרִי
וְהַפְּרִזִּי וְהַחִוִּי
וְהַיְבוּסִי

to the place of the Canaanite

and the Hittite and the Amorite

and the Perizzite and the Hivite

and the Jebusite

(9)

וְעַתָּה הִנֵּה
צַעֲקַת בְּנֵי־יִשְׂרָאֵל
בָּאָה אֵלָי

and now behold

the cry of the children of Israel

is come to Me

וְגַם־רָאִיתִי אֶת־הַלַּחַץ
אֲשֶׁר מִצְרַיִם
לֹחֲצִים אֹתָם

and also I see * the oppression

that Egypt

oppresses * them

Exodus ~ 3

(10)

וְעַתָּה לְכָה

וְאֶשְׁלָחֲךָ אֶל־פַּרְעֹה

וְהוֹצֵא אֶת־עַמִּי

בְנֵי־יִשְׂרָאֵל

מִמִּצְרָיִם

come now therefore

and I will send you to Pharaoh

that you may bring forth* My people

the children of Israel

out of Egypt.

(11) וַיֹּאמֶר מֹשֶׁה אֶל־הָאֱלֹהִים (And Moses said to the Elohim):

"Who am אָנֹכִי (I) that אֵלֵךְ (I should go) אֶל־פַּרְעֹה and that I should bring forth אֶת־בְּנֵי יִשְׂרָאֵל (* the children of Israel) מִמִּצְרָיִם (from Egypt)

(12) וַיֹּאמֶר (And He said):

כִּי־אֶהְיֶה עִמָּךְ

וְזֶה־לְּךָ הָאוֹת

כִּי אָנֹכִי שְׁלַחְתִּיךָ

I will certainly be with you

and this shall be the token to you

that I have sent you

Level Two　　　　　　　　　　　　　　　שְׁמוֹת ~ ג

בְּהוֹצִיאֲךָ אֶת־הָעָם

מִמִּצְרַיִם

תַּעַבְדוּן אֶת־הָאֱלֹהִים

עַל הָהָר הַזֶּה

*when you have brought forth * the people*

out of Egypt

*you shall serve * the Elohim*

on this mountain.

(13) וַיֹּאמֶר מֹשֶׁה אֶל־הָאֱלֹהִים (And Moses said to the Elohim):

"Behold, אָנֹכִי (I go) אֶל־בְּנֵי יִשְׂרָאֵל (to the children of Israel) וְאָמַרְתִּי (and I say) לָהֶם (to them):

אֱלֹהֵי אֲבוֹתֵיכֶם (The Elohim of your fathers) שְׁלָחַנִי (has sent me) אֲלֵיכֶם (to you).'

וְאָמְרוּ (And they say) לִי (to me):

'What is שְׁמוֹ (His name)?'

What אֹמַר (shall I say) אֲלֵהֶם (to them)?"

(14) וַיֹּאמֶר אֱלֹהִים אֶל־מֹשֶׁה (And Elohim said to Moses):

אֶהְיֶה אֲשֶׁר אֶהְיֶה

I AM THAT I AM

וַיֹּאמֶר (And He said):

כֹּה תֹאמַר

לִבְנֵי יִשְׂרָאֵל

אֶהְיֶה שְׁלָחַנִי

אֲלֵיכֶם

Thus shall you say

to the children of Israel

I AM has sent me

to you.

(15) וַיֹּאמֶר אֱלֹהִים אֶל מֹשֶׁה *(And Elohim said to Moses):*

כֹּה־תֹאמַר

אֶל־בְּנֵי יִשְׂרָאֵל

יהוה אֱלֹהֵי אֲבֹתֵיכֶם

Thus you shall say

to the children of Israel

YHVH, the Elohim of our fathers

אֱלֹהֵי אַבְרָהָם

אֱלֹהֵי יִצְחָק

the Elohim of Abraham,

the Elohim of Isaac

Level Two   שְׁמוֹת ~ ג

וֵאלֹהֵי יַעֲקֹב
שְׁלָחַנִי אֲלֵיכֶם

and the Elohim of Jacob
has sent me to you

זֶה-שְּׁמִי לְעֹלָם
וְזֶה זִכְרִי
לְדֹר דֹּר

this is My name forever
and this is My memorial
to all generations

(16)

לֵךְ וְאָסַפְתָּ
אֶת-זִקְנֵי יִשְׂרָאֵל
וְאָמַרְתָּ אֲלֵהֶם

go and gather
* the elders of Israel together
and say to them

יהוה אֱלֹהֵי אֲבֹתֵיכֶם
נִרְאָה אֵלַי

YHVH, the Elohim of your fathers
has appeared to me

Exodus ~ 3

אֱלֹהֵי אַבְרָהָם יִצְחָק
וְיַעֲקֹב לֵאמֹר
פָּקֹד פָּקַדְתִּי אֶתְכֶם
וְאֶת־הֶעָשׂוּי לָכֶם
בְּמִצְרָיִם

the Elohim of Abraham, of Isaac
and of Jacob saying
I have surely noticed * you
and * that which is done to you
in Egypt

(17)

וָאֹמַר
אַעֲלֶה אֶתְכֶם
מֵעֳנִי מִצְרַיִם
אֶל־אֶרֶץ הַכְּנַעֲנִי
וְהַחִתִּי וְהָאֱמֹרִי

And I have said
I will bring * you up
out of the affliction of Egypt
to the land of the Canaanite
and the Hittite and the Amorite

Level Two ~ שְׁמוֹת ~ ג

וְהַפְּרִזִּי וְהַחִוִּי
וְהַיְבוּסִי
אֶל־אֶרֶץ זָבַת
חָלָב וּדְבָשׁ

and the Perizzite and the Hivite
and the Jebusite
to a land flowing with
milk and honey

(18)

וְשָׁמְעוּ לְקֹלֶךָ
וּבָאתָ אַתָּה
וְזִקְנֵי יִשְׂרָאֵל

and they shall listen to your voice
and you shall come * you
and the elders of Israel

אֶל־מֶלֶךְ מִצְרַיִם
וַאֲמַרְתֶּם אֵלָיו
יהוה אֱלֹהֵי הָעִבְרִיִּים

to the king of Egypt
and you shall say to him
YHVH, the Elohim of the Hebrews

נִקְרָה עָלֵינוּ
וְעַתָּה נֵלְכָה-נָּא
דֶּרֶךְ שְׁלֹשֶׁת יָמִים
בַּמִּדְבָּר

has met with us
and now we shall go we pray you
a journey of three days
in the wilderness

וְנִזְבְּחָה
לַיהוה אֱלֹהֵינוּ

that we may sacrifice
YHVH our Elohim

(19)

וַאֲנִי יָדַעְתִּי כִּי
לֹא-יִתֵּן אֶתְכֶם מֶלֶךְ מִצְרַיִם
לַהֲלֹךְ
וְלֹא בְּיָד חֲזָקָה

and I know that
the king of Egypt will not allow * you
to go
except by a mighty hand

Level Two   שְׁמוֹת ~ ג

(20)

וְשָׁלַחְתִּי אֶת־יָדִי

וְהִכֵּיתִי אֶת־מִצְרַיִם

בְּכֹל נִפְלְאֹתַי

אֲשֶׁר אֶעֱשֶׂה בְּקִרְבּוֹ

and I will put forth * My hand

and smite * Egypt

with all My wonders

which I will do in the midst thereof

וְאַחֲרֵי־כֵן

יְשַׁלַּח אֶתְכֶם

and after that

he will let * you go

(21)

וְנָתַתִּי אֶת־חֵן הָעָם־הַזֶּה

בְּעֵינֵי מִצְרָיִם

וְהָיָה כִּי תֵלֵכוּן

לֹא תֵלְכוּ רֵיקָם

and I will give this people * favor

in the sight of Egypt

and it shall be that when you go

you shall not go empty

(22)

וְשָׁאֲלָה אִשָּׁה מִשְּׁכֶנְתָּהּ
וּמִגָּרַת בֵּיתָהּ
כְּלֵי-כֶסֶף וּכְלֵי זָהָב
תִּלְמְשׁוּ

and a woman shall ask of her neighbor
and of her that sojourns in her house
implements of silver and implements of gold
and raiment

וְשַׂמְתֶּם עַל-בְּנֵיכֶם
וְעַל-בְּנֹתֵיכֶם
וְנִצַּלְתֶּם אֶת-מִצְרָיִם

and you shall put them on your sons
and on your daughters
and you shall spoil * Egypt.

Chapter Four

The Staff Becomes A Serpent

(1) And מֹשֶׁה answered וַיֹּאמֶר (*and he said*):

> "But, behold, they will not believe לִי (*me*) וְלֹא יִשְׁמְעוּ (*and they will not listen*) בְּקֹלִי (*in my voice*) for יֹאמְרוּ (*they will say*):
>
> לֹא-נִרְאָה אֵלֶיךָ יהוה (*YHVH has not appeared to you*)."

(2) וַיֹּאמֶר אֵלָיו יהוה (*And YHVH said to him*):

> מַה־זֶּה
>
> בְּיָדֶךָ
>
> *What is that*
> *in your hand?*

וַיֹּאמֶר (*And he said*):

> מַטֶּה (*A staff*).

(3) וַיֹּאמֶר (*And He said*):

> הַשְׁלִיכֵהוּ אַרְצָה
>
> *Cast towards the land.*

And he cast it אַרְצָה (*toward the land*) and it turned לְנָחָשׁ (*to a serpent*); and מֹשֶׁה fled מִפָּנָיו (*from the face of it*).

(4) וַיֹּאמֶר יהוה אֶל-מֹשֶׁה (*And YHVH said to Moses*):

Exodus ~ 4

שְׁלַח יָדְךָ

וֶאֱחֹז בִּזְנָבוֹ

Put forth your hand

and take it by the tail.

וַיִּשְׁלַח יָדוֹ (*And he sent his hand*) and laid hold of it, and it became לְמַטֶּה בְּכַפּוֹ (*a staff in his palm*).

(5)

לְמַעַן יַאֲמִינוּ

כִּי־נִרְאָה אֵלֶיךָ יהוה

That they may believe

that YHVH has appeared to you

אֱלֹהֵי אֲבֹתָם

אֱלֹהֵי אַבְרָהָם

אֱלֹהֵי יִצְחָק

וֵאלֹהֵי יַעֲקֹב

the Elohim of their fathers

the Elohim of Abraham

the Elohim of Isaac

the Elohim of Jacob.

(6) וַיֹּאמֶר יהוה (*And YHVH said*) further לוֹ (*to him*):

Level Two   שְׁמוֹת ~ ד

> הָבֵא-נָא יָדְךָ
> בְּחֵיקֶךָ
>
> *Put now your hand*
> *in your bosom.*

And he put יָדוֹ (*his hand*) בְּחֵיקוֹ (*in his bosom*); and when he took it out, behold יָדוֹ (*his hand*) was leprous, as white as snow.

(7) וַיֹּאמֶר (*And He said*):

> הָשֵׁב יָדְךָ
> אֶל-חֵיקֶךָ
>
> *Put your hand back*
> *to your bosom.*

And he put יָדוֹ (*his hand*) back אֶל-חֵיקוֹ (*to his bosom*); and when he took it מֵחֵיקוֹ (*from his bosom*), behold, it was turned again כִּבְשָׂרוֹ (*as his flesh*).

(8)
> וְהָיָה
> אִם-לֹא יַאֲמִינוּ לָךְ
> וְלֹא יִשְׁמְעוּ לְקֹל
>
> *And it shall be*
> *if they will not believe you*
> *neither hearken to the voice of*

Exodus ~ 4

הָאֹת הָרִאשׁוֹן
וְהֶאֱמִינוּ לְקֹל
הָאֹת הָאַחֲרוֹן

the first sign

that they will believe the voice

of the latter sign

(9)

וְהָיָה
אִם־לֹא יַאֲמִינוּ
גַּם לִשְׁנֵי הָאֹתוֹת הָאֵלֶּה
וְלֹא יִשְׁמְעוּן לְקֹלֶךָ

and it shall be

if they will not believe

even these two signs

neither hearken to your voice

וְלָקַחְתָּ
מִמֵּימֵי הַיְאֹר
וְשָׁפַכְתָּ הַיַּבָּשָׁה

that you shall take

from the water of the river

and pour it on the dry land

Level Two   שְׁמוֹת ~ ד

וְהָיוּ הַמַּיִם אֲשֶׁר
תִּקַּח מִן־הַיְאֹר
וְהָיוּ לְדָם בַּיַּבָּשֶׁת

and the water which

you take from the river

shall become blood on the dry land.

(10) וַיֹּאמֶר מֹשֶׁה אֶל יהוה (*And Moses said to YHVH*):

"Oh אֲדֹנָי לֹא אִישׁ דְּבָרִים אָנֹכִי (*My Lord, I am not a man of words*) גַּם (*also*) heretofore גַּם (*also*) since דַּבֶּרְךָ (*You have spoken*) אֶל- עַבְדֶּךָ (*to Your servant*); *for slow of speech, and* אָנֹכִי (*I*) *am of a slow tongue.*"

(11) וַיֹּאמֶר יהוה אֵלָיו (*And YHVH said to him*):

מִי שָׂם פֶּה לָאָדָם
אוֹ מִי־יָשׂוּם אִלֵּם
אוֹ חֵרֵשׁ אוֹ פִקֵּחַ אוֹ עִוֵּר
הֲלֹא אָנֹכִי יהוה

Who has made a mouth for the man

or who makes a man dumb

or deaf or seeing or blind

is it not I, YHVH

(12)

וְעַתָּ֖ה לֵ֑ךְ

וְאָנֹכִי֙ אֶֽהְיֶ֣ה עִם־פִּ֔יךָ

וְהוֹרֵיתִ֖יךָ

אֲשֶׁ֥ר תְּדַבֵּֽר

now therefore go

and I will be with your mouth

and teach you

what you shall speak.

(13) וַיֹּ֖אמֶר (And he said):

"Oh אֲדֹנָ֖י שְׁלַח (My Lord, send), I pray You בְּיַד־תִּשְׁלָֽח (by the hand of him whom You will send)."

(14) And the anger of יהוה was kindled בְּמֹשֶׁ֗ה וַיֹּ֙אמֶר֙ (and He said):

הֲלֹ֨א אַהֲרֹ֤ן

אָחִ֙יךָ֙ הַלֵּוִ֔י

יָדַ֕עְתִּי כִּֽי־

דַבֵּ֥ר יְדַבֵּ֖ר הֽוּא

There is not Aaron

your brother the Levi

I know that

he can speak well

Level Two — שְׁמוֹת ~ ד

וְגַם הִנֵּה־הוּא יֹצֵא
לִקְרָאתֶךָ
וְרָאֲךָ
וְשָׂמַח בְּלִבּוֹ

and also behold he comes forth
to meet you
and when he sees you
he will be glad in his heart

(15)

וְדִבַּרְתָּ אֵלָיו
וְשַׂמְתָּ אֶת־הַדְּבָרִים בְּפִיו
וְאָנֹכִי אֶהְיֶה עִם־פִּיךָ

and I will be with your mouth
and with his mouth
and you shall speak to him

וְעִם־פִּיהוּ
וְהוֹרֵיתִי אֶתְכֶם
אֵת אֲשֶׁר תַּעֲשׂוּן

*and put * the words in his mouth*
*and will teach * you*
** what you shall do*

Exodus ~ 4

(16)

וְדִבֶּר־הוּא לְךָ
אֶל־הָעָם
וְהָיָה

and he shall be your spokesman
to the people
and it shall be

הוּא יִהְיֶה־לְּךָ לְפֶה
וְאַתָּה תִּהְיֶה־לּוֹ
לֵאלֹהִים

that he shall be to you a mouth
and you shall be to him
for an elohim

(17)

וְאֶת־הַמַּטֶּה הַזֶּה
תִּקַּח בְּיָדֶךָ
אֲשֶׁר תַּעֲשֶׂה־בּוֹ
אֶת־הָאֹתֹת

and this * staff
you shall take in your hand
wherewith you shall do
* the signs.

Level Two   שְׁמוֹת ~ ד

(18) וַיֵּלֶךְ מֹשֶׁה (And Moses went) and returned אֶל-יֶתֶר his in-law (and he said) לוֹ (to him):

אֵלְכָה (I will go), I pray you, and return אֶל-אַחַי (to my brothers) who are בְּמִצְרַיִם (in Egypt) וְאֶרְאֶה (and I will see) whether they are yet חַיִּים (alive)."

וַיֹּאמֶר יִתְרוֹ לְמֹשֶׁה (And Jethro said to Moses):

לֵךְ לְשָׁלוֹם (Go for peace)."

(19) וַיֹּאמֶר יהוה אֶל מֹשֶׁה בְּמִדְיָן (And YHVH said to Moses in Midian):

לֵךְ שֻׁב מִצְרָיִם
כִּי-מֵתוּ כָּל-הָאֲנָשִׁים
הַמְבַקְשִׁים אֶת-נַפְשֶׁךָ

Go return to Egypt
for all the men are dead
that sought * your life.

(20) And מֹשֶׁה took אֶת-אִשְׁתּוֹ (* his wife) וְאֶת בָּנָיו (and * his sons), and set them עַל (on) a donkey and he returned אַרְצָה מִצְרָיִם (to the land of Egypt) and מֹשֶׁה took אֶת-מַטֵּה (* the staff of) הָאֱלֹהִים בְּיָדוֹ (the Elohim in his hand).
(21) וַיֹּאמֶר יהוה אֶל-מֹשֶׁה (And YHVH said to Moses):

בְּלֶכְתְּךָ לָשׁוּב מִצְרַיְמָה

When you go back in Egypt

Exodus ~ 4

רְאֵה כָּל־הַמֹּפְתִים
אֲשֶׁר־שַׂמְתִּי בְיָדֶךָ
וַעֲשִׂיתָם לִפְנֵי פַרְעֹה

see that all the wonders
which I have put in your hand
you do before Pharaoh

וַאֲנִי אֲחַזֵּק אֶת־לִבּוֹ
וְלֹא יְשַׁלַּח אֶת־הָעָם

*and I will harden * his heart*
*and he will not send * the people*

(22)

וְאָמַרְתָּ אֶל־פַּרְעֹה
כֹּה אָמַר יהוה
בְּנִי בְכֹרִי יִשְׂרָאֵל

and you shall say to Pharaoh
Thus says YHVH
Israel is My son, My firstborn

(23)

וָאֹמַר אֵלֶיךָ
שַׁלַּח אֶת־בְּנִי

and I have said to you
*Send * My son*

| Level Two | שְׁמוֹת ~ ד |

וְיַעַבְדֵנִי

וַתְּמָאֵן לְשַׁלְּחוֹ

הִנֵּה אָנֹכִי הֹרֵג אֶת-בִּנְךָ

בְּכֹרֶךָ

and he shall serve Me
and you have refused to let him go
and you have refused to let him go
*behold I will slay * your son*
your firstborn.

(24) And it was on the way at the lodging-place, that יהוה met him and sought to kill him.

Moses' Son Is Circumcised

(25) And צִפֹּרָה took a flint, and cut off אֵת the foreskin of בְּנָהּ (*her son*), and touched it לְרַגְלָיו (*to his feet*) וַתֹּאמֶר (*and she said*):

"Surely a bridegroom of דָּמִים (*bloods*) אַתָּה לִי (* *you are to me*)."

(26) And he let go מִמֶּנּוּ (*from him*) then אָמְרָה (*she said*):

"A bridegroom of דָּמִים (*bloods*) for the circumcision."

Aaron Meets With Moses

(27) וַיֹּאמֶר יהוה אֶל-אַהֲרֹן (*And YHVH said to Aaron*):

Exodus ~ 4

לֵךְ לִקְרַאת מֹשֶׁה
הַמִּדְבָּרָה

Go to meet Moses
in the wilderness.

וַיֵּלֶךְ (*And he went*) and met him בְּהַר הָאֱלֹהִים (*in the mountain of the Elohim*) and kissed לוֹ (*to him*).

(28) And מֹשֶׁה told לְאַהֲרֹן (*to Aaron*) אֵת כָּל־דִּבְרֵי יהוה (* *all the words of YHVH*) wherewith שְׁלָחוֹ (*He sent him*) וְאֵת כָּל (*and * all*) the signs wherewith He had charged him.

Moses Meets With The Elders Of Israel

(29) וַיֵּלֶךְ מֹשֶׁה וְאַהֲרֹן (*And Moses and Aaron went*) and gathered together אֶת־כָּל (* *all*) the elders of בְּנֵי יִשְׂרָאֵל (*the children of Israel*).

(30) וַיְדַבֵּר אַהֲרֹן (*And Aaron spoke*) אֵת כָּל הַדְּבָרִים (* *all the words*) which דִּבֶּר יהוה (*YHVH had spoken*) אֶל מֹשֶׁה and he did the signs לְעֵינֵי (*in the eyes of*) הָעָם (*the people*).

(31) And הָעָם (*the people*) believed וַיִּשְׁמְעוּ (*and they heard*) that יהוה had noticed אֶת־בְּנֵי יִשְׂרָאֵל (* *the children of Israel*), and that רָאָה (*He saw*) אֵת their affliction then they bowed their heads and bowed down.

Chapter Five

Moses Meets With Pharaoh

(1) And afterward מֹשֶׁה וְאַהֲרֹן came וַיֹּאמְרוּ אֶל-פַּרְעֹה (and they said to Pharaoh):

"Thus אָמַר (says) יהוה אֱלֹהֵי יִשְׂרָאֵל

שַׁלַּח אֶת-עַמִּי וְיָחֹגּוּ לִי בַּמִּדְבָּר

Send * My people

that they may hold a feast to Me

in the wilderness.

(2) וַיֹּאמֶר פַּרְעֹה (And Pharaoh said):

"Who is יהוה that אֶשְׁמַע בְּקֹלוֹ (I should listen to His voice) לְשַׁלַּח אֶת- (to let * Israel go)? לֹא יָדַעְתִּי (I do not know) אֶת יִשְׂרָאֵל יהוה moreover אֶת יִשְׂרָאֵל לֹא אֲשַׁלֵּחַ (I will not let * Israel go)."

(3) וַיֹּאמְרוּ (And they said):

"אֱלֹהֵי הָעִבְרִים has met עָלֵינוּ (with us) נֵלְכָה (We shall go), we pray you דֶּרֶךְ (a journey of) three days בַּמִּדְבָּר (in the wilderness) and sacrifice לַיהוה אֱלֹהֵינוּ lest He fall on us with pestilence, or with the sword."

(4) וַיֹּאמֶר מֶלֶךְ מִצְרַיִם (And the king of Egypt said) אֲלֵהֶם (to them):

"Why מֹשֶׁה וְאַהֲרֹן are you causing אֶת הָעָם (* the people) to break loose מִמַּעֲשָׂיו (from their work) לְכוּ (You go) to your burdens."

(5) וַיֹּאמֶר פַּרְעֹה (And Pharaoh said):

"Behold עַם (the people of) הָאָרֶץ (the land) are now many, and will you make אֹתָם rest from their burdens?"

(6) And on the same day פַּרְעֹה commanded אֵת the taskmasters בָּעָם (in the people) and וְאֶת their officers לֵאמֹר (saying):

(7)

"You shall no more give לָעָם (to the people) straw to make brick, heretofore הֵם יֵלְכוּ (They shall go) and gather straw לָהֶם (for themselves)."

(8)

וְאֶת the number of the bricks, which הֵם (they) made heretofore, you shall lay עֲלֵיהֶם (on them); you shall not diminish from it for הֵם (they) are idle; therefore הֵם (they) cry לֵאמֹר (saying):

נֵלְכָה (Let us go) and sacrifice לֵאלֹהֵינוּ

(9)

"Let הָעֲבֹדָה (the service) be heavy עַל הָאֲנָשִׁים (on the men) that they do בָהּ (in it); and let them not regard lying בְּדִבְרֵי (in words)."

(10) And the taskmasters of הָעָם (the people) went forth and their officers וַיֹּאמְרוּ אֶל-הָעָם (and they spoke to the people) לֵאמֹר (saying):

"Thus אָמַר פַּרְעֹה (says Pharaoh):

'I will not give straw לָכֶם (to you).'

(11)

אַתֶּם לְכוּ (* You go) take לָכֶם (for yourselves) straw where you can find it; because none of your work shall not diminished דָּבָר (a thing)."

Level Two   שְׁמוֹת ~ ה

(12) And הָעָם (*the people*) were scattered abroad בְּכָל אֶרֶץ מִצְרָיִם (*in all the land of Egypt*) to gather stubble for straw.

(13)   And the taskmasters were urgent לֵאמֹר (*saying*):

"Finish your work, your daily דְּבַר (*thing*), as when there was straw."

(14) And the officers of בְּנֵי יִשְׂרָאֵל (*the children of Israel*) whom the taskmasters of פַּרְעֹה had set עֲלֵהֶם (*over them*) were beaten לֵאמֹר (*saying*):

"Why have you not finished your appointed task in making brick as heretofore גַּם (*also*) yesterday גַּם (*also*) today?"

(15) And the officers of בְּנֵי יִשְׂרָאֵל (*the children of Israel*) entered and cried אֶל־פַּרְעֹה (*to Pharaoh*) לֵאמֹר (*saying*):

"Why are you doing thus לַעֲבָדֶיךָ (*to your servants*)?"

(16)

"There is no straw given לַעֲבָדֶיךָ (*to your servants*) אֹמְרִים (*and they say*) לָנוּ (*to us*):

'Make brick.'

"And, behold, עֲבָדֶיךָ (*your servants*) are beaten, but the fault is in עַמֶּךָ (*your people*)."

(17) וַיֹּאמֶר (*And he said*):

"Idle אַתֶּם are idle עַל (*on*) thus אַתֶּם אֹמְרִים (* *you say*):

לַיהוה (*We shall go*) and sacrifice נֵלְכָה

(18)

35

Exodus ~ 5

"And now לְכוּ עִבְדוּ (you go work); for there shall no straw be given לָכֶם (to you), yet you shall give the regular number of bricks."

(19) וַיִּרְאוּ שֹׁטְרֵי בְנֵי-יִשְׂרָאֵל (And the officers of the children of Israel saw) אֹתָם set on mischief לֵאמֹר (saying):

"You shall not diminish from your bricks, a daily דְּבַר (thing) in its day."

(20) And they met אֶת-מֹשֶׁה וְאֶת-אַהֲרֹן who stood to meet them as they came forth מֵאֵת פַּרְעֹה (from * Pharaoh)

(21) וַיֹּאמְרוּ (and they said) אֲלֵהֶם (to them):

יֵרֶא יהוה (YHVH look) עֲלֵיכֶם (on you) and judge; because you have made אֵת our scent to stink בְּעֵינֵי פַרְעֹה (in the eyes of Pharaoh) וּבְעֵינֵי (and in the eyes of) עֲבָדָיו (his servants), to give a sword בְּיָדָם (in their hand) to kill us."

(22) And מֹשֶׁה returned אֶל-יהוה (to YHVH) וַיֹּאמַר (and said):

אֲדֹנָי why have You dealt evil לָעָם הַזֶּה (to this people)? Why is it that שְׁלַחְתָּנִי (You have sent me)?"

(23)

"For since I entered אֶל-פַּרְעֹה (to Pharaoh) לְדַבֵּר (to speak) בִּשְׁמֶךָ (in Your name), he has dealt evil לָעָם הַזֶּה (to this people); neither have You rescued אֶת עַמֶּךָ (* Your people)."

Chapter Six

YHVH Speaks Against Pharaoh

(1) וַיֹּאמֶר יהוה אֶל־מֹשֶׁה (*And YHVH said to Moses*):

עַתָּה תִרְאֶה
אֲשֶׁר אֶעֱשֶׂה לְפַרְעֹה

Now you shall see
what I will do to Pharaoh

כִּי בְיָד חֲזָקָה
יְשַׁלְּחֵם
וּבְיָד חֲזָקָה
יְגָרְשֵׁם מֵאַרְצוֹ

for by a strong hand
he shall send them
and by a strong hand
he shall drive them out of his land.

(2) וַיְדַבֵּר אֱלֹהִים אֶל־מֹשֶׁה (*And Elohim spoke to Moses*) וַיֹּאמֶר (*and He said*) אֵלָיו (*to him*):

אֲנִי יהוה

I am YHVH

(3)

וָאֵרָא אֶל־אַבְרָהָם
אֶל־יִצְחָק
וְאֶל־יַעֲקֹב
בְּאֵל שַׁדָּי

and I appeared to Abraham
to Isaac
and to Jacob
in El Almighty

וּשְׁמִי יהוה
לֹא נוֹדַעְתִּי לָהֶם

and My name YHVH
I was not known to them

(4)

וְגַם הֲקִמֹתִי
אֶת־בְּרִיתִי אִתָּם
לָתֵת לָהֶם אֶת־אֶרֶץ כְּנַעַן
אֵת אֶרֶץ מְגֻרֵיהֶם

and I have also established
* My covenant with * them
* the land of their sojournings
to give them * the land of Canaan

Level Two ~ שְׁמוֹת ו

אֲשֶׁר־גָּרוּ בָהּ

wherein they sojourned

(5)

וְגַם אֲנִי שָׁמַעְתִּי

אֶת־נַאֲקַת בְּנֵי יִשְׂרָאֵל

אֲשֶׁר מִצְרַיִם

מַעֲבִדִים אֹתָם

וָאֶזְכֹּר אֶת־בְּרִיתִי

and also I have heard

* the groaning of the children of Israel

whom Egypt,

making servants of * them

and I have remembered * My covenant

(6)

לָכֵן אֱמֹר לִבְנֵי־יִשְׂרָאֵל

אֲנִי יהוה

וְהוֹצֵאתִי אֶתְכֶם

מִתַּחַת סִבְלֹת מִצְרַיִם

therefore say to the children of Israel

I am YHVH

and I will rescue * you out

from under the burdens of Egypt

וְהִצַּלְתִּי אֶתְכֶם

מֵעֲבֹדָתָם

וְגָאַלְתִּי אֶתְכֶם

בִּזְרוֹעַ נְטוּיָה

וּבִשְׁפָטִים גְּדֹלִים

and I will deliver * you

from their bondage

and I will redeem * you

with an outstretched arm

and with great judgments

(7)

וְלָקַחְתִּי אֶתְכֶם

לִי לְעָם

וְהָיִיתִי לָכֶם לֵאלֹהִים

וִידַעְתֶּם כִּי

אֲנִי יהוה אֱלֹהֵיכֶם

and I will take * you

to Me for a people

and I will be to you for Elohim

and you shall know that

I am YHVH your Elohim

Level Two   שְׁמוֹת ~ ו

הַמּוֹצִיא אֶתְכֶם

מִתַּחַת סִבְלוֹת מִצְרָיִם

Who brought * you out

from under the burdens of Egypt

(8)

וְהֵבֵאתִי אֶתְכֶם אֶל־הָאָרֶץ

אֲשֶׁר נָשָׂאתִי אֶת־יָדִי

and I will bring * you to the land

which I lifted up * My hand

לָתֵת אֹתָהּ לְאַבְרָהָם

לְיִצְחָק וּלְיַעֲקֹב

to give * it to Abraham

to Isaac and to Jacob

וְנָתַתִּי אֹתָהּ לָכֶם

מוֹרָשָׁה

אֲנִי יהוה

and I will give * it to you

for a heritage

I am YHVH

(9) Thus וַיְדַבֵּר מֹשֶׁה (*And Moses spoke*) אֶל־בְּנֵי יִשְׂרָאֵל (*to the children of Israel*) וְלֹא שָׁמְעוּ (*and they did not listen*) אֶל־מֹשֶׁה for impatience of רוּחַ

Exodus ~ 6

(spirit) וּמֵעֲבֹדָה קָשָׁה (and from hard work).

(10) וַיְדַבֵּר יהוה אֶל מֹשֶׁה (And YHVH spoke to Moses) לֵּאמֹר (saying):

(11)

בֹּא דַבֵּר אֶל-פַּרְעֹה
מֶלֶךְ מִצְרָיִם
וִישַׁלַּח אֶת-בְּנֵי-יִשְׂרָאֵל
מֵאַרְצוֹ

Go speak to Pharaoh

king of Egypt

and he shall send * the children of Israel

from his land.

(12) וַיְדַבֵּר מֹשֶׁה (And Moses spoke) לִפְנֵי יהוה (before YHVH) לֵּאמֹר (saying): "Behold בְּנֵי-יִשְׂרָאֵל (the children of Israel) לֹא-שָׁמְעוּ (will not listen) אֵלַי (to me); how then יִשְׁמָעֵנִי פַרְעֹה (shall Pharaoh listen to me) וַאֲנִי (and I am of) uncircumcised of lips?"

(13) וַיְדַבֵּר יהוה (And YHVH spoke) אֶל מֹשֶׁה וְאֶל-אַהֲרֹן (to Moses and to Aaron) and gave them a charge אֶל-בְּנֵי יִשְׂרָאֵל (to the children of Israel) -וְאֶל פַּרְעֹה מֶלֶךְ מִצְרָיִם (and to Pharaoh king of Egypt) to bring אֶת בְּנֵי יִשְׂרָאֵל (* the children of Israel) מֵאֶרֶץ מִצְרָיִם (from the land of Egypt).

The Heads Of Israel

(14) These are רָאשֵׁי (the heads of) בֵית (the house of) אֲבֹתָם (their fathers): בְּנֵי רְאוּבֵן (the sons of Reuben) בְּכֹר יִשְׂרָאֵל (the firstborn of Israel)

Level Two   שְׁמוֹת ~ ו

חֲנוֹךְ וּפַלּוּא חֶצְרֹן וְכַרְמִי

These are מִשְׁפְּחֹת רְאוּבֵן (*the families of Reuben*).

(15) וּבְנֵי שִׁמְעוֹן (*And the sons of Simeon*):

יְמוּאֵל וְיָמִין וְאֹהַד וְיָכִין וְצֹחַר וְשָׁאוּל

בֶּן-הַכְּנַעֲנִית (*the son of the Canaanite woman*).

These are מִשְׁפְּחֹת שִׁמְעוֹן (*the families of Simeon*).

(16) And these are שְׁמוֹת (*the names of*) בְּנֵי-לֵוִי (*the sons of Levi*) לְתֹלְדֹתָם (*according to their generations*):

גֵּרְשׁוֹן וּקְהָת וּמְרָרִי

And the years of חַיֵּי לֵוִי (*the life of Levi*) were a hundred and thirty-seven years.

(17) בְּנֵי גֵרְשׁוֹן (*The sons of Gershon*):

לִבְנִי וְשִׁמְעִי

לְמִשְׁפְּחֹתָם (*according to their families*).

(18) וּבְנֵי קְהָת (*And the sons of Kohath*):

עַמְרָם וְיִצְהָר וְחֶבְרוֹן וְעֻזִּיאֵל

And the years of חַיֵּי קְהָת (*the life of Kohath*) were a hundred and thirty-three years.

(19) וּבְנֵי מְרָרִי (*And the sons of Merari*):

מַחְלִי וּמוּשִׁי

Exodus ~ 6

These are מִשְׁפְּחֹת הַלֵּוִי (the families of the Levi) לְתֹלְדֹתָם (according to their generations).

(20) And עַמְרָם took אֶת-יוֹכֶבֶד דֹּדָתוֹ (* Jochebed his aunt) לוֹ (for himself) לְאִשָּׁה (for a wife) וַתֵּלֶד לוֹ (and she bore for him)

אֶת אַהֲרֹן וְאֶת מֹשֶׁה

And the years of חַיֵּי עַמְרָם (the life of Amram) were a hundred and thirty-seven years.

(21) וּבְנֵי יִצְהָר (And the sons of Izhar):

קֹרַח וָנֶפֶג וְזִכְרִי

(22) וּבְנֵי עֻזִּיאֵל (And the sons of Uzziel):

מִישָׁאֵל וְאֶלְצָפָן וְסִתְרִי

(23) And אַהֲרֹן took אֶת-אֱלִישֶׁבַע בַּת עַמִּינָדָב (* Elisheba, the daughter of Amminadab) אֲחוֹת נַחְשׁוֹן (the sister of Nahshon) לוֹ (for himself) לְאִשָּׁה (for a wife) וַתֵּלֶד לוֹ (and she bore for him):

אֶת נָדָב וְאֶת-אֲבִיהוּא אֶת-אֶלְעָזָר וְאֶת-אִיתָמָר

(24) וּבְנֵי קֹרַח (And the sons of Korah):

אַסִּיר וְאֶלְקָנָה וַאֲבִיאָסָף

These are מִשְׁפְּחֹת הַקָּרְחִי (the families of the Korahite).

(25) וְאֶלְעָזָר בֶּן-אַהֲרֹן (And Eleazar son of Aaron) took לוֹ (for him) מִבְּנוֹת

Level Two   שְׁמוֹת ~ ו

וַתֵּלֶד (for a wife) לְאִשָּׁה (for himself) לוֹ (from the daughters of Putiel) פּוּטִיאֵל לוֹ (and she bore for him)

אֶת-פִּינְחָס

These are רָאשֵׁי (the heads of) אֲבוֹת הַלְוִיִּם (the fathers of the Levites) לְמִשְׁפְּחֹתָם (according to their families).

(26) These are that אַהֲרֹן וּמֹשֶׁה to whom אָמַר יהוה (YHVH said) לָהֶם (to them):

הוֹצִיאוּ אֶת-בְּנֵי יִשְׂרָאֵל

Bring out * the children of Israel

מֵאֶרֶץ מִצְרַיִם

עַל-צִבְאֹתָם

from the land of Egypt

according to their armies.

(27) הֵם הַמְדַבְּרִים (They are the ones speaking) אֶל פַּרְעֹה מֶלֶךְ מִצְרַיִם (to Pharaoh king of Egypt), to bring forth אֶת בְּנֵי-יִשְׂרָאֵל מִמִּצְרָיִם (* the children of Israel from Egypt) הוּא (It) is מֹשֶׁה וְאַהֲרֹן.

(28) And it was on a day דִּבֶּר יהוה אֶל-מֹשֶׁה (YHVH spoke to Moses) בְּאֶרֶץ מִצְרָיִם (in the land of Egypt).

YHVH Sends Moses To Pharaoh

(29) וַיְדַבֵּר יהוה אֶל-מֹשֶׁה (And YHVH spoke to Moses) לֵאמֹר (saying):

Exodus ~ 6

אֲנִי יהוה

I am YHVH

דַּבֵּר אֶל־פַּרְעֹה

מֶלֶךְ מִצְרָיִם

אֵת כָּל־אֲשֶׁר אֲנִי דֹּבֵר אֵלֶיךָ

Speak you to Pharaoh

king of Egypt

* all that I speak to you.

(30) וַיֹּאמֶר מֹשֶׁה (*And Moses said*) before יהוה

"Behold, אֲנִי (*I am of*) uncircumcised lips, and how יִשְׁמַע פַּרְעֹה (*shall Pharaoh listen*) אֵלַי (*to me*)?"

Chapter Seven

YHVH Answers Moses

(1) וַיֹּאמֶר יהוה אֶל-מֹשֶׁה (*And YHVH said to Moses*):

רְאֵה נְתַתִּיךָ

אֱלֹהִים לְפַרְעֹה

וְאַהֲרֹן אָחִיךָ

יִהְיֶה נְבִיאֶךָ

See I have set you

in the stead of Elohim to Pharaoh

and Aaron your brother

shall be your prophet

(2)

אַתָּה תְדַבֵּר

אֵת כָּל-אֲשֶׁר אֲצַוֶּךָּ

וְאַהֲרֹן אָחִיךָ

יְדַבֵּר אֶל-פַּרְעֹה

וְשִׁלַּח אֶת-בְּנֵי-יִשְׂרָאֵל מֵאַרְצוֹ

* you shall speak

* all that I command you

and Aaron your brother

shall speak to Pharaoh

that he let * the children of Israel go from his land

Exodus ~ 7

(3)

וַאֲנִי אַקְשֶׁה
אֶת-לֵב פַּרְעֹה
וְהִרְבֵּיתִי אֶת-אֹתֹתַי
וְאֶת-מוֹפְתַי
בְּאֶרֶץ מִצְרָיִם

and I will harden
* the heart of Pharaoh
and multiply * My signs
and * My wonders
in the land of Egypt

(4)

וְלֹא-יִשְׁמַע אֲלֵכֶם פַּרְעֹה
וְנָתַתִּי אֶת-יָדִי בְּמִצְרָיִם
וְהוֹצֵאתִי אֶת-צִבְאֹתַי
אֶת-עַמִּי בְנֵי-יִשְׂרָאֵל
מֵאֶרֶץ מִצְרַיִם בִּשְׁפָטִים גְּדֹלִים

and Pharaoh will not listen to you
and I will lay * My hand on Egypt
and bring forth * My armies
* My people the children of Israel
from the land of Egypt in great judgments

Level Two ~ שְׁמוֹת ז

(5)

וְיָדְעוּ מִצְרַיִם

כִּי־אֲנִי יהוה

בִּנְטֹתִי אֶת־יָדִי עַל־מִצְרָיִם

וְהוֹצֵאתִי אֶת־בְּנֵי־יִשְׂרָאֵל

מִתּוֹכָם

and Egypt shall know

that I am YHVH

in My stretching forth of * My hand on Egypt

and bring forth * the children of Israel

from their midst.

(6) And מֹשֶׁה did וְאַהֲרֹן as יהוה commanded אֹתָם so they did.

(7) וּמֹשֶׁה בֶּן (And Moses was a son of) eighty years וְאַהֲרֹן בֶּן (and Aaron was a son of) eighty-three years, בְּדַבְּרָם (on their speaking) אֶל־פַּרְעֹה

(8) וַיֹּאמֶר יהוה אֶל־מֹשֶׁה וְאֶל־אַהֲרֹן (And YHVH said to Moses and to Aaron) לֵאמֹר (saying):

(9)

כִּי יְדַבֵּר אֲלֵכֶם פַּרְעֹה לֵאמֹר

תְּנוּ לָכֶם מוֹפֵת

וְאָמַרְתָּ אֶל־אַהֲרֹן

When Pharaoh shall speak to you saying

Give a wonder for you.

Then you shall say to Aaron

Exodus ~ 7

קַח אֶת-מַטְּךָ וְהַשְׁלֵךְ

לִפְנֵי-פַרְעֹה

יְהִי לְתַנִּין

Take * your staff and cast down

before Pharaoh

it shall become for a dragon.

Moses Goes To Pharaoh

(10) And מֹשֶׁה went in וְאַהֲרֹן אֶל-פַּרְעֹה and they did so, as יהוה had commanded וַיַּשְׁלֵךְ אַהֲרֹן (and Aaron cast down) אֶת-מַטֵּהוּ (* his staff) לִפְנֵי פַרְעֹה (before Pharaoh) וְלִפְנֵי עֲבָדָיו (and before his servants) and it was לְתַנִּין (for a dragon).

(11) וַיִּקְרָא גַם-פַּרְעֹה (And Pharaoh also called) for the wise men and for the sorcerers and גַם-הֵם (also they) the magicians of מִצְרַיִם did in like manner with their secret arts.

(12) וַיַּשְׁלִיכוּ (And they cast down) אִישׁ מַטֵּהוּ (a man his staff) and they were לְתַנִּינִם (for dragons) and מַטֵּה-אַהֲרֹן (the staff of Aaron) swallowed up אֶת מַטֹּתָם (* their staffs).

(13) And לֵב פַּרְעֹה (the heart of Pharaoh) was hardened וְלֹא שָׁמַע (and he would not listen) אֲלֵהֶם (to them) as דִּבֶּר יהוה (YHVH had spoken).

Blood, Blood, Blood!

(14) וַיֹּאמֶר יהוה אֶל-מֹשֶׁה (And YHVH said to Moses):

כָּבֵד לֵב פַּרְעֹה

מֵאֵן לְשַׁלַּח הָעָם

Level Two   שְׁמוֹת ~ ז

The heart of Pharaoh is stubborn
he refuses to send the people

(15)

לֵךְ אֶל־פַּרְעֹה בַּבֹּקֶר

הִנֵּה יֹצֵא הַמַּיְמָה

וְנִצַּבְתָּ לִקְרָאתוֹ

עַל־שְׂפַת הַיְאֹר

וְהַמַּטֶּה אֲשֶׁר־נֶהְפַּךְ לְנָחָשׁ

תִּקַּח בְּיָדֶךָ

go to Pharaoh in the morning
behold he goes toward the water
and you shall stand to meet him
on the shore of the river
and the staff which was turned to a serpent
you shall take in your hand

(16)

וְאָמַרְתָּ אֵלָיו

יהוה אֱלֹהֵי הָעִבְרִים

שְׁלָחַנִי אֵלֶיךָ לֵאמֹר

and you say to him
YHVH Elohim of the Hebrews
sent me to you saying

Exodus ~ 7

שַׁלַּח אֶת-עַמִּי

וְיַעַבְדֻנִי בַּמִּדְבָּר

וְהִנֵּה לֹא-שָׁמַעְתָּ עַד-כֹּה

Send * My people

and they shall serve Me in the wilderness

and behold you have not listened up to now

(17)

כֹּה אָמַר יהוה

בְּזֹאת תֵּדַע כִּי אֲנִי יהוה

הִנֵּה אָנֹכִי מַכֶּה

בַּמַּטֶּה אֲשֶׁר-בְּיָדִי

עַל-הַמַּיִם אֲשֶׁר בַּיְאֹר

וְנֶהֶפְכוּ לְדָם

Thus says YHVH

In this you shall know that I am YHVH

behold, I will smite

with the staff that is in my hand

on the waters which are in the river

and they shall be turned to blood

(18)

וְהַדָּגָה אֲשֶׁר-בַּיְאֹר תָּמוּת

וּבָאַשׁ הַיְאֹר

Level Two   שְׁמוֹת ~ ז

and the fish that are in the river shall die

and the river shall stink

וְנִלְאוּ מִצְרַיִם

לִשְׁתּוֹת מַיִם מִן-הַיְאֹר

and Egypt shall loathe

to drink water from the river.

(19) וַיֹּאמֶר יהוה אֶל-מֹשֶׁה *(And YHVH said to Moses):*

אֱמֹר אֶל-אַהֲרֹן

קַח מַטְּךָ וּנְטֵה-יָדְךָ

Say to Aaron

Take your staff and stretch out your hand

עַל-מֵימֵי מִצְרַיִם

עַל-נַהֲרֹתָם

עַל-יְאֹרֵיהֶם

וְעַל-אַגְמֵיהֶם

וְעַל כָּל-מִקְוֵה מֵימֵיהֶם

over the waters of Egypt

over their rivers

over their streams

and over their pools

and over all their ponds of water

וְיִהְיוּ־דָם

וְהָיָה דָם

בְּכָל־אֶרֶץ מִצְרַיִם

וּבָעֵצִים וּבָאֲבָנִים

that they may become blood

and there shall be blood

throughout all the land of Egypt

and in wooden vessels and in stone vessels.

(20) And מֹשֶׁה וְאַהֲרֹן did so, as יהוה commanded and he held high בַּמַּטֶּה (*on the staff*) and smote אֶת־הַמַּיִם (** the waters*) that were in the river לְעֵינֵי פַרְעֹה (*for the eyes of Pharaoh*) וּלְעֵינֵי (*and for the eyes of*) עֲבָדָיו (*his servants*); and כָּל הַמַּיִם (*all the waters*) that were in the river were turned לְדָם (*to blood*).

(21) And the fish that were in the river died; and the river stank and מִצְרַיִם could not drink מַיִם (*water*) מִן (*from*) the river; and הַדָּם (*the blood*) was בְּכָל־אֶרֶץ מִצְרָיִם (*in all the land of Egypt*).

(22) And the magicians of מִצְרַיִם did so with their secret arts; and לֵב פַּרְעֹה (*the heart of Pharaoh*) was hardened וְלֹא שָׁמַע (*and he did not listen*) אֲלֵהֶם (*to them*); as דִּבֶּר יהוה (*YHVH had spoken*).

(23) And פַּרְעֹה turned and went אֶל־בֵּיתוֹ (*to his house*) neither did he lay לִבּוֹ גַּם־לָזֹאת (*to his heart also to this*).

(24) And כָּל־מִצְרַיִם (*all Egypt*) dug around about the river for מַיִם (*water*) to drink; for they could not drink מִמֵּימֵי (*from the water of*) the river.

(25) And seven days were fulfilled, after יהוה smote אֵת the river.

Chapter Eight

Frogs, Frogs, Frogs!

(1) (7:26) וַיֹּאמֶר יהוה אֶל־מֹשֶׁה (And YHVH said to Moses):

בֹּא אֶל־פַּרְעֹה וְאָמַרְתָּ אֵלָיו

כֹּה אָמַר יהוה

שַׁלַּח אֶת־עַמִּי

וְיַעַבְדֻנִי

Go to Pharaoh and say to him

Thus says YHVH

Send * My people

and they shall serve Me

(2) (7:27)

וְאִם־מָאֵן אַתָּה לְשַׁלֵּחַ

הִנֵּה אָנֹכִי נֹגֵף

אֶת־כָּל־גְּבוּלְךָ בַּצְפַרְדְּעִים

and if * you refuse to send them

behold I will smite

* all your borders with frogs

(3) (7:28)

וְשָׁרַץ הַיְאֹר צְפַרְדְּעִים

וְעָלוּ

and the river shall swarm with frogs

and they shall go up

Exodus ~ 8

וּבָ֣אוּ בְּבֵיתֶ֔ךָ

וּבַחֲדַ֥ר מִשְׁכָּבְךָ֖

וְעַל־מִטָּתֶ֑ךָ

and go in your house

and in your bed-chamber

and on your couch

וּבְבֵ֥ית עֲבָדֶ֖יךָ

וּבְעַמֶּ֑ךָ

וּבְתַנּוּרֶ֖יךָ

וּבְמִשְׁאֲרוֹתֶֽיךָ

and in the house of your servants

and on your people

and in your ovens

and in your kneading-troughs

(4) (7:29)

וּבְכָ֥ה וּבְעַמְּךָ֖

וּבְכָל־עֲבָדֶֽיךָ

יַעֲל֖וּ הַֽצְפַרְדְּעִֽים

and on you and on your people

and on all your servants

the frogs shall ascend.

(5) (8:1) וַיֹּ֤אמֶר יהוה אֶל־מֹשֶׁה֙ (*And YHVH said to Moses*):

Level Two   שְׁמוֹת ~ ח

אֱמֹר אֶל-אַהֲרֹן

נְטֵה אֶת-יָדְךָ בְּמַטֶּךָ

עַל-הַנְּהָרֹת עַל-הַיְאֹרִים וְעַל-הָאֲגַמִּים

וְהַעַל אֶת-הַצְפַרְדְּעִים

עַל-אֶרֶץ מִצְרָיִם

Say to Aaron

Stretch forth * your hand with your staff

over the rivers, over the canals, and over the pools

and bring up * the frogs

on the land of Egypt.

(6) (8:2)   And אַהֲרֹן stretched out אֶת-יָדוֹ (* *his hand*) עַל מֵימֵי מִצְרָיִם (*over the waters of Egypt*) וַתַּעַל (*and she came up*) הַצְפַרְדֵּעַ (*the frog*) וַתְּכַס (*and she covered*) אֶת אֶרֶץ מִצְרָיִם (* *the land of Egypt*).

(7) (8:3)   And the magicians did so with their secret arts, and they brought up אֶת הַצְפַרְדְּעִים (* *the frogs*) עַל אֶרֶץ מִצְרָיִם (*over the land of Egypt*).

(8) (8:4)   וַיִּקְרָא פַרְעֹה לְמֹשֶׁה וּלְאַהֲרֹן (*And Pharaoh called for Moses and for Aaron*) וַיֹּאמֶר (*and he said*):

"Entreat אֶל-יהוה that He take away הַצְפַרְדְּעִים (*the frogs*) מִמֶּנִּי (*from me*) וּמֵעַמִּי (*and from my people*) וַאֲשַׁלְּחָה (*and I will send*) אֶת הָעָם (* *the people*) that they may sacrifice לַיהוה

(9) (8:5)   וַיֹּאמֶר מֹשֶׁה לְפַרְעֹה (*And Moses said to Pharaoh*):

"Glory עָלַי (*over me*); for when shall I entreat לְךָ (*for you*)

Exodus ~ 8

וְלַעֲבָדֶיךָ (and for your servants) וּלְעַמְּךָ (and for your people) that וּמִבָּתֶּיךָ (and your houses) מִמְּךָ (from you) הַצְפַרְדְּעִים (the frogs) be destroyed, but they shall remain in the river?"

(10) (8:6) וַיֹּאמֶר (And he said):
"Tomorrow."

וַיֹּאמֶר (And he said):

כִּדְבָרְךָ (As your word) that you may know that there is none כַּיהוה אֱלֹהֵינוּ (like YHVH our Elohim.)"

(11) (8:7)

"And הַצְפַרְדְּעִים (the frogs) shall withdraw מִמְּךָ (from you) וּמִבָּתֶּיךָ (and from your houses) וּמֵעֲבָדֶיךָ (and from your servants), וּמֵעַמְּךָ (and from your people); they shall remain in the river only."

(12) (8:8) And מֹשֶׁה וְאַהֲרֹן went forth מֵעִם פַּרְעֹה (from with Pharaoh) and מֹשֶׁה cried אֶל יהוה (to YHVH) עַל דְּבַר הַצְפַרְדְּעִים (over the matter of frogs) which He had brought לְפַרְעֹה

(13) (8:9) And יהוה did כִּדְבַר מֹשֶׁה (as the word of Moses). And הַצְפַרְדְּעִים (the frogs) died מִן הַבָּתִּים (from the houses) מִן־הַחֲצֵרֹת (from the courts) וּמִן (and from) the fields.

(14) (8:10) And they gathered אֹתָם together in heaps; and הָאָרֶץ (the land) stank.

(15) (8:11) וַיַּרְא פַּרְעֹה (And Pharaoh saw) that there was the interval, he hardened לִבּוֹ אֶת־ (* his heart) וְלֹא שָׁמַע (and did not listen) אֲלֵהֶם (to them) as דִּבֶּר יהוה (YHVH had spoken).

58

Level Two   שְׁמוֹת ~ ח

Lice, Lice, Lice!

(16) (8:12) וַיֹּאמֶר יהוה אֶל-מֹשֶׁה (And YHVH said to Moses):

אֱמֹר אֶל-אַהֲרֹן

נְטֵה אֶת-מַטְּךָ

וְהַךְ אֶת-עֲפַר הָאָרֶץ

Say to Aaron

*Stretch out * your staff*

*and smite * the soil of the land*

וְהָיָה לְכִנִּם

בְּכָל-אֶרֶץ מִצְרָיִם

he/it will be for lice

in all the land of Egypt

(17) (8:13) And they did so, and אַהֲרֹן stretched out אֶת יָדוֹ בְמַטֵּהוּ (* his hand with his staff) and smote אֶת the soil of הָאָרֶץ (the land) וַתְּהִי הַכִּנָּם (and she/it was the louse) בָּאָדָם (on the man) וּבַבְּהֵמָה (and on the animal); and כָּל (all) the soil of הָאָרֶץ (the land) הָיָה כִנִּים (he/it became lice) בְּכָל-אֶרֶץ מִצְרָיִם (in all the land of Egypt).

(18) (8:14) And the magicians did so with their secret arts to bring forth אֶת הַכִּנִּים (* the lice), and they could not. וַתְּהִי הַכִּנָּם (and she/it was the louse) בָּאָדָם (on the man) וּבַבְּהֵמָה (and on the animal).

(19) (8:15) And the magicians וַיֹּאמְרוּ (they said) אֶל-פַּרְעֹה

אֶצְבַּע אֱלֹהִים הוּא (She is the finger of Elohim!)

Exodus ~ 8

And לֶב-פַּרְעֹה (the heart of Pharaoh) was hardened, וְלֹא שָׁמַע (and he did not listen) אֲלֵהֶם (to them) as דִּבֶּר יהוה (YHVH had spoken).

Swarms, Swarms, Swarms!

(20) (8:16) וַיֹּאמֶר יהוה אֶל-מֹשֶׁה (And YHVH said to Moses):

הַשְׁכֵּם בַּבֹּקֶר

וְהִתְיַצֵּב לִפְנֵי פַרְעֹה

הִנֵּה יוֹצֵא הַמָּיְמָה

וְאָמַרְתָּ אֵלָיו

כֹּה אָמַר יהוה

שַׁלַּח עַמִּי וְיַעַבְדֻנִי

Rise up early in the morning

and stand before Pharaoh

behold he goes forth to the water

and say to him

Thus says YHVH

Send My people and they shall serve Me

(21) (8:17)

כִּי אִם-אֵינְךָ

מְשַׁלֵּחַ אֶת-עַמִּי

הִנְנִי מַשְׁלִיחַ

בְּךָ וּבַעֲבָדֶיךָ וּבְעַמְּךָ

Level Two

שְׁמוֹת ~ ח

else if you will not
send * My people
behold I will send
on you and on your servantsand on your people

וּבְבָתֶּיךָ אֶת־הֶעָרֹב

וּמָלְאוּ בָּתֵּי מִצְרַיִם

אֶת־הֶעָרֹב

וְגַם הָאֲדָמָה
אֲשֶׁר־הֵם עָלֶיהָ

and in your houses * the mixture
and the houses of Egypt shall be full of
* the mixture
and also the ground
whereon they are

(22) (8:18)

וְהִפְלֵיתִי בַיּוֹם הַהוּא

אֶת־אֶרֶץ גֹּשֶׁן

אֲשֶׁר עַמִּי עֹמֵד עָלֶיהָ

לְבִלְתִּי הֱיוֹת־שָׁם עָרֹב

and I will set apart in that day
* the land of Goshen
in which My people dwell
that no mixture shall be there

Exodus ~ 8

לְמַעַן תֵּדַע

כִּי אֲנִי יהוה בְּקֶרֶב הָאָרֶץ

to the end that you may know

that I am YHVH in the midst of the land

(23) (8:19)

וְשַׂמְתִּי פְדֻת

and I will put a division

בֵּין עַמִּי וּבֵין עַמֶּךָ

לְמָחָר יִהְיֶה הָאֹת הַזֶּה

between My people and your people

by tomorrow shall this sign be.

(24) (8:20)   And יהוה did so, and there came עָרֹב כָּבֵד (*a grievous mixture*) בֵּיתָה פַרְעֹה (*in the house of Pharaoh*) וּבֵית (*and in houses of*) עֲבָדָיו (*his servants*) וּבְכָל-אֶרֶץ מִצְרַיִם (*and in all the land of Egypt*) הָאָרֶץ (*the land*) was ruined מִפְּנֵי הֶעָרֹב (*from the face of the mixture*).

(25) (8:21)   וַיִּקְרָא פַרְעֹה (*And Pharaoh called*) אֶל מֹשֶׁה וּלְאַהֲרֹן וַיֹּאמֶר (*and he said*):

לְכוּ (*You go!*) Sacrifice לֵאלֹהֵיכֶם (*to your Elohim*) בָּאָרֶץ (*in the land*)."

(26) (8:22)   וַיֹּאמֶר מֹשֶׁה (*And Moses said*):

"It is not meet to do so; for we shall sacrifice the abomination

Level Two   שְׁמוֹת ~ ח

אֶת Behold, we shall sacrifice מִצְרַיִם לַיהוה אֱלֹהֵינוּ of abomination of מִצְרַיִם (Egypt) לְעֵינֵיהֶם (to their eyes) will they not stone us?"

(27) (8:23)

דֶּרֶךְ (A journey of) three days נֵלֵךְ (we will go) בַּמִּדְבָּר (in the wilderness) and we shall sacrifice לַיהוה אֱלֹהֵינוּ as which יֹאמַר (He shall say) אֵלֵינוּ (to us)."

(28) (8:24) וַיֹּאמֶר פַּרְעֹה (And Pharaoh said):

אָנֹכִי (I) אֲשַׁלַּח אֶתְכֶם (I will send * you) and you may sacrifice לַיהוה אֱלֹהֵיכֶם בַּמִּדְבָּר (to YHVH your Elohim in the wilderness); but לָלֶכֶת (to go) you shall not go very far. Entreat about me."

(29) (8:25) וַיֹּאמֶר מֹשֶׁה (And Moses said):

"Behold, אָנֹכִי (I) go forth מֵעִמָּךְ (from you), and I will entreat אֶל־יהוה and He shall withdraw הֶעָרֹב (the mixture) מִפַּרְעֹה (from Pharaoh) מֵעֲבָדָיו (from his servants) וּמֵעַמּוֹ (and from his people) tomorrow; but פַּרְעֹה must not deal deceitfully any more so as not שַׁלַּח (to send) אֶת־הָעָם (* the people) to sacrifice לַיהוה

(30) (8:26) And מֹשֶׁה went forth מֵעִם פַּרְעֹה (from with Pharaoh), and entreated יהוה

(31) (8:27) And יהוה did כִּדְבַר מֹשֶׁה (as the word of Moses) and He removed הֶעָרֹב מִפַּרְעֹה (the mixture from Pharaoh) מֵעֲבָדָיו (from his servants) וּמֵעַמּוֹ (and from his people). Not one remained.

(32) (8:28) And פַּרְעֹה hardened אֶת לִבּוֹ (* his heart) גַּם (also) this time וְלֹא שִׁלַּח (and he did not send) אֶת־הָעָם (* the people).

63

Chapter Nine

Cattle Disease!

(1) וַיֹּ֤אמֶר יהוה אֶל־מֹשֶׁ֔ה (*And YHVH said to Moses*):

בֹּ֖א אֶל־פַּרְעֹ֑ה וְדִבַּרְתָּ֣ אֵלָ֔יו

כֹּֽה־אָמַ֥ר יהוה

אֱלֹהֵ֣י הָעִבְרִ֑ים

שַׁלַּ֥ח אֶת־עַמִּ֖י

וְיַֽעַבְדֻֽנִי

Go to Pharaoh and speak to him

Thus says YHVH

the Elohim of the Hebrews

Send * My people

that they may serve Me

(2)

כִּ֛י אִם־מָאֵ֥ן אַתָּ֖ה לְשַׁלֵּ֑חַ

וְעֽוֹדְךָ֖ מַחֲזִ֥יק בָּֽם

for if * you refuse to send them

and will hold them still

(3)

הִנֵּ֨ה יַד־יהוה

הוֹיָ֗ה בְּמִקְנְךָ֙ אֲשֶׁ֣ר בַּשָּׂדֶ֔ה

behold the hand of YHVH

is on your cattle which are in the field

Level Two   שְׁמוֹת ~ ט

בַּסּוּסִים בַּחֲמֹרִים
בַּגְּמַלִּים בַּבָּקָר וּבַצֹּאן
דֶּבֶר כָּבֵד מְאֹד

on the horses on the donkeys
on the camels, on the herds, and on the flocks
a very grievous plague

(4)

וְהִפְלָה יהוה
בֵּין מִקְנֵה יִשְׂרָאֵל
וּבֵין מִקְנֵה מִצְרָיִם
וְלֹא יָמוּת
מִכָּל לִבְנֵי יִשְׂרָאֵל דָּבָר

and YHVH shall make a division
between the cattle of Israel
and the cattle of Egypt
and not shall
a thing from all to the children of Israel.

(5) And יהוה made מוֹעֵד (*an appointment*) לֵאמֹר (*saying*):

מָחָר יַעֲשֶׂה יהוה
הַדָּבָר הַזֶּה--בָּאָרֶץ

Tomorrow YHVH shall do
this thing in the land.

65

Exodus ~ 9

(6) And יהוה did אֶת-הַדָּבָר הַזֶּה (*this * thing*) on the morrow, and כֹּל (*all*) the cattle of מִצְרַיִם died; but of the cattle of בְּנֵי-יִשְׂרָאֵל (*the children of Israel*) died not one.

(7) וַיִּשְׁלַח פַּרְעֹה (*And Pharaoh sent*), and behold, there was not so much as one of the cattle of יִשְׂרָאֵל dead. But לֵב פַּרְעֹה (*the heart of Pharaoh*) was stubborn וְלֹא שִׁלַּח (*and he would not send*) אֶת הָעָם (** the people*).

Boils, Boils, Boils!

(8) וַיֹּאמֶר יהוה אֶל-מֹשֶׁה וְאֶל-אַהֲרֹן (*And YHVH said to Moses and to Aaron*):

קְחוּ לָכֶם מְלֹא חָפְנֵיכֶם

פִּיחַ כִּבְשָׁן

וּזְרָקוֹ מֹשֶׁה הַשָּׁמַיְמָה

לְעֵינֵי פַרְעֹה

Take for yourself fullness of both hands

of ash of a furnace

and let Moses scatter it towards the sky

for the eyes of Pharaoh

(9)

וְהָיָה לְאָבָק

עַל כָּל-אֶרֶץ מִצְרָיִם

וְהָיָה עַל-הָאָדָם וְעַל-הַבְּהֵמָה

לִשְׁחִין פֹּרֵחַ אֲבַעְבֻּעֹת

בְּכָל-אֶרֶץ מִצְרָיִם

| Level Two | שְׁמוֹת ~ ט |

and it shall become small dust

over all the land of Egypt

and it shall be on the man and on the animal

a boil breaking forth with pustules

in all the land of Egypt.

(10) And they took אֶת ash of the furnace, and they stood לִפְנֵי פַרְעֹה (before Pharaoh) and מֹשֶׁה scattered אֹתוֹ (* him/it) הַשָּׁמַיְמָה (towards the sky) and it became שְׁחִין (a boil) breaking forth with pustules בָּאָדָם (on the man) וּבַבְּהֵמָה (and on the animal).

(11) And the magicians could not stand לִפְנֵי מֹשֶׁה (before Moses) because of הַשְּׁחִין (the boil) because הַשְּׁחִין (the boil) was on the magicians וּבְכָל-מִצְרָיִם (and on all Egypt).

(12) And יהוה hardened אֶת-לֵב פַּרְעֹה (* the heart of Pharaoh) וְלֹא שָׁמַע (and he would not listen) אֲלֵהֶם (to them) as דִּבֶּר יהוה (YHVH had spoken) אֶל- מֹשֶׁה

Hail, Hail, Hail!

(13) וַיֹּאמֶר יהוה אֶל-מֹשֶׁה (And YHVH said to Moses):

הַשְׁכֵּם בַּבֹּקֶר

וְהִתְיַצֵּב לִפְנֵי פַרְעֹה

וְאָמַרְתָּ אֵלָיו

Rise up early in the morning

and stand before Pharaoh

and say to him

כֹּה־אָמַר יהוה אֱלֹהֵי הָעִבְרִים
שַׁלַּח אֶת־עַמִּי
וְיַעַבְדֻנִי

Thus says YHVH the Elohim of the Hebrews
Send * My people,
and they shall serve Me

(14)

כִּי בַּפַּעַם הַזֹּאת אֲנִי שֹׁלֵחַ
אֶת־כָּל־מַגֵּפֹתַי אֶל־לִבְּךָ
וּבַעֲבָדֶיךָ וּבְעַמֶּךָ
בַּעֲבוּר תֵּדַע
כִּי אֵין כָּמֹנִי בְּכָל־הָאָרֶץ

for this time I will send
* all My plagues to your heart
and on your servants and on your people
in order that you may know
that there is none like Me in all the land

(15)

כִּי עַתָּה שָׁלַחְתִּי אֶת־יָדִי
וָאַךְ אוֹתְךָ
וְאֶת־עַמְּךָ בַּדָּבֶר
וַתִּכָּחֵד מִן־הָאָרֶץ

Level Two   שְׁמוֹת ~ ט

for now I have put forth * My hand
and smitten * you
and * your people with pestilence
and you have been cut off from the land

(16)

וְאוּלָם בַּעֲבוּר זֹאת

הֶעֱמַדְתִּיךָ

בַּעֲבוּר הַרְאֹתְךָ אֶת-כֹּחִי

וּלְמַעַן סַפֵּר שְׁמִי

בְּכָל-הָאָרֶץ

and nevertheless, in this cause
I have made you to stand
to show you * My power
and that My name may be declared
in all the land

(17)

עוֹדְךָ מִסְתּוֹלֵל בְּעַמִּי לְבִלְתִּי שַׁלְּחָם

till you exalt yourself in My people so as not to send them

(18)

הִנְנִי מַמְטִיר

כָּעֵת מָחָר

behold I will cause it to rain
tomorrow about this time

Exodus ~ 9

בָּרָד כָּבֵד מְאֹד

אֲשֶׁר לֹא־הָיָה כָמֹהוּ בְּמִצְרַיִם

לְמִן־הַיּוֹם הִוָּסְדָה וְעַד־עָתָּה

a very heavy hail

such as has not been in Egypt

since the day it was found even until now

(19)

וְעַתָּה שְׁלַח

הָעֵז אֶת־מִקְנְךָ

וְאֵת כָּל־אֲשֶׁר לְךָ בַּשָּׂדֶה

כָּל־הָאָדָם וְהַבְּהֵמָה

אֲשֶׁר־יִמָּצֵא בַשָּׂדֶה

now therefore send

*hasten in * your cattle*

*and * all that you have in the field*

all of the man and the animal

that shall be found in the field

וְלֹא יֵאָסֵף הַבַּיְתָה

וְיָרַד עֲלֵהֶם הַבָּרָד וָמֵתוּ

and shall not be brought to the house

the hail shall descend on them and they shall die.

Level Two   שְׁמוֹת ~ ט

(20) He that feared אֶת-דְּבַר יהוה (* *the word of YHVH*) מֵעַבְדֵי פַּרְעֹה (*from the servants of Pharaoh*) made עֲבָדָיו (* *his servants*) וְאֶת his cattle flee -אֶל הַבָּתִּים (*to the houses*);

(21) and he that directed not לִבּוֹ (*his heart*) אֶל-דְּבַר יהוה (*to the word of YHVH*) left עֲבָדָיו-אֶת (* *his servants*) וְאֶת his cattle in the field.

(22) וַיֹּאמֶר יהוה אֶל-מֹשֶׁה (*And YHVH said to Moses*):

נְטֵה אֶת-יָדְךָ עַל-הַשָּׁמַיִם

וִיהִי בָרָד

בְּכָל-אֶרֶץ מִצְרָיִם

עַל-הָאָדָם וְעַל-הַבְּהֵמָה

וְעַל כָּל-עֵשֶׂב הַשָּׂדֶה

בְּאֶרֶץ מִצְרָיִם

*Stretch forth * your hand to the sky*

and there shall be hail

in all the land of Egypt

on the man and on the animal

and on all herbage of the field

in the land of Egypt

(23) And מֹשֶׁה stretched forth אֶת-מַטֵּהוּ (* *his staff*) עַל הַשָּׁמַיִם (*to the sky*) and יהוה gave קֹלֹת (*voices*) וּבָרָד (*and hail*) וַתִּהֲלַךְ אֵשׁ (*and fire went*) אַרְצָה (*towards the land*); and יהוה caused it to rain בָּרָד (*hail*) עַל-אֶרֶץ מִצְרָיִם (*on the land of Egypt*).

(24) And it was בָּרָד (*hail*) וְאֵשׁ (*and fire*) flashing in the midst of הַבָּרָד (*the*

71

Exodus ~ 9

hail) very heavy, such as had not been בְּכָל-אֶרֶץ מִצְרַיִם *(in all the land of Egypt)* since it became a nation.

(25) And הַבָּרָד *(the hail)* smote בְּכָל-אֶרֶץ מִצְרַיִם *(in all the land of Egypt)* אֵת כָּל *(* all)* that was in the field מֵאָדָם *(from human)* וְעַד בְּהֵמָה *(and as far as animal)* הַבָּרָד *(the hail)* smote וְאֵת כָּל *(and * every)* herb of the field וְאֶת-כָּל *(and * every)* tree of the field, it broke.

(26) Only בְּאֶרֶץ גֹּשֶׁן *(in the land of Goshen)* where בְּנֵי יִשְׂרָאֵל *(the children of Israel)* were there was no בָּרָד *(hail)*.

(27) וַיִּשְׁלַח פַּרְעֹה *(And Pharaoh sent)* וַיִּקְרָא לְמֹשֶׁה וּלְאַהֲרֹן *(and called for Moses and for Aaron)* וַיֹּאמֶר *(and he said)* אֲלֵהֶם *(to them):*

"I have sinned this time יהוה is righteous וַאֲנִי *(and I)* וְעַמִּי *(and my people)* are wicked."

(28)

"Entreat יהוה and let there be enough of these קֹלֹת אֱלֹהִים *(voices of Elohim)* וּבָרָד *(and hail)* וַאֲשַׁלְּחָה *(and I will send)* אֶתְכֶם and you shall stay no longer."

(29) וַיֹּאמֶר מֹשֶׁה *(And Moses said)* אֵלָיו *(to him):*

"As soon as I am gone out of אֶת הָעִיר *(* the city)*, I will spread forth אֶת כַּפַּי אֶל יהוה *(* my palms to YHVH)* הַקֹּלוֹת *(the voices)* shall cease וְהַבָּרָד *(and the hail)* will not be continuing; that you may know that לַיהוה הָאָרֶץ *(the land is for YHVH).*"

(30)

וְאַתָּה וַעֲבָדֶיךָ *(And * you and your servants)* I know that you will not yet fear מִפְּנֵי יהוה אֱלֹהִים *(from the face of YHVH Elohim)*."

Level Two ~ שְׁמוֹת ~ ט

(31) And the flax and the barley were smitten; for the barley was pollinated, and the flax was in pod.

(32) But the wheat and the spelt were not smitten; for they were in blade.

(33) And מֹשֶׁה went forth מֵעִם פַּרְעֹה (from with Pharaoh) אֶת-הָעִיר (* the city) and spread כַּפָּיו (his palms) אֶל-יהוה and הַקֹּלוֹת (the voices) וְהַבָּרָד (and the hail) they ceased, and וּמָטָר (the rain) was not poured אָרְצָה (landward).

(34) וַיַּרְא פַּרְעֹה (And Pharaoh saw) that הַמָּטָר (the rain) וְהַבָּרָד (and the hail) וְהַקֹּלֹת (and the voices) ceased, he sinned yet more, and hardened לִבּוֹ (his heart) הוּא (he) וַעֲבָדָיו (and his servants).

(35) And לֵב פַּרְעֹה (the heart of Pharaoh) was hardened וְלֹא שִׁלַּח (and he did not send) אֶת-בְּנֵי יִשְׂרָאֵל (* the children of Israel) as דִּבֶּר יהוה (YHVH had spoken) בְּיַד מֹשֶׁה (in the hand of Moses).

Chapter Ten

Locust, Locust, Locust!

(1) וַיֹּאמֶר יהוה אֶל־מֹשֶׁה (*And YHVH said to Moses*):

בֹּא אֶל־פַּרְעֹה

כִּי־אֲנִי הִכְבַּדְתִּי אֶת־לִבּוֹ

וְאֶת־לֵב עֲבָדָיו

לְמַעַן שִׁתִי אֹתֹתַי אֵלֶּה

בְּקִרְבּוֹ

Go to Pharaoh

*for I have hardened * his heart*

*and * the heart of his servants*

so that I set these My signs

in the midst of him

(2)

וּלְמַעַן תְּסַפֵּר

אָזְנֵי בִנְךָ וּבֶן־בִּנְךָ

and that you may relate

in the ears of your son and of your son's son

אֵת אֲשֶׁר הִתְעַלַּלְתִּי בְּמִצְרַיִם

וְאֶת־אֹתֹתַי אֲשֶׁר־שַׂמְתִּי בָם

וִידַעְתֶּם כִּי־אֲנִי יהוה

Level Two שְׁמוֹת ~ י

* what I set in action in Egypt
and * My signs that I have placed on them
that you may know that I am YHVH

(3) And מֹשֶׁה וְאַהֲרֹן entered in אֶל-פַּרְעֹה (to Pharaoh) וַיֹּאמְרוּ (and they said) אֵלָיו (to him):

אֱלֹהֵי הָעִבְרִים (Thus says YHVH) כֹּה-אָמַר יהוה

עַד-מָתַי מֵאַנְתָּ
לֵעָנֹת מִפָּנָי
שַׁלַּח עַמִּי
וְיַעַבְדֻנִי

How long will you refuse
to be humbled from My face?
Send My people
and they shall serve Me

(4)

כִּי אִם-מָאֵן אַתָּה
לְשַׁלֵּחַ אֶת-עַמִּי
הִנְנִי מֵבִיא מָחָר אַרְבֶּה
בִּגְבֻלֶךָ

because if * you refuse
to send * My people
behold tomorrow will I bring locust
in your border

Exodus ~ 10

(5)

וְכִסָּה אֶת־עֵין הָאָרֶץ

וְלֹא יוּכַל לִרְאֹת אֶת־הָאָרֶץ

וְאָכַל אֶת־יֶתֶר הַפְּלֵטָה

הַנִּשְׁאֶרֶת לָכֶם מִן־הַבָּרָד

וְאָכַל אֶת־כָּל־הָעֵץ

הַצֹּמֵחַ לָכֶם מִן־הַשָּׂדֶה

and he shall cover * the eye of the land
and he shall not be able to see * the land
and he shall eat * the residue of what escaped
the remaining for you from the hail
and he shall eat * every tree
the one sprouting for you from the field

(6)

וּמָלְאוּ בָתֶּיךָ

וּבָתֵּי כָל־עֲבָדֶיךָ

וּבָתֵּי כָל־מִצְרַיִם

אֲשֶׁר לֹא־רָאוּ אֲבֹתֶיךָ

and your houses shall be filled
and the houses of all your servants
and the houses of all Egypt
which neither your fathers saw

Level Two שְׁמוֹת ~ י

וַאֲבוֹת אֲבֹתֶיךָ

מִיּוֹם הֱיוֹתָם עַל-הָאֲדָמָה

עַד הַיּוֹם הַזֶּה

and the fathers of your fathers

from the day that they were on the ground

to this day.

And he turned, and went forth מֵעִם פַּרְעֹה (from with Pharaoh).

(7) וַיֹּאמְרוּ עַבְדֵי פַרְעֹה (And the servants of Pharaoh said) אֵלָיו (to him):

"How long shall this be a snare לָנוּ (to us)? שַׁלַּח (Send) אֶת- אֶת יהוה אֱלֹהֵיהֶם and they shall serve (* the men) הָאֲנָשִׁים Do you not yet know that מִצְרָיִם is destroyed?"

(8) And וַיֹּאמֶר again אֶל-פַּרְעֹה were brought אֶת-מֹשֶׁה וְאֶת-אַהֲרֹן (and he said) אֲלֵהֶם (to them):

לְכוּ (Go) serve אֶת-יהוה אֱלֹהֵיכֶם but who are הַהֹלְכִים (the ones going)?"

(9) וַיֹּאמֶר מֹשֶׁה (And Moses said):

נֵלֵךְ (We will go) with our young and with our old בִּבְנֵינוּ (with our sons) וּבִבְנוֹתֵנוּ (and with our daughters) with our flocks and with our herds נֵלֵךְ (we will go) לָנוּ (for we) must hold a feast to יהוה

(10) וַיֹּאמֶר (And he said) אֲלֵהֶם (to them):

"So יהוה be עִמָּכֶם (with you) as which אֲשַׁלַּח (I will send) אֶתְכֶם

Exodus ~ 10

וְאֶת your little ones רְאוּ (See) that evil is in front of פְּנֵיכֶם (your faces)."

(11)

"Not so לְכוּ (you go) now that are mighty men וְעִבְדוּ (and serve) אֶת-יהוה for אֹתָהּ (* it is) אַתֶּם desire."

And he drove אֹתָם out מֵאֵת פְּנֵי פַרְעֹה (from * the face of Pharaoh).

(12) וַיֹּאמֶר יהוה אֶל-מֹשֶׁה (And YHVH said to Moses):

נְטֵה יָדְךָ
עַל-אֶרֶץ מִצְרַיִם בָּאַרְבֶּה
וְיַעַל עַל-אֶרֶץ מִצְרָיִם
וְיֹאכַל אֶת-כָּל-עֵשֶׂב הָאָרֶץ
אֵת כָּל-אֲשֶׁר הִשְׁאִיר הַבָּרָד

Stretch out your hand
over the land of Egypt on the locust
and he shall ascend on the land of Egypt
and he shall eat * every herb of the land
* all that was left by the hail

(13) And מֹשֶׁה stretched forth אֶת-מַטֵּהוּ (* his staff) עַל אֶרֶץ מִצְרַיִם (over the land of Egypt) וַיהוה brought רוּחַ קָדִים (an east wind) בָּאָרֶץ (on the land) כָּל (all) that day וְכָל (and all) the night; and when it was morning וְרוּחַ הַקָּדִים (and the east wind) brought אֶת-הָאַרְבֶּה (* the locust).

78

Level Two   שְׁמוֹת ~ י

(14) And הָאַרְבֶּה (*the locust*) ascended עַל כָּל-אֶרֶץ מִצְרַיִם (*on all the land of Egypt*) and rested בְּכֹל (*in all*) the borders of מִצְרַיִם very grievous לְפָנָיו (*before him*) there were no such אַרְבֶּה (*locust*) like him neither after him shall be such.

(15) וַיְכַס (*And he covered*) אֶת-עֵין (** the eye of*) כָּל-הָאָרֶץ (*the whole land*) and הָאָרֶץ (*the land*) was darkened וַיֹּאכַל (*and he ate*) אֵת כָּל (** every*) herb of הָאָרֶץ (*the land*) וְאֵת כָּל (** all*) the fruit of the tree which הַבָּרָד (*the hail*) had left; and there remained none of כָּל (*all*) green either tree or herb of the field בְּכָל אֶרֶץ מִצְרָיִם (*in all the land of Egypt*).

(16) And פַּרְעֹה hastened לִקְרֹא (*to call*) לְמֹשֶׁה וּלְאַהֲרֹן (*for Moses and for Aaron*) וַיֹּאמֶר (*and he said*):

"I have sinned לַיהוה אֱלֹהֵיכֶם (*to YHVH your Elohim*) וְלָכֶם (*and to you*)."

(17)

"Now therefore forgive, I pray you, my sin only this once, and entreat לַיהוה אֱלֹהֵיכֶם that He may take away מֵעָלַי (*from on me*) this אֶת death only."

(18) And he went forth מֵעִם פַּרְעֹה (*from with Pharaoh*) and entreated אֶל- יהוה

(19) And יהוה turned an exceeding strong רוּחַ-יָם (*sea spirit/wind*) and He carried away אֶת-הָאַרְבֶּה (** the locust*) and He blew him יָמָּה סוּף (*towards the Red Sea*) there did not remain one אַרְבֶּה (*locust*) בְּכֹל (*in all*) the border of מִצְרָיִם

(20) But יהוה hardened אֶת-לֵב פַּרְעֹה (** the heart of Pharaoh*) וְלֹא שִׁלַּח (*and he did not send*) אֶת בְּנֵי יִשְׂרָאֵל (** the children of Israel*).

Exodus ~ 10

Darkness, Darkness, Darkness!

(21) וַיֹּאמֶר יהוה אֶל-מֹשֶׁה (*And YHVH said to Moses*):

נְטֵה יָדְךָ עַל-הַשָּׁמַיִם

וִיהִי חֹשֶׁךְ

עַל-אֶרֶץ מִצְרָיִם

וְיָמֵשׁ חֹשֶׁךְ

Stretch out your hand to the sky

and darkness will be

over the land of Egypt

even darkness which may be felt.

(22) And מֹשֶׁה stretched forth אֶת-יָדוֹ (* *his hand*) עַל הַשָּׁמַיִם (*to the sky*) and there was a thick חֹשֶׁךְ-אֲפֵלָה (*gloomy darkness*) בְּכָל-אֶרֶץ מִצְרַיִם (*in all the land of Egypt*) three days.

(23) לֹא-רָאוּ (*They did not see*) אִישׁ (*a man*) אֶת אָחִיו (* *his brother*) neither rose אִישׁ (*a man*) from his place for three days וּלְכָל-בְּנֵי יִשְׂרָאֵל (*and for all the children of Israel*) light was in their dwellings.

(24) וַיִּקְרָא פַרְעֹה (*And Pharaoh called*) אֶל מֹשֶׁה וַיֹּאמֶר (*and he said*):

לְכוּ (*You go*) עִבְדוּ (*serve*) אֶת-יהוה only let your flocks and your herds stay put גַּם (*also*) your little one יֵלֵךְ (*he shall go*) עִמָּכֶם (*with you*)."

(25) וַיֹּאמֶר מֹשֶׁה (*And Moses said*):

גַּם (*also*) אַתָּה must give בְּיָדֵנוּ (*in our hand*) sacrifices and burnt-

Level Two   שְׁמוֹת ~ י

    offerings, that we may sacrifice to יהוה אֱלֹהֵינוּ

(26)

    וְגַם *(And also) our cattle* יֵלֵךְ *(he shall go)* עִמָּנוּ *(with us). There shall not a hoof be left behind; for we must take from it* אֶת לַעֲבֹד יהוה אֱלֹהֵינוּ *(to serve * YHVH our Elohim) and we do not know* מַה-נַּעֲבֹד *(what we shall serve)* אֶת-יהוה *until we come to there."*

(27) *And* יהוה *hardened* אֶת-לֵב פַּרְעֹה *(* the heart of Pharaoh) and he would not comply* לְשַׁלְּחָם *(to send them).*

(28) וַיֹּאמֶר-לוֹ פַרְעֹה *(And Pharaoh said to him):*

    לֵךְ *(Go)* מֵעָלָי *(from on me)* הִשָּׁמֶר *(guard yourself)* לְךָ *(for you) must not* רְאוֹת *(be seeing)* פָּנַי *(my face) no more; for in the day of* רְאֹתְךָ *(your seeing)* פָנַי *(my face) you shall die."*

(29) וַיֹּאמֶר מֹשֶׁה *(And Moses said):*

    "So דִּבַּרְתָּ *(You have spoken); I will no more* רְאוֹת *(be seeing)* פָּנֶיךָ *(your face)."*

Chapter Eleven

Death, Death, Death!

(1) וַיֹּאמֶר יהוה אֶל־מֹשֶׁה (And YHVH said to Moses):

> עוֹד נֶגַע אֶחָד
> אָבִיא עַל־פַּרְעֹה וְעַל־מִצְרַיִם
> אַחֲרֵי־כֵן יְשַׁלַּח אֶתְכֶם מִזֶּה כְּשַׁלְּחוֹ
> כָּלָה גָּרֵשׁ יְגָרֵשׁ אֶתְכֶם מִזֶּה

> *Yet one more plague*
> *will I bring on Pharaoh and on Egypt*
> *afterwards he will send * you from here as to his sending*
> *altogether he shall surely drive * you from here*

(2)

> דַּבֶּר־נָא בְּאָזְנֵי הָעָם
> וְיִשְׁאֲלוּ אִישׁ מֵאֵת רֵעֵהוּ
> וְאִשָּׁה מֵאֵת רְעוּתָהּ
> כְּלֵי־כֶסֶף וּכְלֵי זָהָב

> *Speak now in the ears of the people*
> *and they shall ask a man from * his neighbor*
> *and a woman from * her neighbor*
> *implements of silver and implements of gold.*

(3) And יהוה gave הָעָם (the people) אֶת favor בְּעֵינֵי מִצְרָיִם (in the eyes of Egypt) גַּם הָאִישׁ (also the man) מֹשֶׁה was very great בְּאֶרֶץ מִצְרַיִם (in the land

Level Two שְׁמוֹת ~ יא

of Egypt) בְּעֵינֵי עַבְדֵי פַרְעֹה (*in the eyes of the servants of Pharaoh*) וּבְעֵינֵי הָעָם (*and in the eyes of the people*).

(4) וַיֹּאמֶר מֹשֶׁה (*And Moses said*):

"Thus אָמַר יהוה (*says YHVH*)

כַּחֲצֹת הַלַּיְלָה

אֲנִי יוֹצֵא בְּתוֹךְ מִצְרָיִם

About midnight

will I go out in the midst of Egypt

(5)

וּמֵת כָּל־בְּכוֹר בְּאֶרֶץ מִצְרַיִם

מִבְּכוֹר פַּרְעֹה

הַיֹּשֵׁב עַל־כִּסְאוֹ

and every firstborn dies in the land of Egypt

from the firstborn of Pharaoh

the one sitting on his throne

עַד בְּכוֹר הַשִּׁפְחָה

אֲשֶׁר אַחַר הָרֵחָיִם

וְכֹל בְּכוֹר בְּהֵמָה

unto the firstborn of the maid

who is behind the millstones

and every firstborn of animal

(6)

וְהָיְתָה צְעָקָה גְדֹלָה
בְּכָל־אֶרֶץ מִצְרָיִם
אֲשֶׁר כָּמֹהוּ לֹא נִהְיָתָה
וְכָמֹהוּ לֹא תֹסִף

and there shall be a great cry
in all the land of Egypt
such as there has been none like it
nor shall be like it any more

(7)

וּלְכֹל בְּנֵי יִשְׂרָאֵל
לֹא יֶחֱרַץ־כֶּלֶב לְשֹׁנוֹ
לְמֵאִישׁ וְעַד־בְּהֵמָה

and for all the children of Israel
a dog shall not sharpen his tongue
against man or animal

לְמַעַן תֵּדְעוּן
אֲשֶׁר יַפְלֶה יהוה
בֵּין מִצְרַיִם וּבֵין יִשְׂרָאֵל

so that you may know
that YHVH is distinguishing
between Egypt and between Israel

Level Two   שְׁמוֹת ~ יא

(8)

וְיָרְדוּ כָל־עֲבָדֶיךָ אֵלֶּה אֵלַי

וְהִשְׁתַּחֲווּ־לִי לֵאמֹר

צֵא אַתָּה וְכָל־הָעָם

אֲשֶׁר־בְּרַגְלֶיךָ

וְאַחֲרֵי־כֵן אֵצֵא

And all these your servants shall descend to Me

and bow down to Me saying:

Go forth * you and all the people

who are at your feet/who follow you

and after that I will go forth.

And he went out מֵעִם־פַּרְעֹה (*from with Pharaoh*) in hot anger.

(9) וַיֹּאמֶר יהוה אֶל־מֹשֶׁה (*And YHVH said to Moses*):

לֹא־יִשְׁמַע אֲלֵיכֶם פַּרְעֹה

לְמַעַן רְבוֹת מוֹפְתַי

בְּאֶרֶץ מִצְרָיִם

Pharaoh will not listen to you

so that My wonders may be multiplied

in the land of Egypt.

(10) וּמֹשֶׁה וְאַהֲרֹן did אֶת־כָּל (* *all*) these wonders לִפְנֵי פַרְעֹה (*before Pharaoh*) and יהוה hardened אֶת לֵב פַּרְעֹה (* *the heart of Pharaoh*) וְלֹא־שִׁלַּח (*and he did not send*) אֶת בְּנֵי־יִשְׂרָאֵל (* *the children of Israel*) מֵאַרְצוֹ (*from his land*).

Chapter Twelve

First Of The Year

(1) וַיֹּאמֶר יהוה אֶל-מֹשֶׁה וְאֶל-אַהֲרֹן (*And YHVH said to Moses and to Aaron*) בְּאֶרֶץ מִצְרַיִם (*in the land of Egypt*) לֵאמֹר (*saying*):

(2)

הַחֹדֶשׁ הַזֶּה לָכֶם

רֹאשׁ חֳדָשִׁים

רִאשׁוֹן הוּא לָכֶם

לְחָדְשֵׁי הַשָּׁנָה

This month shall be to you

the beginning of months

it shall be the first for you

for months of the year

The Passover

(3)

דַּבְּרוּ אֶל-כָּל-עֲדַת יִשְׂרָאֵל לֵאמֹר

בֶּעָשֹׂר לַחֹדֶשׁ הַזֶּה

וְיִקְחוּ לָהֶם אִישׁ שֶׂה

לְבֵית-אָבֹת שֶׂה לַבָּיִת

Speak to all the congregation of Israel saying

On the tenth of this month

they shall take to them - a man a flockling

for the house of fathers, a flockling for a house

Level Two — שְׁמוֹת ~ יב

(4)

וְאִם־יִמְעַט הַבַּיִת

מִהְיוֹת מִשֶּׂה

וְלָקַח הוּא

וּשְׁכֵנוֹ הַקָּרֹב אֶל־בֵּיתוֹ

and if the house few

from being from a flockling

and he shall take

and his neighbor next to his house

בְּמִכְסַת נְפָשֹׁת

אִישׁ לְפִי אָכְלוֹ

תָּכֹסּוּ עַל־הַשֶּׂה

in accordance of souls

a man for a mouth of his eating

you shall assess on the flockling

(5)

שֶׂה תָמִים זָכָר

בֶּן־שָׁנָה יִהְיֶה לָכֶם

מִן־הַכְּבָשִׂים וּמִן־הָעִזִּים תִּקָּחוּ

a flawless male

son of a year he shall be for you

from the lambs and from the goatsyou shall take

(6)

וְהָיָה לָכֶם לְמִשְׁמֶרֶת

עַד אַרְבָּעָה עָשָׂר יוֹם

לַחֹדֶשׁ הַזֶּה

וְשָׁחֲטוּ אֹתוֹ

כֹּל קְהַל עֲדַת־יִשְׂרָאֵל

בֵּין הָעַרְבָּיִם

and he is for you for guarding

until the fourteenth day

for this month

and they shall slay * him

all the assembly of the congregation of Israel

between the evenings

(7)

וְלָקְחוּ מִן־הַדָּם

וְנָתְנוּ עַל־שְׁתֵּי הַמְּזוּזֹת

וְעַל־הַמַּשְׁקוֹף עַל הַבָּתִּים

אֲשֶׁר־יֹאכְלוּ אֹתוֹ בָּהֶם

And they shall take from the blood

and put it on two of the doorposts

and on the lintel, on the houses

wherein they are eating * him

Level Two   שְׁמוֹת ~ יב

(8)

וְאָכְלוּ אֶת־הַבָּשָׂר בַּלַּיְלָה הַזֶּה
צְלִי־אֵשׁ וּמַצּוֹת
עַל־מְרֹרִים יֹאכְלֻהוּ

and they shall eat * the flesh on this night
roasted with fire and unleavened bread
with bitter herbs they shall eat him

(9)

אַל־תֹּאכְלוּ מִמֶּנּוּ נָא
וּבָשֵׁל מְבֻשָּׁל בַּמָּיִם
כִּי אִם־צְלִי־אֵשׁ
רֹאשׁוֹ עַל־כְּרָעָיו
וְעַל־קִרְבּוֹ

you must not eat not from him uncooked
and cooked at all in water
but rather roasted with fire
its head with its legs
and with the inwards

(10)

וְלֹא־תוֹתִירוּ מִמֶּנּוּ
עַד־בֹּקֶר

and you shall not reserve from him
until the morning

89

Exodus ~ 12

וְהַנֹּתָר מִמֶּנּוּ עַד־בֹּקֶר
בָּאֵשׁ תִּשְׂרֹפוּ

and the leftovers from him until the morning
you shall burn in the fire

(11)

וְכָכָה תֹּאכְלוּ אֹתוֹ
מָתְנֵיכֶם חֲגֻרִים
נַעֲלֵיכֶם בְּרַגְלֵיכֶם
וּמַקֶּלְכֶם בְּיֶדְכֶם
וַאֲכַלְתֶּם אֹתוֹ בְּחִפָּזוֹן
פֶּסַח הוּא לַיהוה

and as thus you shall eat * him
your waist being girded
your shoes on your feet
and your staff in your hand
and you shall eat * him in haste
it is a Passover to YHVH

(12)

וְעָבַרְתִּי בְאֶרֶץ־מִצְרַיִם
בַּלַּיְלָה הַזֶּה
וְהִכֵּיתִי כָל־בְּכוֹר בְּאֶרֶץ מִצְרַיִם
מֵאָדָם וְעַד־בְּהֵמָה

Level Two

שְׁמוֹת ~ יב

for I will pass in the land of Egypt
on this night
and I will strike every firstborn in the land of Egypt
from man and unto animal

וּבְכָל־אֱלֹהֵי מִצְרַיִם
אֶעֱשֶׂה שְׁפָטִים
אֲנִי יהוה

and on all the elohim of Egypt
I will execute judgments:
I am YHVH

(13)

וְהָיָה הַדָּם לָכֶם לְאֹת
עַל הַבָּתִּים אֲשֶׁר אַתֶּם שָׁם
וְרָאִיתִי אֶת־הַדָּם

and the blood shall be for you for a sign
on the houses that * you are there
and I will see * the blood

וּפָסַחְתִּי עֲלֵכֶם
וְלֹא־יִהְיֶה בָכֶם

I will pass over on you
and there shall not be on you

Exodus ~ 12

נֶגֶף לְמַשְׁחִית

בְּהַכֹּתִי בְּאֶרֶץ מִצְרָיִם

a destructive plague

in My striking in the land of Egypt

(14)

וְהָיָה הַיּוֹם הַזֶּה

לָכֶם לְזִכָּרוֹן

וְחַגֹּתֶם אֹתוֹ חַג לַיהוה

and this day shall be

to you for a memorial

*and you shall celebrate * it a feast to YHVH*

לְדֹרֹתֵיכֶם

חֻקַּת עוֹלָם

תְּחָגֻּהוּ

for your generations

a statute forever

you shall celebrate it

Unleavened Bread

(15)

שִׁבְעַת יָמִים

מַצּוֹת תֹּאכֵלוּ

אַךְ בַּיּוֹם הָרִאשׁוֹן

Level Two ~ שְׁמוֹת ~ יב

seven days
you shall eat unleavened bread
yea, in the first day

תַּשְׁבִּיתוּ שְּׂאֹר מִבָּתֵּיכֶם
כִּי כָּל־אֹכֵל חָמֵץ
וְנִכְרְתָה הַנֶּפֶשׁ הַהִוא
מִיִּשְׂרָאֵל מִיּוֹם הָרִאשֹׁן
עַד־יוֹם הַשְּׁבִעִי

you shall eradicate leaven from your houses
because anyone eating leaven
and that soul shall be cut off
from Israel from the first day
until the seventh day

(16)

וּבַיּוֹם הָרִאשׁוֹן
מִקְרָא־קֹדֶשׁ
וּבַיּוֹם הַשְּׁבִיעִי
מִקְרָא־קֹדֶשׁ יִהְיֶה לָכֶם

and on the first day
a holy meeting
and on the seventh day
a holy meeting shall be for you

כָּל-מְלָאכָה לֹא-יֵעָשֶׂה בָהֶם
אַךְ אֲשֶׁר יֵאָכֵל לְכָל-נֶפֶשׁ
הוּא לְבַדּוֹ יֵעָשֶׂה לָכֶם

all work shall not be done in them
but which for every soul he eats
it only may be done for you

(17)

וּשְׁמַרְתֶּם אֶת-הַמַּצּוֹת
כִּי בְּעֶצֶם הַיּוֹם הַזֶּה
הוֹצֵאתִי אֶת-צִבְאוֹתֵיכֶם
מֵאֶרֶץ מִצְרָיִם

*and you shall keep * the unleavened*
because on this very day
*I brought forth * your armies*
from the land of Egypt

וּשְׁמַרְתֶּם אֶת-הַיּוֹם הַזֶּה
לְדֹרֹתֵיכֶם
חֻקַּת עוֹלָם

*and you shall keep this * day*
for your generations
a statute forever

Level Two   שְׁמוֹת ~ יב

(18)

בָּרִאשֹׁן

בְּאַרְבָּעָה עָשָׂר יוֹם לַחֹדֶשׁ

בָּעֶרֶב

תֹּאכְלוּ מַצֹּת

עַד יוֹם הָאֶחָד וְעֶשְׂרִים לַחֹדֶשׁ

בָּעָרֶב

in the first

on the fourteenth day to the month

in the evening

you shall eat unleavened breads

until the one and twentieth day to the month

in the evening

(19)

שִׁבְעַת יָמִים

שְׂאֹר לֹא יִמָּצֵא בְּבָתֵּיכֶם

כִּי כָּל־אֹכֵל מַחְמֶצֶת

וְנִכְרְתָה הַנֶּפֶשׁ הַהִוא

seven days

leaven shall not be found in your houses

because anyone eating leaven

and that soul shall be cut off

Exodus ~ 12

מֵעֲדַת יִשְׂרָאֵל

בַּגֵּר וּבְאֶזְרַח הָאָרֶץ

from the congregation of Israel

in the sojourner and in the native of the land

(20)

כָּל־מַחְמֶצֶת

לֹא תֹאכֵלוּ

בְּכֹל מוֹשְׁבֹתֵיכֶם

תֹּאכְלוּ מַצּוֹת

any of leavened

you shall not eat

in all your dwellings

shall you eat unleavened breads.

Moses Speaks Of Passover

(21) וַיִּקְרָא מֹשֶׁה (And Moses called) לְכָל (for all) the elders of יִשְׂרָאֵל (Israel) וַיֹּאמֶר (and he said) אֲלֵהֶם (to them):

"Draw out, and take לָכֶם (for yourselves) flock לְמִשְׁפְּחֹתֵיכֶם (for your families) and slay the passover."

(22)

"And you shall take a bunch of hyssop, and dip it בַּדָּם (in the blood) that is in the basin, and strike the lintel and two of the doorposts

Level Two   שְׁמוֹת ~ יב

מִן-הַדָּם (from the blood) that is in the basin; and * you shall not go forth אִישׁ (a man) from the door of בֵּיתוֹ (his house) until morning."

(23) "For יהוה will pass through to strike אֶת מִצְרַיִם (* Egypt) וְרָאָה (and He will see) אֶת-הַדָּם (* the blood) עַל (on) the lintel וְעַל (and on) two of the doorposts יהוה will pass עַל (over) the door, and He will not allow the destroyer to enter אֶל-בָּתֵּיכֶם (in your houses) to strike."

(24) וּשְׁמַרְתֶּם (And you shall keep) אֶת הַדָּבָר הַזֶּה (this * thing) for a statute לְךָ (for you) וּלְבָנֶיךָ (and for your sons) forever."

(25) "And it shall be, when you come אֶל-הָאָרֶץ (to the land) which יהוה will give לָכֶם (to you) as which דִּבֵּר (He spoke) וּשְׁמַרְתֶּם (and you shall keep) אֶת-הָעֲבֹדָה הַזֹּאת (this * service)."

(26) "And it shall be that יֹאמְרוּ אֲלֵיכֶם בְּנֵיכֶם (your children say to you):

'What is הָעֲבֹדָה הַזֹּאת (this work) לָכֶם (to you)?'

(27) וַאֲמַרְתֶּם (And you shall say):

'It is the sacrifice of passover לַיהוה Who passed over עַל בָּתֵּי (on the houses of) בְּנֵי יִשְׂרָאֵל (the children of Israel) בְּמִצְרַיִם (in Egypt) in His striking אֶת מִצְרַיִם and delivered וְאֶת בָּתֵּינוּ (and * our houses).'"

Exodus ~ 12

And הָעָם (the people) bowed the head and bowed themselves down.

(28) וַיֵּלְכוּ (And they went) בְּנֵי יִשְׂרָאֵל (the children of Israel) and did so; as יהוה had instructed אֶת מֹשֶׁה וְאַהֲרֹן so did they.

Death Of The Firstborn

(29) And it was at midnight וַיהוה smote כָּל-בְּכוֹר (all the firstborn) בְּאֶרֶץ מִצְרַיִם (in the land of Egypt) מִבְּכֹר פַּרְעֹה (from the firstborn of Pharaoh) that sat עַל (on) his throne to בְּכוֹר (the firstborn) of the captive that was בְּבֵית (in the house) the pit וְכֹל בְּכוֹר בְּהֵמָה (and all the firstborn of animal).

Pharaoh Releases Israel

(30) And פַּרְעֹה rose up in the night הוּא (he) וְכָל-עֲבָדָיו (and all his servants) וְכָל-מִצְרַיִם (and all Egypt) and there was a great cry בְּמִצְרָיִם for there was not בַּיִת (a house) where there was not one dead.

(31) וַיִּקְרָא (And he called) לְמֹשֶׁה וּלְאַהֲרֹן by night וַיֹּאמֶר (and he said):

"Rise up, go forth from the midst of עַמִּי (my people) גַּם-אַתֶּם (also * you) גַּם בְּנֵי יִשְׂרָאֵל (also the children of Israel) וּלְכוּ (and you go) עִבְדוּ (serve) אֶת יהוה (* YHVH) כְּדַבֶּרְכֶם (as you have said)."

(32)

"Take גַּם (also) your flocks גַּם (also) your herds דִּבַּרְתֶּם (as you have said) וָלֵכוּ (and go) and bless אֹתִי-גַם (also * me)."

(33) And מִצְרַיִם was urgent עַל-הָעָם (on the people) לְשַׁלְּחָם (to send them) מִן-הָאָרֶץ (from the land) in haste for אָמְרוּ (they said):

Level Two

שְׁמוֹת ~ יב

כֻּלָּנוּ (All of us) are dying."

(34) And הָעָם (the people) took אֵת their dough before it was leavened, their kneading-troughs being bound up in their clothes עַל (on) their shoulders.

(35) וּבְנֵי-יִשְׂרָאֵל (And the children of Israel) did כִּדְבַר מֹשֶׁה (as the word of Moses) and מִמִּצְרַיִם they asked כְּלֵי-כֶסֶף (implements of silver) וּכְלֵי זָהָב (and implements of gold), and raiment.

(36) וַיהוה gave הָעָם (the people) אֵת favor בְּעֵינֵי מִצְרַיִם (in the sight of Egypt) so that they let them have what they asked. And they despoiled אֶת-מִצְרָיִם.

(37) And בְּנֵי-יִשְׂרָאֵל (the children of Israel) journeyed מֵרַעְמְסֵס (from Rameses) סֻכֹּתָה (towards Succoth) about six hundred thousand, the mighty footmen, beside little ones.

(38) וְגַם (And also) a mixed multitude went up also אִתָּם and flocks, and herds, even very much cattle.

(39) And they baked מַצּוֹת (unleavened) cakes of אֵת the dough which they brought forth מִמִּצְרַיִם for it was not leavened; because they were thrust out מִמִּצְרַיִם and could not tarry וְגַם (and also) they had not prepared provision לָהֶם (for themselves).

(40) Now the time that בְּנֵי יִשְׂרָאֵל (the children of Israel) dwelt בְּמִצְרַיִם was four hundred and thirty years.

(41) And it was at the end of four hundred and thirty years, it was in this very day, that כָּל (all) the host of יהוה went forth מֵאֶרֶץ מִצְרָיִם (from the land of Egypt).

(42) הוּא (It) was a night of observances לַיהוה to bring them forth מֵאֶרֶץ מִצְרַיִם (from the land of Egypt) הוּא (it) is this night לַיהוה observances לְכָל-בְּנֵי יִשְׂרָאֵל (for all the children of Israel) לְדֹרֹתָם (for their generations).

99

Exodus ~ 12

Passover Protocol

(43) וַיֹּאמֶר יהוה אֶל-מֹשֶׁה וְאַהֲרֹן (And YHVH said to Moses and Aaron):

זֹאת חֻקַּת הַפָּסַח

כָּל-בֶּן-נֵכָר לֹא-יֹאכַל בּוֹ

This is the statute of the Passover

every son of a foreigner shall not eat on it

(44)

וְכָל-עֶבֶד אִישׁ

מִקְנַת-כָּסֶף

וּמַלְתָּה אֹתוֹ

אָז יֹאכַל בּוֹ

and every sevant of a man

acquired by money

and you circumcised * him

then he shall eat on it

(45)

תּוֹשָׁב וְשָׂכִיר לֹא-יֹאכַל בּוֹ

a sojourner and a hired servant shall not eat on it

(46)

בְּבַיִת אֶחָד יֵאָכֵל

לֹא-תוֹצִיא מִן-הַבַּיִת

מִן-הַבָּשָׂר חוּצָה

וְעֶצֶם לֹא תִשְׁבְּרוּ-בוֹ

Level Two שְׁמוֹת ~ יב

in one house, it shall be eaten
you shall not bring forth from the house
from the flesh towards the outside
neither shall you break a bone on it

(47)

כָּל־עֲדַת יִשְׂרָאֵל
יַעֲשׂוּ אֹתוֹ

all the congregation of Israel
shall do * it

(48)

וְכִי־יָגוּר אִתְּךָ גֵּר
וְעָשָׂה פֶסַח לַיהוה
הִמּוֹל לוֹ כָל־זָכָר

and stranger that is sojourning with * you
and he does Passover to YHVH
let all his males be circumcised

וְאָז יִקְרַב לַעֲשֹׂתוֹ
וְהָיָה כְּאֶזְרַח הָאָרֶץ
וְכָל־עָרֵל לֹא־יֹאכַל בּוֹ

and then he shall draw near and do it
and he shall be as the native of the land
and every uncircumcised person shall not eat on it

(49)

תּוֹרָה אַחַת
יִהְיֶה לָאֶזְרָח וְלַגֵּר
הַגָּר בְּתוֹכְכֶם

one law

shall be to the native and to the sojourner

the on sojourning in your midst.

(50) וַיַּעֲשׂוּ כָּל-בְּנֵי יִשְׂרָאֵל (*And all the children of Israel did*) as יהוה commanded אֶת-מֹשֶׁה וְאֶת-אַהֲרֹן so did they.

(51) And it was on this very day that יהוה brought forth אֶת בְּנֵי יִשְׂרָאֵל (** the children of Israel*) מֵאֶרֶץ מִצְרָיִם (*from the land of Egypt*) עַל (*on*) their hosts.

Chapter Thirteen

Sanctification Of The Firstborns

(1) וַיְדַבֵּר יהוה אֶל-מֹשֶׁה (And YHVH spoke to Moses) לֵּאמֹר (saying):

(2)

קַדֶּשׁ-לִי כָל-בְּכוֹר

פֶּטֶר כָּל-רֶחֶם

בִּבְנֵי יִשְׂרָאֵל

בָּאָדָם וּבַבְּהֵמָה לִי הוּא

Sanctify to Me all the firstborn

opening up every womb

in the children of Israel

in the man and in the animal it is for Me.

(3) וַיֹּאמֶר מֹשֶׁה אֶל-הָעָם (And Moses said to the people):

זָכוֹר (Remember) this אֶת day which you went forth מִמִּצְרַיִם (from Egypt) מִבֵּית עֲבָדִים (from the house of servants) for by strength of יָד (hand) יהוה brought אֶתְכֶם from here; and leaven shall not be eaten."

(4)

"Today אַתֶּם go forth in the month of הָאָבִיב

(5)

"And it shall be that יהוה shall bring you אֶל-אֶרֶץ (to the land of) הַכְּנַעֲנִי וְהַחִתִּי וְהָאֱמֹרִי וְהַחִוִּי וְהַיְבוּסִי which He swore לַאֲבֹתֶיךָ (to your fathers) to give לָךְ (to you) אֶרֶץ (a land) flowing with milk and honey וְעָבַדְתָּ (and you shall serve) אֶת הָעֲבֹדָה הַזֹּאת (this * service) in this month."

Exodus ~ 13

(6)

"Seven days you shall eat מַצֹּת (unleavened breads) and on the seventh day a feast לַיהוה

(7)

וְלֹא- מַצֹּת (Unleavened breads) shall be eaten the אֵת seven days יֵרָאֶה לְךָ (and it shall not be seen for you) leaven וְלֹא יֵרָאֶה לְךָ (and it shall not be seen for you) yeast בְּכָל (in all) of your borders."

(8)

"And you shall tell לְבִנְךָ (to your son) in that day לֵאמֹר (saying):

'Because of what יהוה did לִי (for me) in my going forth מִמִּצְרָיִם

(9)

"And it shall be for a sign לְךָ (to you) עַל יָדְךָ (on your hand) וּלְזִכָּרוֹן (and for a remembrance) בֵּין עֵינֶיךָ (between your eyes) that the law of יהוה may be בְּפִיךָ (in your mouth) for בְּיָד חֲזָקָה (in a strong hand) יהוה brought you forth מִמִּצְרָיִם

(10)

וְשָׁמַרְתָּ (And you shall keep) this אֵת statute לְמוֹעֲדָהּ (for its appointed time) from days to days."

(11)

"And it shall be that יהוה shall bring you אֶל-אֶרֶץ (to the land of) הַכְּנַעֲנִי as He swore לְךָ (to you) וְלַאֲבֹתֶיךָ (and to your fathers) and shall give it לְךָ (to you)."

(12)

"And you shall set apart כָּל (all) that opens the womb לַיהוה (to YHVH) וְכָל (and every) firstling בְּהֵמָה (animal) that is לְךָ (to

Level Two   שְׁמוֹת ~ יג

you) the males לַיהוה

(13)

וְכָל (*And every) firstling of a donkey you shall redeem with a flockling; and if you will not redeem it, then you shall break its neck;* וְכֹל בְּכוֹר אָדָם (*and every firstborn human*) בְּבָנֶיךָ (*in your sons) you shall redeem.*"

(14)

"*And it shall be that* בִּנְךָ (*your son) asks you tomorrow* לֵאמֹר (*saying):*

'*What is this?*'

וְאָמַרְתָּ אֵלָיו (*And you shall say to him):*
'*By strength of* יָד (*hand)* יהוה *brought us forth* מִמִּצְרַיִם (*from Egypt)* מִבֵּית עֲבָדִים (*from the house of servants).*'

(15)

'*And it was that* פַּרְעֹה *was obstinate* לְשַׁלְּחֵנוּ (*to send us) and* יהוה *slew* כָּל־בְּכוֹר (*all the firstborn)* בְּאֶרֶץ מִצְרַיִם (*in the land of Egypt)* מִבְּכֹר אָדָם (*from the firstborn of human)* וְעַד בְּכוֹר בְּהֵמָה (*and to the firstborn of animal).* עַל (*On) thus* אֲנִי (*I) sacrifice* לַיהוה (*to YHVH)* כָּל (*all) the males that open the womb* וְכָל־בְּכוֹר בָּנַי (*and all the firstborn of my sons) I redeem.*'"

(16)

"*And it shall be for a sign* עַל יָדְכָה (*on your hand) and for frontlets* בֵּין עֵינֶיךָ (*between your eyes) for by strength of* יָד (*hand)* יהוה *brought us forth* מִמִּצְרָיִם

Exodus ~ 13

(17) And it was בְּשַׁלַּח פַּרְעֹה אֶת-הָעָם (in Pharaoh sending * the people) that אֱלֹהִים did not guide them דֶּרֶךְ אֶרֶץ פְּלִשְׁתִּים (the way of the land of Philistines) because הוּא (it) was near; because אָמַר אֱלֹהִים (Elohim said):

פֶּן-יִנָּחֵם הָעָם

בִּרְאֹתָם מִלְחָמָה

וְשָׁבוּ מִצְרָיְמָה

Lest the people regret

In their seeing war

and they return to Egypt.

(18) But אֱלֹהִים led אֶת-הָעָם (* the people) דֶּרֶךְ הַמִּדְבָּר (the way of the wilderness) יַם-סוּף (the Sea of Reed) and in battle array בְּנֵי יִשְׂרָאֵל (the children of Israel) ascended מֵאֶרֶץ מִצְרָיִם (from the land of Egypt).

(19) And מֹשֶׁה took אֶת-עַצְמוֹת יוֹסֵף (* the bones of Joseph) עִמּוֹ (with him) for he had surely adjured אֶת בְּנֵי יִשְׂרָאֵל (* the children of Israel) לֵאמֹר (saying):

אֱלֹהִים will surely notice אֶתְכֶם and you shall bring up אֶת-עַצְמֹתַי (* my bones) מִזֶּה אִתְּכֶם (from here with * you).

(20) And they took their journey מִסֻּכֹּת (from Succoth) and encamped בְאֵתָם (in Etham) on the edge of הַמִּדְבָּר (the wilderness).

(21) וַיהוה הֹלֵךְ לִפְנֵיהֶם (And YHVH went before them) בְּעַמּוּד עָנָן (in a pillar of a cloud) by day to guide them הַדֶּרֶךְ (the way) and בְּעַמּוּד אֵשׁ (in a pillar of fire) by night to give light לָהֶם (to them) לָלֶכֶת (to go) by day and night.

(22) עַמּוּד הֶעָנָן (The pillar of the cloud) by day וְעַמּוּד הָאֵשׁ (and the pillar of the fire) by night, was not removed לִפְנֵי הָעָם (before the people).

Chapter Fourteen

Pharaoh Pursues Israel

(1) וַיְדַבֵּר יהוה אֶל-מֹשֶׁה *(And YHVH spoke to Moses)* לֵּאמֹר *(saying)*:

(2)

דַּבֵּר אֶל-בְּנֵי יִשְׂרָאֵל

וְיָשֻׁבוּ וְיַחֲנוּ

לִפְנֵי פִּי~הַחִירֹת

בֵּין מִגְדֹּל וּבֵין הַיָּם

לִפְנֵי בַּעַל~צְפֹן

נִכְחוֹ תַחֲנוּ עַל-הַיָּם

Speak to the children of Israel

and they shall turn back and encamp

before Pi-hahiroth

between Migdol and the sea

before Baal-zephon

you shall encamp opposite it by the sea

(3)

וְאָמַר פַּרְעֹה לִבְנֵי יִשְׂרָאֵל

נְבֻכִים הֵם בָּאָרֶץ

סָגַר עֲלֵיהֶם הַמִּדְבָּר

And Pharaoh will say of the children of Israel

They are entangled in the land

the wilderness has shut them in.

(4)

וְחִזַּקְתִּי אֶת-לֵב-פַּרְעֹה

וְרָדַף אַחֲרֵיהֶם

וְאִכָּבְדָה בְּפַרְעֹה

וּבְכָל-חֵילוֹ

וְיָדְעוּ מִצְרַיִם כִּי-אֲנִי יהוה

*And I will harden * the heart of Pharaoh*

and he shall pursue after them

and I will be glorified in Pharaoh

and in all his army

and Egypt shall know that I am YHVH

And they did so.

(5) And it was told לְמֶלֶךְ מִצְרַיִם (the king of Egypt) that הָעָם (the people) fled and לְבַב פַּרְעֹה (the heart of Pharaoh) וַעֲבָדָיו (and his servants) was turned אֶל-הָעָם (to the people) וַיֹּאמְרוּ (and they said):

"What is this we have done כִּי שִׁלַּחְנוּ אֶת יִשְׂרָאֵל (because we sent * Israel) מֵעָבְדֵנוּ (from serving us)?

(6) And he made ready אֶת his chariots וְאֶת עַמּוֹ (and * his people) he took עַמּוֹ (with him).

(7) And he took six hundred chosen chariots וְכֹל (and all) the chariots of מִצְרָיִם and captains עַל-כֻּלּוֹ (over all).

(8) And יהוה hardened אֶת-לֵב פַּרְעֹה (* the heart of Pharaoh) מֶלֶךְ מִצְרַיִם (king of Egypt) and he pursued after בְּנֵי יִשְׂרָאֵל (the children of Israel) וּבְנֵי

Level Two ~ שְׁמוֹת ~ יד

יִשְׂרָאֵל (and the children of Israel) went forth בְּיָד רָמָה (in a high hand).

(9) And מִצְרַיִם pursued after them כָּל (all) the horses and chariots of פַּרְעֹה and his horsemen, and his army, and overtook אוֹתָם encamping עַל-הַיָּם (by the sea) עַל (on) פִּי-הַחִירֹת before בַּעַל-צְפֹן.

(10) וּפַרְעֹה (And Pharaoh) drew near בְּנֵי יִשְׂרָאֵל (the children of Israel) lifted up אֵת עֵינֵיהֶם (* their eyes) and behold מִצְרַיִם was marching after them; and they were sore afraid; and בְּנֵי יִשְׂרָאֵל (the children of Israel) cried out אֶל יהוה

(11) וַיֹּאמְרוּ (And they said) אֶל-מֹשֶׁה

"Because there are no tombs בְּמִצְרַיִם you take us to die בַּמִּדְבָּר (in the wilderness)? What is this you are doing לָנוּ (to us) to bring us forth מִמִּצְרָיִם (from Egypt)?"

(12)

"Is this not הַדָּבָר (the word) that דִּבַּרְנוּ אֵלֶיךָ בְמִצְרַיִם (we spoke to you in Egypt) לֵאמֹר (saying):

'Leave מִמֶּנּוּ (from us) וְנַעַבְדָה אֶת מִצְרָיִם (and we will serve * Egypt)? For it were better לָנוּ עֲבֹד (for us to serve) אֶת מִצְרַיִם than us dying בַּמִּדְבָּר (in the wilderness).'"

(13) וַיֹּאמֶר מֹשֶׁה אֶל-הָעָם (And Moses said to the people):
"Do not fear, stand still וּרְאוּ (and you will see) אֵת the salvation of יהוה which He will work לָכֶם (for you) today; for whereas רְאִיתֶם (you have seen) אֵת מִצְרַיִם today, no more will you לִרְאֹתָם (be seeing) them again forever."

(14)

יהוה will fight לָכֶם (for you) וְאַתֶּם be silent."

Exodus ~ 14

(15) וַיֹּאמֶר יהוה אֶל־מֹשֶׁה *(And YHVH said to Moses):*

מַה־תִּצְעַק אֵלָי

דַּבֵּר אֶל־בְּנֵי־יִשְׂרָאֵל

וְיִסָּעוּ

What are you crying to Me

speak to the children of Israel

and they shall journey

(16)

וְאַתָּה הָרֵם אֶת־מַטְּךָ

וּנְטֵה אֶת־יָדְךָ עַל־הַיָּם

וּבְקָעֵהוּ

וְיָבֹאוּ בְנֵי־יִשְׂרָאֵל

בְּתוֹךְ הַיָּם בַּיַּבָּשָׁה

and * you lift up * your staff

and stretch out * your hand over the sea

and divide it

and the children of Israel shall go

in the midst of the sea on the dry ground.

(17)

וַאֲנִי הִנְנִי מְחַזֵּק

אֶת־לֵב מִצְרַיִם

וְיָבֹאוּ אַחֲרֵיהֶם

Level Two   שְׁמוֹת ~ יד

And I, behold I will harden
* the heart of Egypt
and they shall go in after them

וְאִכָּבְדָה בְּפַרְעֹה
וּבְכָל-חֵילוֹ
בְּרִכְבּוֹ וּבְפָרָשָׁיו

and I shall be glorified in Pharaoh
and in all his army
in his chariots and in his horsemen

(18)

וְיָדְעוּ מִצְרַיִם כִּי-אֲנִי יהוה
בְּהִכָּבְדִי בְּפַרְעֹה
בְּרִכְבּוֹ וּבְפָרָשָׁיו

And Egypt shall know that I am YHVH
in My being glorified in Pharaoh
in his chariots and in his horsemen.

(19) And מַלְאַךְ הָאֱלֹהִים הַהֹלֵךְ (the messenger of the Elohim who went) לִפְנֵי מַחֲנֵה יִשְׂרָאֵל (before the camp of Israel) journeyed וַיֵּלֶךְ (and he went) behind them; and עַמּוּד הֶעָנָן (the pillar of the cloud) journeyed מִפְּנֵיהֶם (from their faces) and stood behind them;

(20) and it came between מַחֲנֵה מִצְרַיִם (the camp of Egypt) מַחֲנֵה יִשְׂרָאֵל (and the camp of Israel) and there was הֶעָנָן (the cloud) וְהַחֹשֶׁךְ (and the darkness) and it lit up אֶת the night; and this one did not come near to the other one כָּל (all) the night.

Exodus ~ 14

(21) And מֹשֶׁה stretched out אֶת-יָדוֹ (* his hand) עַל הַיָּם (over the sea); and יהוה caused אֶת-הַיָּם (* the sea) to go back by בְּרוּחַ קָדִים עַזָּה (a strong east wind) כָּל (all) the night, and made אֶת-הַיָּם (* the sea) dry ground, and הַמָּיִם (the waters) were divided.

(22) And בְּנֵי יִשְׂרָאֵל (the children of Israel) entered in the midst of הַיָּם (the sea) on the dry ground וְהַמַּיִם (and the waters) were a wall לָהֶם (to them) from their right and from their left.

(23) And מִצְרַיִם pursued, and entered after them in the midst of הַיָּם (the sea) כֹּל (every) horse of פַּרְעֹה his chariots, and his horsemen.

(24) And it was in the morning watch, that יהוה gazed אֶל-מַחֲנֵה מִצְרַיִם (to the camp of Egypt) בְּעַמּוּד אֵשׁ (through the pillar of fire) וְעָנָן (and cloud) and discomfited אֵת מַחֲנֵה מִצְרָיִם (* the camp of Egypt).

(25) And He clogged אֵת the wheels of his chariots, and made them to drive heavily. וַיֹּאמֶר מִצְרַיִם (And Egypt said):

"I shall flee מִפְּנֵי יִשְׂרָאֵל (from the face of Israel) for יהוה is fighting בְּמִצְרָיִם (for them) לָהֶם

(26) וַיֹּאמֶר יהוה אֶל-מֹשֶׁה (And YHVH said to Moses):

> נְטֵה אֶת-יָדְךָ עַל-הַיָּם
>
> וְיָשֻׁבוּ הַמַּיִם עַל-מִצְרַיִם
>
> עַל-רִכְבּוֹ וְעַל-פָּרָשָׁיו

*Stretch out * your hand over the sea*

that the waters may return on Egypt

on his chariots, and on his horsemen.

Level Two שְׁמוֹת ~ יד

(27) And מֹשֶׁה stretched forth אֶת-יָדוֹ (* his hand) עַל הַיָּם (over the sea), and הַיָּם (the sea) returned to its strength לִפְנוֹת (before) the morning appeared וּמִצְרַיִם fled against it; and יהוה overthrew אֶת-מִצְרַיִם in the midst of הַיָּם (the sea).

(28) And הַמַּיִם (the waters) returned, and covered אֵת the chariots וְאֵת the horsemen לְכֹל (to all) the army of פַּרְעֹה that entered after them בַּיָּם (in the sea); there did not remain בָּהֶם (in them) even one.

(29) וּבְנֵי יִשְׂרָאֵל הָלְכוּ (And the children of Israel walked) on dry ground in the midst of הַיָּם (the sea) וְהַמַּיִם (and the waters) were a wall לָהֶם (to them) from their right, and from their left.

(30) And יהוה saved אֶת-יִשְׂרָאֵל in that day מִיַּד מִצְרָיִם (from the hand of Egypt) וַיַּרְא יִשְׂרָאֵל (and Israel saw) אֶת מִצְרַיִם dead עַל (on) the shore of הַיָּם (the sea).

(31) וַיַּרְא יִשְׂרָאֵל (and Israel saw) אֶת הַיָּד הַגְּדֹלָה (the great * hand) which יהוה did בְּמִצְרַיִם and הָעָם (the people) feared אֶת-יהוה and they believed בַּיהוה וּבְמֹשֶׁה עַבְדּוֹ (in YHVH and in Moses His servant).

Chapter Fifteen

Song Of Praise

(1) Then מֹשֶׁה sang וּבְנֵי יִשְׂרָאֵל (and the children of Israel) this אֶת song לַיהוה וַיֹּאמְרוּ (and they spoke) לֵאמֹר (saying):

"I will sing לַיהוה for He is surely exalted; a horse and his rider He has thrown in the sea."

(2)

"My strength and melody is of יָהּ and He is becoming לִי (to me) for salvation; this is אֵלִי and I will glorify Him אֱלֹהֵי אָבִי (Elohim of my father) and I will exalt Him."

(3)

יהוה is אִישׁ (a man of) war שְׁמוֹ יהוה (YHVH is His name)."

(4)

"The chariots of פַּרְעֹה and his army He has cast in the sea, and his chosen fighters they sank בְיַם-סוּף (in the Red Sea)."

(5)

"Abysses covered them - they descended in the depths like אָבֶן (a stone)."

(6)

"Your right hand יהוה is glorious in power, Your right hand יהוה crushes the enemy."

(7)

"And in the vastness of Your excellency, You overthrow them that rise up against You תְּשַׁלַּח (You send) Your wrath, it consumes them as the stubble."

Level Two ~ שְׁמוֹת ~ טו

(8)

וּבְרוּחַ (And with the spirit/breath of) Your nostrils מַיִם (waters) piled up - floods stood like a waterspout; abysses were congealed בְּלֶב (in the heart of) the sea."

(9)

"The enemy אָמַר (said):
'I will pursue, I will overtake, I will divide the spoil נַפְשִׁי (my soul) shall be satisfied on them; I will draw my sword יָדִי (my hand) shall seize them.'"

(10)

"You blew בְרוּחֲךָ (with Your Spirit) the sea covered them; they sank as lead בְּמַיִם אַדִּירִים (in majestic waters).

(11)

מִי-כָמֹכָה (Who is like to You) בָּאֵלִם יהוה (YHVH in the mighty) מִי כָּמֹכָה (Who is like to You) נֶאְדָּר בַּקֹּדֶשׁ (glorious in holiness) נוֹרָא תְהִלֹּת (fearful in praises) עֹשֵׂה פֶלֶא (doing wonders)?"

(12)

"You stretched out Your right hand אֶרֶץ (land) is swallowing them up."

(13)

"In Your kindness, You guided עַם-זוּ (this people) that You redeemed. In Your strength, You conduct them to the homestead of your holiness."

(14)

שָׁמְעוּ עַמִּים (Peoples heard) they tremble; travail holds the inhabitants of פְּלָשֶׁת

(15)

"Then the sheiks of אֱדוֹם are flustered; the leaders of מוֹאָב trembling takes hold of them כֹּל (all) the inhabitants of כְּנַעַן are melted away."

(16)

"Terror and dread falls עֲלֵיהֶם (on them) by the greatness of Your arm they are as still כָּאָבֶן (as a stone) till עַמְּךָ (Your people) pass over יהוה till עַם-זוּ (this people) pass over that You acquired."

(17)

"You brought them in, and planted them בְּהַר (in the mountain of) Your inheritance, the place יהוה which You made for You to dwell מִקְּדָשׁ (from the sanctuary) אֲדֹנָי which יָדֶיךָ (Your hands) have established."

(18)

יהוה יִמְלֹךְ (YHVH shall reign) forever and ever."

(19)

For the horses of פַּרְעֹה entered with his chariots and with his horsemen בַּיָּם (in the sea), and יהוה brought back אֶת מֵי הַיָּם (* the waters of the sea) עֲלֵהֶם (on them) but וּבְנֵי יִשְׂרָאֵל הָלְכוּ (and the children of Israel walked) on dry ground in the midst of הַיָּם (the sea).

(20) And מִרְיָם the prophetess אֲחוֹת אַהֲרֹן (the sister of Aaron) took אֶת the timbrel בְּיָדָהּ (in her hand) and כָּל הַנָּשִׁים (all the women) went forth after her with timbrels and with dances.

(21) And מִרְיָם shouted לָהֶם (to them):

Level Two   שְׁמוֹת ~ טו

"Sing לַיהוה *for He is surely exalted: the horse and his rider He has thrown in the sea!*"

The Bitter Water

(22) And מֹשֶׁה caused אֶת יִשְׂרָאֵל to journey מִיַּם סוּף *(from the Red Sea)* and they went forth אֶל-מִדְבַּר-שׁוּר *(to the wilderness of Shur)* וַיֵּלְכוּ *(and they went)* three days בַּמִּדְבָּר *(in the wilderness)* and found no מָיִם *(water)*.

(23) And when they came מָרָתָה *(toward Marah)* they could not drink of מַיִם מִמָּרָה *(waters from Marah)* for הֵם *(they)* were bitter עַל *(on)* thus קָרָא שְׁמָהּ מָרָה *(he called the name of it Marah)*.

(24) And הָעָם *(the people)* murmured עַל מֹשֶׁה *(against Moses)* לֵאמֹר *(saying)*:

"What shall we drink?"

(25) And he cried אֶל-יהוה and יהוה directed him to a tree, and he cast it אֶל-הַמַּיִם *(to the waters)*, and הַמַּיִם *(the waters)* were made sweet. He made לוֹ *(for him)* there a statute and an ordinance, and there He proved him;

(26) וַיֹּאמֶר *(and He said)*:

אִם-שָׁמוֹעַ תִּשְׁמַע
לְקוֹל יהוה אֱלֹהֶיךָ
וְהַיָּשָׁר בְּעֵינָיו תַּעֲשֶׂה

*If you will diligently listen
to the voice of YHVH your Elohim
and do what is right in His eyes*

וְהַאֲזַנְתָּ לְמִצְוֹתָיו

וְשָׁמַרְתָּ כָּל־חֻקָּיו

כָּל־הַמַּחֲלָה

אֲשֶׁר־שַׂמְתִּי בְמִצְרַיִם

לֹא־אָשִׂים עָלֶיךָ

and will give ear to His commandments

and keep all His statutes

all the diseases

that I have put on Egypt

I shall not put on you

כִּי אֲנִי יהוה רֹפְאֶךָ

for I am YHVH your Healer.

(27) And they came אֵילִמָה (*towards Elim*) and there were twelve springs of מַיִם (*water*) and seventy palm trees; and they encamped there עַל־הַמָּיִם (*on the waters*).

Chapter Sixteen

The Congregation Murmurs

(1) And they journeyed מֵאֵילִם (from Elim) and כָּל־עֲדַת בְּנֵי־יִשְׂרָאֵל (all the congregation of the children of Israel) came אֶל־מִדְבַּר סִין (to the wilderness of Sin) which is בֵּין אֵילִם וּבֵין סִינָי (between Elim and Sinai) on the fifteenth day of the second month after their departing מֵאֶרֶץ מִצְרָיִם (from the land of Egypt).

(2) And כָּל־עֲדַת בְּנֵי־יִשְׂרָאֵל (all the congregation of the children of Israel) murmured עַל מֹשֶׁה וְעַל אַהֲרֹן (against Moses and against Aaron) בַּמִּדְבָּר (in the wilderness).

(3) וַיֹּאמְרוּ אֲלֵהֶם בְּנֵי יִשְׂרָאֵל (And the children of Israel said to them):

"If only we had died בְּיַד־יהוה (in the hand of YHVH) בְּאֶרֶץ מִצְרַיִם (in the land of Egypt) when we sat עַל (over) the pots of הַבָּשָׂר (the flesh) when we ate לֶחֶם (bread) to satisfaction; for you have brought אֹתָנוּ forth אֶל הַמִּדְבָּר הַזֶּה (to this wilderness) to kill this אֵת כָּל הַקָּהָל הַזֶּה (* all this assembly) with hunger."

Quails And Manna

(4) וַיֹּאמֶר יהוה אֶל־מֹשֶׁה (And YHVH said to Moses):

הִנְנִי מַמְטִיר לָכֶם

לֶחֶם מִן־הַשָּׁמָיִם

וְיָצָא הָעָם

Behold, I will rain for you
bread from sky for you;
and the people shall go forth

Exodus ~ 16

וְלָקְט֞וּ דְּבַר־י֥וֹם בְּיוֹמ֖וֹ
לְמַ֧עַן אֲנַסֶּ֛נּוּ
הֲיֵלֵ֥ךְ בְּתוֹרָתִ֖י אִם־לֹֽא

and pick up a day's portion every day
that I may prove him
whether he will walk in My law or not

(5)

וְהָיָה֙ בַּיּ֣וֹם הַשִּׁשִּׁ֔י
וְהֵכִ֖ינוּ אֵ֣ת אֲשֶׁר־יָבִ֑יאוּ
וְהָיָ֣ה מִשְׁנֶ֔ה
עַ֥ל אֲשֶֽׁר־יִלְקְט֖וּ י֥וֹם ׀ יֽוֹם

and it shall be on the sixth day
and they shall prepare * what they bring in
and it shall be double
over what they pick up daily

(6) וַיֹּ֤אמֶר מֹשֶׁה֙ וְאַהֲרֹ֔ן (And Moses said and Aaron) אֶֽל־כָּל־בְּנֵ֖י יִשְׂרָאֵ֑ל (to all the children of Israel):

"Evening, and you will know that יהוה has brought אֶתְכֶ֖ם forth מֵאֶ֥רֶץ מִצְרָֽיִם (from the land of Egypt)."

(7)

"And morning וּרְאִיתֶם֙ (and you shall see) אֶת־כְּב֣וֹד יהוה (* the glory of YHVH) בְּשָׁמְע֥וֹ (on His hearing) אֶת your murmurings עַל־יהוה (about YHVH) וְנַ֣חְנוּ (and we) are what that you murmur

Level Two   שְׁמוֹת ~ טז

עָלֵינוּ (about us)?"

(8) וַיֹּאמֶר מֹשֶׁה (And Moses said):

"In יהוה giving לָכֶם (to you) בָּשָׂר (flesh) to eat in the evening וְלֶחֶם (and bread) to satisfaction in the morning בִּשְׁמֹעַ יהוה (on YHVH hearing of) אֶת your murmurings which אַתֶּם murmur עָלָיו (against Him) וְנַחְנוּ (and we) are what? Your murmurings are לֹא עָלֵינוּ (not against us) but עַל יהוה (against YHVH)."

(9) וַיֹּאמֶר מֹשֶׁה (And Moses said) אֶל-אַהֲרֹן

אֱמֹר אֶל-כָּל-עֲדַת בְּנֵי יִשְׂרָאֵל (say to all the congregation of the children of Israel)

'Come near לִפְנֵי יהוה (before YHVH) for שָׁמַע (He has heard) אֵת your murmurings.'"

(10) And it was כְּדַבֵּר אַהֲרֹן (as Aaron spoke) אֶל-כָּל-עֲדַת בְּנֵי יִשְׂרָאֵל (to all the congregation of the children of Israel) וַיִּפְנוּ אֶל הַמִּדְבָּר (and they faced toward the wilderness) and, behold כְּבוֹד יהוה (the glory of YHVH) נִרְאָה (was seen) בֶּעָנָן (in the cloud).

(11) וַיְדַבֵּר יהוה אֶל-מֹשֶׁה (And YHVH spoke to Moses) לֵּאמֹר (saying):

(12)

שָׁמַעְתִּי אֶת-תְּלוּנֹת בְּנֵי יִשְׂרָאֵל
דַּבֵּר אֲלֵהֶם לֵאמֹר

I have heard * the murmurings of the children of Israel
Speak to them saying

121

בֵּין הָעַרְבַּיִם

תֹּאכְלוּ בָשָׂר

וּבַבֹּקֶר

תִּשְׂבְּעוּ-לָחֶם

וִידַעְתֶּם כִּי

אֲנִי יהוה אֱלֹהֵיכֶם

between the evenings

you shall eat flesh

and in the morning

you shall be satisfied with bread

and you shall know that

I am YHVH your Elohim.

(13) And it was in the evening, that the quails came up, and covered אֶת the camp; and in the morning, there was a layer of dew round about לַמַּחֲנֶה (to the camp).

(14) And when the layer of dew was gone up, behold עַל פְּנֵי הַמִּדְבָּר (on the face of the wilderness) a thin, flaking, thin as the hoar-frost עַל הָאָרֶץ (on the land).

(15) וַיִּרְאוּ בְּנֵי יִשְׂרָאֵל (And the children of Israel saw) וַיֹּאמְרוּ (and they said) אִישׁ (a man) אֶל-אָחִיו (to his brother):

מָן הוּא (What is it)?"

For they did not know מַה-הוּא (what it was) וַיֹּאמֶר מֹשֶׁה (And Moses said) אֲלֵהֶם (to them):

Level Two   שְׁמוֹת ~ טז

הוּא הַלֶּחֶם (It is the bread) which יהוה has given לָכֶם (to you) to eat."

(16) "This is הַדָּבָר (the thing) which יהוה has commanded:

לִקְטוּ מִמֶּנּוּ
אִישׁ לְפִי אָכְלוֹ
עֹמֶר לַגֻּלְגֹּלֶת
מִסְפַּר נַפְשֹׁתֵיכֶם
אִישׁ לַאֲשֶׁר בְּאָהֳלוֹ תִּקָּחוּ

You gather from it

a man according to his eating

an omer for a poll

number of your persons

a man for who is in his tent you shall take.

(17) And בְּנֵי יִשְׂרָאֵל (the children of Israel) did so, and gathered some more, some less.

(18) And they measured in an omer, he with much had nothing left over, and he with little had no lack; they gathered אִישׁ (a man) according to his eating.

Rotten Manna

(19) וַיֹּאמֶר מֹשֶׁה (And Moses said) אֲלֵהֶם (to them):

אִישׁ (A man) must not reserve מִמֶּנּוּ (from it) till the morning."

123

Exodus ~ 16 — The Progressive Torah

(20) וְלֹא־שָׁמְעוּ *(And they did not listen)* אֶל־מֹשֶׁה and אֲנָשִׁים *(men)* reserved מִמֶּנּוּ *(from it)* until the morning, and it bred worms, and stank; and מֹשֶׁה was furious עֲלֵהֶם *(with them)*.

(21) And they gathered אֹתוֹ morning by morning אִישׁ *(a man)* according to his eating; and the sun warmed, and it melted.

(22) And it was on the sixth day they gathered twice as much לֶחֶם *(bread)* two omers for one; and כָּל *(all)* the rulers of הָעֵדָה *(the congregation)* came and reported לְמֹשֶׁה

Food For The Sabbath

(23) וַיֹּאמֶר אֲלֵהֶם *(And he said to them):*

הוּא *(It) is that* דִּבֶּר יהוה *(YHVH spoke).*

שַׁבָּתוֹן שַׁבַּת־קֹדֶשׁ

לַיהוה מָחָר

אֵת אֲשֶׁר־תֹּאפוּ אֵפוּ

וְאֵת אֲשֶׁר־תְּבַשְּׁלוּ בַּשֵּׁלוּ

A rest, a holy Sabbath

to YHVH is tomorrow*

what you are baking, bake

and * what you are cooking, cook

וְאֵת כָּל־הָעֹדֵף

הַנִּיחוּ לָכֶם

לְמִשְׁמֶרֶת עַד־הַבֹּקֶר

Level Two

שְׁמוֹת ~ טז

and * all the leftovers

you leave for you

to be kept until the morning.

(24) And they left אֹתוֹ till the morning as מֹשֶׁה instructed, and it did not stink, and there was not a worm בּוֹ (in it).

(25) וַיֹּאמֶר מֹשֶׁה (And Moses said):

"Eat it today כִּי־שַׁבָּת הַיּוֹם (because today is a Sabbath) לַיהוה today you shall not find it in the field."

(26)

"Six days you shall gather it; and on the seventh day is שַׁבָּת (a Sabbath) none shall be בּוֹ (in it)."

(27) And it was on the seventh day, that there went forth מִן־הָעָם (from the people) to gather, and they found none.

(28) וַיֹּאמֶר יהוה אֶל־מֹשֶׁה (And YHVH said to Moses):

עַד־אָנָה מֵאַנְתֶּם

לִשְׁמֹר מִצְוֹתַי וְתוֹרֹתָי

Until when will you refuse

to keep My commandments and My laws

(29)

רְאוּ כִּי־יהוה נָתַן לָכֶם הַשַּׁבָּת

עַל־כֵּן הוּא נֹתֵן

you see that YHVH, He gave to you the Sabbath

therefore, He gives

125

Exodus ~ 16

לָכֶם בַּיּוֹם הַשִּׁשִּׁי

לֶחֶם יוֹמָיִם

שְׁבוּ אִישׁ תַּחְתָּיו

אַל-יֵצֵא אִישׁ מִמְּקֹמוֹ

בַּיּוֹם הַשְּׁבִיעִי

to you on the sixth day

bread of days

you sit, a man on his bottom

a man must not go forth from his place

on the seventh day.

(30) And הָעָם *(the people)* rested on the seventh day.

(31) וַיִּקְרְאוּ בֵית-יִשְׂרָאֵל *(And the house of Israel called)* אֶת-שְׁמוֹ *(the name of it)* מָן *(manna)* וְהוּא *(and it)* was like coriander seed, white; and the taste of it was like cakes in honey.

Manna For Future Generations

(32) וַיֹּאמֶר מֹשֶׁה *(And Moses said):*

'This is הַדָּבָר *(the word)* which יהוה has commanded:

מְלֹא הָעֹמֶר מִמֶּנּוּ

לְמִשְׁמֶרֶת לְדֹרֹתֵיכֶם

לְמַעַן יִרְאוּ אֶת-הַלֶּחֶם

אֲשֶׁר הֶאֱכַלְתִּי אֶתְכֶם בַּמִּדְבָּר

Level Two   שְׁמוֹת ~ טז

A full omer from it
for keeping for your generations
that they shall see * the bread
that I fed * you in the wilderness

בְּהוֹצִיאִי אֶתְכֶם
מֵאֶרֶץ מִצְרָיִם

in My bringing forth of * you
from the land of Egypt

(33) וַיֹּאמֶר מֹשֶׁה (And Moses said) אֶל-אַהֲרֹן

"Take one urn, and put a full omer of מָן (manna) therein, and leave אֹתוֹ (* it) לִפְנֵי יהוה (before YHVH) לְמִשְׁמֶרֶת (for a keeping) לְדֹרֹתֵיכֶם (for your generations)."

(34) As יהוה commanded אֶל-מֹשֶׁה and אַהֲרֹן laid it up לִפְנֵי הָעֵדֻת (before the Testimony) לְמִשְׁמָרֶת (for a keeping).

(35) וּבְנֵי יִשְׂרָאֵל (And the children of Israel) ate אֶת-הַמָּן (* the manna) forty years, until they came אֶל-אֶרֶץ (to a land) inhabited; they ate אֶת-הַמָּן (* the manna) until they came to the fringe of אֶרֶץ כְּנָעַן (the land of Canaan).

(36) And the omer הוּא (it) is the tenth of the ephah.

Chapter Seventeen

Water From The Rock

(1) And כָּל־עֲדַת בְּנֵי־יִשְׂרָאֵל (all the congregation of the children of Israel) journeyed מִמִּדְבַּר־סִין (from the wilderness of Sin) for their journeys עַל (on) the bidding of יהוה and they encamped בִּרְפִידִים (in Rephidim) and there was no מַיִם (water) for הָעָם (the people) to drink.

(2) And הָעָם (the people) contended עִם־מֹשֶׁה (with Moses) וַיֹּאמְרוּ (and they said):

"Give לָנוּ (to us) מַיִם (water) and we shall drink."

וַיֹּאמֶר לָהֶם מֹשֶׁה (And Moses said to them):

"What? You contend עִמָּדִי (with me)? What? You test אֶת־יהוה"

(3) And הָעָם (the people) thirsted there לַמַּיִם (for water) and הָעָם (the people) murmured עַל־מֹשֶׁה (against Moses) וַיֹּאמֶר (and said):

"Why is this you brought us up מִמִּצְרַיִם to kill וְאֶת־בָּנַי אֹתִי (* me and * my sons) וְאֶת my cattle with thirst?"

(4) And מֹשֶׁה cried אֶל־יהוה (to YHVH) לֵאמֹר (saying):

"What shall I do לָעָם הַזֶּה (to this people)? They are almost ready to stone me."

(5) וַיֹּאמֶר יהוה אֶל־מֹשֶׁה (And YHVH said to Moses):

עֲבֹר לִפְנֵי הָעָם

Pass before the people

Level Two   שְׁמוֹת ~ יז

וְקַח אִתְּךָ

מִזִּקְנֵי יִשְׂרָאֵל

וּמַטְּךָ אֲשֶׁר הִכִּיתָ

בּוֹ אֶת־הַיְאֹר

קַח בְּיָדְךָ וְהָלָכְתָּ

and take with * you

from the elders of Israel

and your staff which you smote

with it * the river

take in your hand and go.

(6)

הִנְנִי עֹמֵד לְפָנֶיךָ

שָּׁם עַל־הַצּוּר בְּחֹרֵב

וְהִכִּיתָ בַצּוּר

וְיָצְאוּ מִמֶּנּוּ מַיִם

וְשָׁתָה הָעָם

behold, I will stand before you

there on the rock in Horeb

and you smite the rock

and water shall come forth from it

and the people may drink.

Exodus ~ 17

And מֹשֶׁה did so לְעֵינֵי (for the eyes of) the elders of יִשְׂרָאֵל.

(7) וַיִּקְרָא שֵׁם (And he called the name of) the place מַסָּה וּמְרִיבָה (Massah, and Meribah) וְעַל (over) the contention of בְּנֵי יִשְׂרָאֵל (the children of Israel) (and over) their testing אֶת-יהוה (* YHVH) לֵאמֹר (saying):

"Is יהוה among us, or not?"

Amalek Attacks

(8) And עֲמָלֵק came, and fought עִם-יִשְׂרָאֵל (with Israel) בִּרְפִידִם (in Rephidim).

(9) וַיֹּאמֶר מֹשֶׁה (And Moses said) אֶל-יְהוֹשֻׁעַ (to Joshua):

"Choose לָנוּ (for us) אֲנָשִׁים (men) and go forth. Fight בַּעֲמָלֵק (with Amalek). Tomorrow אָנֹכִי (I) will stand עַל רֹאשׁ (on the top of) the hill וּמַטֵּה הָאֱלֹהִים בְּיָדִי (and the staff of the Elohim in my hand)."

(10) And יְהוֹשֻׁעַ did as which אָמַר-לוֹ מֹשֶׁה (Moses said to him) and fought בַּעֲמָלֵק וּמֹשֶׁה אַהֲרֹן וְחוּר ascended רֹאשׁ (the top of) the hill.

(11) And it was, when מֹשֶׁה held up יָדוֹ (his hand) that יִשְׂרָאֵל prevailed; and when he let down יָדוֹ (his hand) עֲמָלֵק prevailed.

(12) וִידֵי מֹשֶׁה (And the hands of Moses) were heavy; and they took אֶבֶן (a stone) and put it under him, and he sat עָלֶיהָ (on it) וְאַהֲרֹן וְחוּר held בְּיָדָיו (on his hands) מִזֶּה (from this) one וּמִזֶּה (and from that) one; and יָדָיו (his hands) were steady until the setting of the sun.

(13) And יְהוֹשֻׁעַ defeated אֶת-עֲמָלֵק וְאֶת-עַמּוֹ (* Amalek and * his people) with the edge of the sword.

Level Two   שְׁמוֹת ~ יז

(14) וַיֹּאמֶר יהוה אֶל־מֹשֶׁה (And YHVH said to Moses):

> כְּתֹב זֹאת זִכָּרוֹן בַּסֵּפֶר
>
> וְשִׂים בְּאָזְנֵי יְהוֹשֻׁעַ
>
> כִּי־מָחֹה אֶמְחֶה
>
> אֶת־זֵכֶר עֲמָלֵק
>
> מִתַּחַת הַשָּׁמָיִם

> Write this a memorial in the book
>
> and put it in the ears of Joshua
>
> for I will surely wipe out
>
> * the memory of Amalek
>
> from under sky.

(15) And מֹשֶׁה built מִזְבֵּחַ (an altar) וַיִּקְרָא שְׁמוֹ (and called the name of it) יהוה נִסִּי (YHVH my banner).

(16) וַיֹּאמֶר (And he said):

"For יָד (a hand) עַל (on) the throne of לַיהוה -- יָהּ will have war בַּעֲמָלֵק (with Amalek) מִדֹּר דֹּר (from generation to generation)."

Chapter Eighteen

Jethro Visits Moses

(1) וַיִּשְׁמַע יִתְרוֹ (And Jethro heard) -- the priest of מִדְיָן the in-law of מֹשֶׁה -- of אֶת כָּל (* all) that אֱלֹהִים had done לְמֹשֶׁה וּלְיִשְׂרָאֵל עַמּוֹ (for Moses and for Israel His people) that יהוה had brought forth אֶת יִשְׂרָאֵל מִמִּצְרָיִם

(2) And יִתְרוֹ the in-law of מֹשֶׁה took אֶת צִפֹּרָה אֵשֶׁת מֹשֶׁה (* Zipporah the wife of Moses) after שִׁלּוּחֶיהָ (her sending away).

(3) וְאֵת two of בָנֶיהָ (her sons) of whom שֵׁם (the name of) the one was גֵּרְשֹׁם for אָמַר (he said):

"I have been גֵּר (a sojourner) בְּאֶרֶץ נָכְרִיָּה (in a foreign land)."

(4) וְשֵׁם (And the name) of the other was אֱלִיעֶזֶר

"For אֱלֹהֵי אָבִי (the Elohim of my father) in my helper and He rescued me from the sword of פַּרְעֹה

(5) And יִתְרוֹ the in-law of מֹשֶׁה came וּבָנָיו (and his sons) וְאִשְׁתּוֹ (and his wife) אֶל-מֹשֶׁה (to Moses) אֶל-הַמִּדְבָּר (to the wilderness) where הוּא (he) was encamped there הַר הָאֱלֹהִים (the mountain of the Elohim).

(6) וַיֹּאמֶר אֶל-מֹשֶׁה (and he said to Moses):

אֲנִי (I) יִתְרוֹ your in-law וְאִשְׁתְּךָ (and your wife) and two of בָנֶיהָ (her sons) עִמָּהּ (with her) are coming אֵלֶיךָ (to you)."

(7) And מֹשֶׁה went forth to meet his in-law, and bowed down and kissed לוֹ (to him) and they asked אִישׁ (a man) his associate לְשָׁלוֹם (for peace) and they came הָאֹהֱלָה (to the tent).

(8) And מֹשֶׁה told his in-law אֶת כָּל (* all) that יהוה had done לְפַרְעֹה וּלְמִצְרַיִם (to Pharaoh and to the Egypt) עַל (on) account of יִשְׂרָאֵל (Israel) אֶת כָּל (* all)

Level Two   שְׁמוֹת ~ יח

the tiredness that had come on them בַּדֶּרֶךְ (on the way) and יהוה delivered them.

(9) And יִתְרוֹ rejoiced עַל כָּל (over all) the goodness which יהוה had done לְיִשְׂרָאֵל in that He had delivered them מִיַּד מִצְרָיִם (from the hand of Egypt).

(10) וַיֹּאמֶר יִתְרוֹ (And Jethro said):

בָּרוּךְ יהוה (Blessed is YHVH) Who has delivered אֶתְכֶם (* you) מִיַּד מִצְרָיִם (from the hand of Egypt) וּמִיַּד פַּרְעֹה (and from the hand of Pharaoh) who has delivered אֶת הָעָם (* the people) from under יַד מִצְרָיִם (the hand of Egypt)."

(11)

Now I know that יהוה is greatest מִכָּל הָאֱלֹהִים (from all the elohim) because בַּדָּבָר (in the thing) which they were arrogant עֲלֵיהֶם (against them)."

(12) And יִתְרוֹ the in-law of מֹשֶׁה took a burnt-offering and sacrifices לֵאלֹהִים and אַהֲרֹן came וְכֹל (and all) the elders of יִשְׂרָאֵל to eat לֶחֶם (bread) with the in-law of מֹשֶׁה before הָאֱלֹהִים

(13) And it was on the morrow, that מֹשֶׁה sat to judge אֶת הָעָם (* the people) and הָעָם (the people) stood עַל-מֹשֶׁה (about Moses) מִן (from) the morning to the evening.

(14) וַיַּרְא חֹתֵן מֹשֶׁה (And the in-law of Moses saw) אֵת כָּל (* all) that הוּא (he) did לָעָם (for the people) וַיֹּאמֶר (he said):

מָה-הַדָּבָר הַזֶּה (What is this thing) that אַתָּה do לָעָם (for the people)? What reason are אַתָּה sitting alone וְכָל-הָעָם (and all the people) stand עָלֶיךָ (about you) from morning to even?"

(15) וַיֹּאמֶר מֹשֶׁה (And Moses said) to his in-law:

(16) "Because אֱלֹהִים (to inquire of) come (the people) הָעָם (to me) אֵלַי.

"Because לָהֶם (to them) it is דָּבָר (a thing) one comes אֵלַי (to me) and I judge between אִישׁ (a man) and his neighbor, and I make them know אֵת the statutes of הָאֱלֹהִים (the Elohim) וְאֵת His laws."

(17) וַיֹּאמֶר חֹתֵן מֹשֶׁה (And the in-law of Moses said) אֵלָיו (to him):

הַדָּבָר (The thing) that אַתָּה are doing is not good."

(18) "You will surely wear away גַּם-אַתָּה (also * you) גַּם-הָעָם הַזֶּה (also this people) that is עִמָּךְ (with you) for מִמְּךָ (from you) הַדָּבָר (the word) is too heavy; you are not able to do it by yourself."

(19) "Now שְׁמַע בְּקֹלִי (listen in my voice) I will counsel you and אֱלֹהִים be עִמָּךְ (with you). אַתָּה be לָעָם (for the people) before הָאֱלֹהִים and אַתָּה bring אֶת הַדְּבָרִים (* the things) אֶל-הָאֱלֹהִים

(20) "And you shall teach אֶתְהֶם (*them) אֵת the statutes וְאֵת the laws, and shall show לָהֶם (to them) אֶת-הַדֶּרֶךְ יֵלְכוּ (* the way they should walk) in it וְאֵת the deed that they should do."

(21) וְאַתָּה shall perceive מִכָּל-הָעָם (from of all the people) אַנְשֵׁי-חַיִל (men of ability) ones fearing אֱלֹהִים (Elohim) אַנְשֵׁי אֱמֶת (men of truth) ones hating gain; and place עֲלֵהֶם (over them) rulers of thousands, rulers of hundreds, rulers of fifties, and rulers of tens."

Level Two

שְׁמוֹת ~ יח

(22)
"And they shall judge אֶת-הָעָם (* the people) בְּכָל (in every) season. And it shall be כָּל הַדָּבָר הַגָּדֹל (every great thing) they shall bring אֵלֶיךָ (to you) וְכָל הַדָּבָר הַקָּטֹן (and every small thing) הֵם (they) shall judge themselves and lighten מֵעָלֶיךָ (from on you) and bear אִתָּךְ (with * you)."

(23)
"If you shall do אֶת-הַדָּבָר הַזֶּה (this * thing) and אֱלֹהִים instruct you, then you shall be able to stand וְגַם (and also) כָּל-הָעָם הַזֶּה (all this people) עַל (on) his place he shall go בְּשָׁלוֹם (in peace)."

Moses Sets Up Judges

(24) וַיִּשְׁמַע מֹשֶׁה לְקוֹל (And Moses listened to the voice of) his in-law, and he did כֹּל (all) that אָמָר (he said).

(25) And מֹשֶׁה chose אַנְשֵׁי-חַיִל (men of ability) מִכָּל יִשְׂרָאֵל (from all Israel) and he gave אֹתָם (* them) רָאשִׁים (heads) עַל-הָעָם (over the people) rulers of thousands, rulers of hundreds, rulers of fifties, and rulers of tens.

(26) And they judged אֶת-הָעָם (* the people) בְּכָל (in every) season: אֶת וְכָל-הַדָּבָר (the hard * thing) they brought to אֶל-מֹשֶׁה (to Moses) הַדָּבָר הַקָּשֶׁה וְכָל-הַדָּבָר הַקָּטֹן (and every small thing) הֵם (they judged) themselves.

(27) וַיְשַׁלַּח מֹשֶׁה (And Moses sent) אֶת his in-law וַיֵּלֶךְ (and he went) לוֹ (for him) אֶל-אַרְצוֹ (to his land).

Chapter Nineteen

Arriving At Sinai

(1) In the third month after בְּנֵי יִשְׂרָאֵל (the children of Israel) had gone forth מֵאֶרֶץ מִצְרָיִם (from the land of Egypt) on this day they entered מִדְבַּר סִינָי (the wilderness of Sinai).

(2) And they journeyed מֵרְפִידִים (from Rephidim) and they entered מִדְבַּר סִינָי (the wilderness of Sinai) and they encamped בַּמִּדְבָּר (in the wilderness). And there יִשְׂרָאֵל encamped in front of הָהָר (the mountain).

(3) וּמֹשֶׁה ascended אֶל-הָאֱלֹהִים (to the Elohim) וַיִּקְרָא יהוה (and YHVH called) אֵלָיו (to him) מִן-הָהָר (from the mountain) לֵאמֹר (saying):

כֹּה תֹאמַר לְבֵית יַעֲקֹב

וְתַגֵּיד לִבְנֵי יִשְׂרָאֵל

Thus shall you say to the house of Jacob

and tell to the children of Israel

(4)

אַתֶּם רְאִיתֶם אֲשֶׁר עָשִׂיתִי לְמִצְרָיִם

וָאֶשָּׂא אֶתְכֶם

עַל-כַּנְפֵי נְשָׁרִים

וָאָבִא אֶתְכֶם אֵלָי

* you have seen what I did to Egypt

and I carried * you

on wings of eagles

and brought * you to Myself

Level Two   שְׁמוֹת ~ יט

(5)

וְעַתָּה אִם-שָׁמוֹעַ

תִּשְׁמְעוּ בְּקֹלִי

וּשְׁמַרְתֶּם אֶת-בְּרִיתִי

and now if listening

you will listen in My voice

and keep * My covenant

וִהְיִיתֶם לִי סְגֻלָּה

מִכָּל-הָעַמִּים

כִּי-לִי כָּל-הָאָרֶץ

and you shall be for Me a treasure

from all peoples

for all the land for Me

(6)

וְאַתֶּם תִּהְיוּ-לִי

מַמְלֶכֶת כֹּהֲנִים וְגוֹי קָדוֹשׁ

אֵלֶּה הַדְּבָרִים אֲשֶׁר תְּדַבֵּר

אֶל-בְּנֵי יִשְׂרָאֵל

and * you shall be for Me

a kingdom of priests and a holy nation

these are the words which you shall speak

to the children of Israel.

Exodus ~ 19

The People Submit

(7) And מֹשֶׁה came וַיִּקְרָא (and he called) for the elders of הָעָם (the people) and set לִפְנֵיהֶם (to the faces of them) אֵת כָּל-הַדְּבָרִים הָאֵלֶּה (* all these words) which יהוה commanded him.

(8) And כָּל-הָעָם (all the people) answered together וַיֹּאמְרוּ (and they said):

כֹּל אֲשֶׁר-דִּבֶּר יהוה (All that YHVH speaks) נַעֲשֶׂה (we will do)."

And מֹשֶׁה reported אֶת-דִּבְרֵי (* the words of) הָעָם (the people) אֶל-יהוה

(9) וַיֹּאמֶר יהוה אֶל-מֹשֶׁה (And YHVH said to Moses):

הִנֵּה אָנֹכִי בָּא אֵלֶיךָ

בְּעַב הֶעָנָן

בַּעֲבוּר יִשְׁמַע הָעָם

בְּדַבְּרִי עִמָּךְ

וְגַם-בְּךָ יַאֲמִינוּ לְעוֹלָם

Behold, I am coming to you

in the thickness of the cloud

in order that the people will hear

in My speaking with you

and also they shall believe you forever

And מֹשֶׁה told אֶת-דִּבְרֵי (* the words of) הָעָם (the people) אֶל-יהוה

(10) וַיֹּאמֶר יהוה אֶל-מֹשֶׁה (And YHVH said to Moses):

לֵךְ אֶל-הָעָם וְקִדַּשְׁתָּם

Go to the people and sanctify them

Level Two ~ שְׁמוֹת ~ יט

הַיּוֹם וּמָחָר
וְכִבְּסוּ שִׂמְלֹתָם

today and tomorrow
and they shall wash their garments

(11)

וְהָיוּ נְכֹנִים
לַיּוֹם הַשְּׁלִישִׁי
כִּי בַּיּוֹם הַשְּׁלִשִׁי
יֵרֵד יהוה
לְעֵינֵי כָל-הָעָם עַל-הַר סִינָי

and they shall be prepared
for the third day
because the third day
YHVH will descend
for the eyes of all the people on Mount Sinai

(12)

וְהִגְבַּלְתָּ
אֶת-הָעָם סָבִיב לֵאמֹר
הִשָּׁמְרוּ לָכֶם

and you shall boundary
* the people round about saying
Guard for yourselves

Exodus ~ 19

עֲלוֹת בָּהָר
וּנְגֹעַ בְּקָצֵהוּ
כָּל־הַנֹּגֵעַ בָּהָר
מוֹת יוּמָת

to ascend on the mountain
and to touch the border of it
everyone touching on the mountain
shall surely be put to death

(13)

לֹא־תִגַּע בּוֹ יָד
כִּי־סָקוֹל יִסָּקֵל
אוֹ־יָרֹה יִיָּרֶה

no hand shall touch on it
because he shall surely be stoned
or he shall surely be shot

אִם־בְּהֵמָה אִם־אִישׁ לֹא יִחְיֶה
בִּמְשֹׁךְ הַיֹּבֵל
הֵמָּה יַעֲלוּ בָהָר

if animal if man, he shall not live
in sounding the ram's horn
they shall ascend on the mountain.

Level Two ~ שְׁמוֹת ~ יט

(14) And מֹשֶׁה descended מִן-הָהָר (from the mountain) אֶל-הָעָם (to the people) and sanctified אֶת-הָעָם (* the people) and they washed their garments.

(15) וַיֹּאמֶר (And he said) אֶל-הָעָם (to the people):

"Be prepared for three days you must not come close אֶל-אִשָּׁה (to a woman)."

YHVH Comes Down

(16) And it was on the third day, and it was the morning and it was קֹלֹת (voices) and lightnings וְעָנָן כָּבֵד (and a thick cloud) עַל הָהָר (on the mountain) וְקֹל (and a voice) of a horn exceeding loud כָּל-הָעָם (and all the people) that were בַּמַּחֲנֶה (in the camp) trembled.

(17) And מֹשֶׁה brought forth אֶת-הָעָם (* the people) מִן הַמַּחֲנֶה (from the camp) to meet הָאֱלֹהִים and they stood at the lowest part of הָהָר (the mountain).

(18) וְהַר סִינַי (And Mount Sinai) smoked כֻּלּוֹ מִפְּנֵי (from all of its faces) because יהוה descended עָלָיו (on it) בָּאֵשׁ (in fire); and his smoke ascended as the smoke of a furnace, and כָּל-הָהָר (all the mountain) trembled exceedingly.

(19) And when קוֹל (the voice of) the horn הוֹלֵךְ (went) very loud מֹשֶׁה יְדַבֵּר (Moses spoke) וְהָאֱלֹהִים answered him בְקוֹל (in a voice).

(20) And יהוה descended עַל-הַר סִינַי (on Mount Sinai) אֶל-רֹאשׁ הָהָר (to the top of the mountain) וַיִּקְרָא יהוה לְמֹשֶׁה (and called for Moses) אֶל-רֹאשׁ הָהָר (to the top of the mountain) and מֹשֶׁה ascended.

(21) וַיֹּאמֶר יהוה אֶל-מֹשֶׁה (And YHVH said to Moses):

רֵד הָעֵד בָּעָם

Go down warn on the people

Exodus ~ 19

פֶּן־יֶהֶרְסוּ
אֶל־יהוה לִרְאוֹת
וְנָפַל מִמֶּנּוּ רָב

lest they break through
to YHVH to see
and many fall from it

(22)

וְגַם הַכֹּהֲנִים
הַנִּגָּשִׁים אֶל־יהוה
יִתְקַדָּשׁוּ
פֶּן־יִפְרֹץ בָּהֶם יהוה

and also the priests
the ones coming close to YHVH
they shall sanctify themselves
lest YHVH break forth on them.

(23) וַיֹּאמֶר מֹשֶׁה (And Moses said) אֶל־יהוה

הָעָם (The people) are not able to ascend אֶל־הַר סִינָי (to Mount Sinai) because אַתָּה charged בָּנוּ (on us) לֵאמֹר (saying):

הַגְבֵּל אֶת־הָהָר
וְקִדַּשְׁתּוֹ

Level Two   שְׁמוֹת ~ יט

Set bounds about * the mountain

and sanctify it.

(24) וַיֹּאמֶר אֵלָיו יהוה (And YHVH said to him):

לֶךְ-רֵד

וְעָלִיתָ

אַתָּה וְאַהֲרֹן עִמָּךְ

Go, descend

and you shall ascend

* you and Aaron with you

וְהַכֹּהֲנִים וְהָעָם

אַל-יֶהֶרְסוּ

לַעֲלֹת אֶל-יהוה

פֶּן-יִפְרָץ-בָּם

and the priests and the people

must not break through

to ascend to YHVH

lest He break forth on them.

(25) So מֹשֶׁה descended אֶל-הָעָם (to the people) וַיֹּאמֶר אֲלֵהֶם (and spoke to them).

Chapter 20

The Ten Commandments

(1) וַיְדַבֵּר אֱלֹהִים (And Elohim spoke) אֵת כָּל-הַדְּבָרִים הָאֵלֶּה (*all these words) לֵאמֹר (saying):

(2)
אָנֹכִי יהוה אֱלֹהֶיךָ

אֲשֶׁר הוֹצֵאתִיךָ

מֵאֶרֶץ מִצְרַיִם

מִבֵּית עֲבָדִים

I am YHVH your Elohim

Who brought you forth

the land of Egypt

from the house of bondage

(3)
לֹא-יִהְיֶה לְךָ

אֱלֹהִים אֲחֵרִים

עַל-פָּנָי

it shall not be to you

other elohim

against My face

(4)
לֹא-תַעֲשֶׂה לְךָ

פֶּסֶל וְכָל-תְּמוּנָה

Level Two

שְׁמוֹת ~ כ

you shall not make for you
a carving and any representation

אֲשֶׁר בַּשָּׁמַיִם מִמַּעַל
וַאֲשֶׁר בָּאָרֶץ מִתָּחַת
וַאֲשֶׁר בַּמַּיִם
מִתַּחַת לָאָרֶץ

that is in the skies above
and that is in the land below
or that is in the water
under the land

(5)

לֹא-תִשְׁתַּחֲוֶה לָהֶם
וְלֹא תָעָבְדֵם
כִּי אָנֹכִי יהוה אֱלֹהֶיךָ
אֵל קַנָּא
פֹּקֵד עֲוֹן אָבֹת עַל-בָּנִים

you shall not bow down to them
and you shall not serve them
for I am YHVH your Elohim
a jealous El
visiting the iniquity of the fathers on the sons

Exodus ~ 20

עַל־שִׁלֵּשִׁים וְעַל־רִבֵּעִים

לְשֹׂנְאָי

on the third and on fourth

to them that hate Me

(6)

וְעֹשֶׂה חֶסֶד לַאֲלָפִים

לְאֹהֲבַי

וּלְשֹׁמְרֵי מִצְוֹתָי

and doing kindness to thousands

to them that love Me

and keep My commandments

(7)

לֹא תִשָּׂא

אֶת־שֵׁם־יהוה אֱלֹהֶיךָ

לַשָּׁוְא

you shall not lift up

* the name of YHVH your Elohim

for the futility

כִּי לֹא יְנַקֶּה יהוה

אֵת אֲשֶׁר־יִשָּׂא

אֶת־שְׁמוֹ לַשָּׁוְא

146

Level Two שְׁמוֹת ~ כ

for YHVH will not hold him innocent
* who lifts up
* His name in futility

(8)

זָכוֹר אֶת־יוֹם הַשַּׁבָּת לְקַדְּשׁוֹ

remember * the day of the Sabbath, to keep it holy

(9)

שֵׁשֶׁת יָמִים תַּעֲבֹד
וְעָשִׂיתָ כָּל־מְלַאכְתֶּךָ

six days you shall work
and do all your occupation

(10)

וְיוֹם הַשְּׁבִיעִי
שַׁבָּת לַיהוה אֱלֹהֶיךָ
לֹא־תַעֲשֶׂה כָל־מְלָאכָה
אַתָּה וּבִנְךָ וּבִתֶּךָ
עַבְדְּךָ וַאֲמָתְךָ

and the seventh day
a Sabbath to YHVH your Elohim
you shall not do all occupation
* you and your son and your daughter
your servant and your handmaid

Exodus ~ 20

וּבְהֶמְתֶּ֙ךָ֙ וְגֵרְךָ֔
אֲשֶׁ֖ר בִּשְׁעָרֶֽיךָ

and your animal and your sojourner
who is in your gates

(11)

כִּ֣י שֵֽׁשֶׁת־יָמִ֡ים
עָשָׂ֣ה יהוה אֶת־הַשָּׁמַ֣יִם
וְאֶת־הָאָ֜רֶץ אֶת־הַיָּ֗ם
וְאֶת־כָּל־אֲשֶׁר־בָּ֔ם

because in six days
YHVH made * the sky
and *the land * the sea and
* all that in them is

וַיָּ֖נַח בַּיּ֣וֹם הַשְּׁבִיעִ֑י
עַל־כֵּ֗ן בֵּרַ֧ךְ יהוה
אֶת־י֥וֹם הַשַּׁבָּ֖ת
וַֽיְקַדְּשֵֽׁהוּ

and stopped on the seventh day
therefore YHVH blessed
* the day of the Sabbath
and He made it holy

(12)

Level Two   שְׁמוֹת ~ כ

כַּבֵּד אֶת־אָבִיךָ וְאֶת־אִמֶּךָ
לְמַעַן יַאֲרִכוּן יָמֶיךָ
עַל הָאֲדָמָה
אֲשֶׁר־יהוה אֱלֹהֶיךָ נֹתֵן לָךְ

*glorify * your father and * your mother*

for the purpose your days may be long

on the ground

which YHVH your Elohim is giving to you

(13)

לֹא תִּרְצָח

You shall not murder

(14) (20:13)

לֹא תִּנְאָף

You shall not commit adultery.

(15) (20:13)

לֹא תִּגְנֹב

You shall not steal

(16) (20:13)

לֹא־תַעֲנֶה בְרֵעֲךָ
עֵד שָׁקֶר

You shall not answer on your neighbor

a testimony of falsehood

149

Exodus ~ 20

(17) (20:14)

לֹא תַחְמֹד

בֵּית רֵעֶךָ

You shall not desire
the house of your neighbor

לֹא־תַחְמֹד

אֵשֶׁת רֵעֶךָ

you shall not desire
the wife of your neighbor

וְעַבְדּוֹ וַאֲמָתוֹ

וְשׁוֹרוֹ וַחֲמֹרוֹ

וְכֹל אֲשֶׁר לְרֵעֶךָ

and his servant and his handmaid
and his ox and his donkey
and all that is for your neighbor

The People Send Moses

(18) (20:15) וְכָל־הָעָם רֹאִים (And all the people saw) אֶת הַקּוֹלֹת (* the voices) וְאֶת the lightnings וְאֵת קוֹל (and * the voice of) the horn וְאֶת הָהָר (and * the mountain) smoking. וַיַּרְא הָעָם (and he people saw) and they trembled, and stood afar off.

(19) (20:16) וַיֹּאמְרוּ אֶל־מֹשֶׁה (And they said to Moses):

150

Level Two ~ שְׁמוֹת ~ כ

דַּבֶּר-אַתָּה (* You speak) עִמָּנוּ (with us) וְנִשְׁמָעָה (and we will hear) וְאַל יְדַבֵּר אֱלֹהִים (and Elohim must not speak) עִמָּנוּ (with us) lest we die."

(20) (20:17) וַיֹּאמֶר מֹשֶׁה (And Moses said) אֶל-הָעָם (to the people):

"You must not fear for הָאֱלֹהִים came in order to test אֶתְכֶם and in order that His fear may be עַל-פְּנֵיכֶם (on your faces) that you do not sin."

Moses Draws Near

(21) (20:18) And הָעָם (the people) stood afar off. וּמֹשֶׁה drew near to the thick darkness where הָאֱלֹהִים was.

(22) (20:19) וַיֹּאמֶר יהוה אֶל-מֹשֶׁה (And YHVH said to Moses):

כֹּה תֹאמַר

לִ-בְנֵי יִשְׂרָאֵל

אַתֶּם רְאִיתֶם

כִּי מִן-הַשָּׁמַיִם

דִּבַּרְתִּי עִמָּכֶם

Thus you shall say

to the children of Israel

* You yourselves saw

that from the sky

I spoke with you

Exodus ~ 20

(23) (20:20)

לֹא תַעֲשׂוּן אִתִּי

אֱלֹהֵי כֶסֶף וֵאלֹהֵי זָהָב

לֹא תַעֲשׂוּ לָכֶם

you shall not make with Me

elohim of silver and elohim of gold

you shall not make for you

Making An Alter

(24) (20:21)

מִזְבַּח אֲדָמָה תַּעֲשֶׂה-לִּי

וְזָבַחְתָּ עָלָיו

an altar of ground you shall make for Me

and shall sacrifice on it

אֶת-עֹלֹתֶיךָ וְאֶת-שְׁלָמֶיךָ

אֶת-צֹאנְךָ וְאֶת-בְּקָרֶךָ

* your burnt-offerings and * your peace-offerings

* your flock and * your herd

בְּכָל-הַמָּקוֹם

אֲשֶׁר אַזְכִּיר אֶת-שְׁמִי

אָבוֹא אֵלֶיךָ

וּבֵרַכְתִּיךָ

Level Two   שְׁמוֹת ~ כ

in every place

where I remember * My name

and I will come to you

and bless you

(25) (20:22)

וְאִם־מִזְבַּח אֲבָנִים

תַּעֲשֶׂה־לִּי

לֹא־תִבְנֶה

אֶתְהֶן גָּזִית

כִּי חַרְבְּךָ הֵנַפְתָּ עָלֶיהָ

וַתְּחַלְלֶהָ

And if an altar of stones

you make for Me

you shall not build

* them of cut stones

for if you weild your sword on it

you have profaned it

(26) (20:23)

וְלֹא־תַעֲלֶה בְמַעֲלֹת עַל־מִזְבְּחִי

אֲשֶׁר לֹא־תִגָּלֶה עֶרְוָתְךָ עָלָיו

and you shall not ascend on stairs on My altar

that your nakedness not be exposed on it.

Chapter Twenty-One

Instructions From YHVH

(1)

וְאֵלֶּה הַמִּשְׁפָּטִים

אֲשֶׁר תָּשִׂים לִפְנֵיהֶם

And these are the judgments

which you shall set to their faces

(2)

כִּי תִקְנֶה עֶבֶד עִבְרִי

שֵׁשׁ שָׁנִים יַעֲבֹד

וּבַשְּׁבִעֵת יֵצֵא

לַחָפְשִׁי חִנָּם

that you buy a Hebrew servant

six years he shall serve

and in the seventh he shall go forth

to the free for nothing

(3)

אִם־בְּגַפּוֹ יָבֹא

בְּגַפּוֹ יֵצֵא

If he come in his singleness

he shall go forth in his singleness.

אִם־בַּעַל אִשָּׁה הוּא

וְיָצְאָה אִשְׁתּוֹ עִמּוֹ

Level Two   שְׁמוֹת ~ כא

If he is a husband of a woman
and his wife shall go out with him.

(4)

אִם-אֲדֹנָיו יִתֶּן-לוֹ אִשָּׁה
וְיָלְדָה-לוֹ בָנִים אוֹ בָנוֹת
הָאִשָּׁה וִילָדֶיהָ
תִּהְיֶה לַאדֹנֶיהָ
וְהוּא יֵצֵא בְגַפּוֹ

If his master give him a wife
and she bear for him sons or daughters,
the wife and her children
she shall be for her master
and he shall go forth by himself.

(5)

וְאִם-אָמֹר יֹאמַר הָעֶבֶד
אָהַבְתִּי אֶת-אֲדֹנִי
אֶת-אִשְׁתִּי וְאֶת-בָּנָי
לֹא אֵצֵא חָפְשִׁי

And if speaking the servant shall say,
*I love * my master*
*my * wife, and * my children*
I will not go forth free

Exodus ~ 21

(6)

וְהִגִּישׁוֹ אֲדֹנָיו אֶל־הָאֱלֹהִים

וְהִגִּישׁוֹ אֶל־הַדֶּלֶת

אוֹ אֶל־הַמְּזוּזָה

and his master shall bring him close to the Elohim

and shall bring him close to the door

or to the doorpost

וְרָצַע אֲדֹנָיו

אֶת־אָזְנוֹ בַּמַּרְצֵעַ

וַעֲבָדוֹ לְעֹלָם

and his master shall bore

* his ear with an awl

and he shall serve him forever.

(7)

וְכִי־יִמְכֹּר אִישׁ

אֶת־בִּתּוֹ לְאָמָה

לֹא תֵצֵא

כְּצֵאת הָעֲבָדִים

And that a man sells

* his daughter to be a maidservant

She shall not go fort

as the servants do.

Level Two שְׁמוֹת ~ כא

(8)

אִם־רָעָה

בְּעֵינֵי אֲדֹנֶיהָ

אֲשֶׁר־לוֹ יְעָדָהּ

וְהֶפְדָּהּ

If an evil one

in the eyes of her master

that has not appointed her to him

and he let her be ransomed.

לְעַם נָכְרִי

לֹא־יִמְשֹׁל לְמָכְרָהּ

בְּבִגְדוֹ־בָהּ

To a foreign people,

he shall not rule to sell her

in his being treacherous with her.

(9)

וְאִם־לִבְנוֹ יִיעָדֶנָּה

כְּמִשְׁפַּט הַבָּנוֹת

יַעֲשֶׂה־לָּהּ

and if he has appointed her for his son

as the custom of the daughters

he shall do for her.

157

Exodus ~ 21

(10)

אִם-אַחֶרֶת יִקַּח-לוֹ
שְׁאֵרָהּ כְּסוּתָהּ
וְעֹנָתָהּ
לֹא יִגְרָע

If he take another for himself
her meat her covering
and her marital rights
he shall he not diminish.

(11)

וְאִם-שְׁלָשׁ-אֵלֶּה
לֹא יַעֲשֶׂה לָהּ
וְיָצְאָה חִנָּם
אֵין כָּסֶף

And if these three
he does not do for her
and shall she go forth for nothing
without money.

(12)

מַכֵּה אִישׁ וָמֵת
מוֹת יוּמָת

He that smites a man and he dies
shall surely be put to death.

Level Two   שְׁמוֹת ~ כא

(13)

וַאֲשֶׁר לֹא צָדָה
וְהָאֱלֹהִים אִנָּה לְיָדוֹ
וְשַׂמְתִּי לְךָ מָקוֹם
אֲשֶׁר יָנוּס שָׁמָּה

And who does not lie in wait
then the Elohim allowed for his hand.
And I will appoint for you a place
where he may flee to there.

(14)

וְכִי־יָזִד אִישׁ
עַל־רֵעֵהוּ
לְהָרְגוֹ בְעָרְמָה
מֵעִם מִזְבְּחִי
תִּקָּחֶנּוּ לָמוּת

And if a man act presumptuously
on his neighbor
to slay him with guile
from with My altar
you shall take him to die.

(15)

וּמַכֵּה אָבִיו וְאִמּוֹ

And he who smites his father or his mother

Exodus ~ 21

מוֹת יוּמָת

shall be surely put to death.

(16)

וְגֹנֵב אִישׁ

וּמְכָרוֹ

וְנִמְצָא בְיָדוֹ

מוֹת יוּמָת

And he that steales a man

and sells him

or he is found in his hand

he shall surely be put to death.

(17)

וּמְקַלֵּל אָבִיו וְאִמּוֹ

מוֹת יוּמָת

And he that slights his father or his mother

shall surely be put to death.

(18)

וְכִי־יְרִיבֻן אֲנָשִׁים

וְהִכָּה־אִישׁ אֶת־רֵעֵהוּ

בְּאֶבֶן אוֹ בְאֶגְרֹף

וְלֹא יָמוּת

וְנָפַל לְמִשְׁכָּב

Level Two

שְׁמוֹת ~ כא

And when men contend

and a man smites his neighbor

with a stone or with his fist

and he does not die

and he falls to his bed

(19)

אִם־יָקוּם וְהִתְהַלֵּךְ

בַּחוּץ עַל־מִשְׁעַנְתּוֹ

וְנִקָּה הַמַּכֶּה

רַק שִׁבְתּוֹ יִתֵּן

וְרַפֹּא יְרַפֵּא

if he rises and he walks

in the outside on his staff

then the one that smote is innocent.

but he shall pay for his rest

and he shall cause him to be thoroughly healed.

(20)

וְכִי־יַכֶּה אִישׁ אֶת־עַבְדּוֹ אוֹ אֶת־אֲמָתוֹ בַּשֵּׁבֶט

וּמֵת תַּחַת יָדוֹ

נָקֹם יִנָּקֵם

And if a man smites * his servant or his maidservant with a staff

and he dies under his hand

he shall surely be punished.

(21)

Exodus ~ 21

אַךְ אִם־יוֹם אוֹ יוֹמַיִם יַעֲמֹד

לֹא יֻקַּם

כִּי כַסְפּוֹ הוּא

Yea, if a day or days he stands

he shall not be avenged

for he is his money.

(22)

וְכִי־יִנָּצוּ אֲנָשִׁים

וְנָגְפוּ אִשָּׁה הָרָה

וְיָצְאוּ יְלָדֶיהָ

וְלֹא יִהְיֶה אָסוֹן

And if men strive

and hurt a woman with child

and her children come forth

and there is no mishap

עָנוֹשׁ יֵעָנֵשׁ

כַּאֲשֶׁר יָשִׁית עָלָיו בַּעַל הָאִשָּׁה

וְנָתַן בִּפְלִלִים

he shall be surely fined

as which the woman's husband imposes on him

and he shall give through the mediators.

Level Two — שְׁמוֹת ~ כא

(23)

וְאִם־אָסוֹן יִהְיֶה
וְנָתַתָּה נֶפֶשׁ תַּחַת נָפֶשׁ

But if it was a mishap
then you shall give soul for soul,

(24)

עַיִן תַּחַת עַיִן שֵׁן תַּחַת שֵׁן
יָד תַּחַת יָד רֶגֶל תַּחַת רָגֶל

eye for eye, tooth for tooth
hand for hand, foot for foot,

(25)

כְּוִיָּה תַּחַת כְּוִיָּה פֶּצַע תַּחַת פָּצַע
חַבּוּרָה תַּחַת חַבּוּרָה

burning for burning, wound for wound,
stripe for stripe.

(26)

וְכִי־יַכֶּה אִישׁ אֶת־עֵין עַבְדּוֹ
אוֹ־אֶת־עֵין אֲמָתוֹ וְשִׁחֲתָהּ
לַחָפְשִׁי יְשַׁלְּחֶנּוּ תַּחַת עֵינוֹ

*And if a man smite * the eye of his servant*
*or * the eye of his maidservant, and destroy it,*
he shall send him to the free for his eye.

Exodus ~ 21

(27)

וְאִם־שֵׁן עַבְדּוֹ
אוֹ־שֵׁן אֲמָתוֹ יַפִּיל
לַחָפְשִׁי יְשַׁלְּחֶנּוּ
תַּחַת שִׁנּוֹ

And if a tooth of his servant
or a tooth of his maidservant, he causes to fall out
he shall send him to the free
for his tooth.

(28)

וְכִי־יִגַּח שׁוֹר אֶת־אִישׁ אוֹ אֶת־אִשָּׁה
וָמֵת סָקוֹל יִסָּקֵל הַשּׁוֹר
וְלֹא יֵאָכֵל אֶת־בְּשָׂרוֹ
וּבַעַל הַשּׁוֹר נָקִי

And if an ox gore * a man or * a woman,
and he dies, the ox shall be surely stoned,
and * the flesh of it shall not be eaten;
and the owner of the ox shall be innocent.

(29)

וְאִם שׁוֹר נַגָּח הוּא
מִתְּמֹל שִׁלְשֹׁם
וְהוּעַד בִּבְעָלָיו

Level Two

שְׁמוֹת ~ כא

But if the ox, he was going
heretofore
and it has been testified on its owner,

וְלֹא יִשְׁמְרֶנּוּ

וְהֵמִית אִישׁ אוֹ אִשָּׁה

הַשּׁוֹר יִסָּקֵל

וְגַם־בְּעָלָיו יוּמָת

and he is not keeping it,
but it has killed a man or a woman;
the ox shall be stoned,
and also its owner shall be put to death.

(30)

אִם־כֹּפֶר יוּשַׁת עָלָיו

וְנָתַן פִּדְיֹן נַפְשׁוֹ

כְּכֹל אֲשֶׁר־יוּשַׁת עָלָיו

If a ransom is imposed on him,
then he shall give a redemption of his soul
as all which is imposed on him.

(31)

אוֹ־בֵן יִגָּח אוֹ־בַת יִגָּח

כַּמִּשְׁפָּט הַזֶּה יֵעָשֶׂה לּוֹ

Whether it gored a son, or gored a daughter,
as this judgment, it shall be done to him.

Exodus ~ 21

(32)

אִם־עֶ֛בֶד יִגַּ֥ח הַשּׁ֖וֹר א֣וֹ אָמָ֑ה
כֶּ֣סֶף ׀ שְׁלֹשִׁ֣ים שְׁקָלִ֗ים
יִתֵּן֙ לַֽאדֹנָ֔יו וְהַשּׁ֖וֹר יִסָּקֵֽל

If the ox gore a servant or a maidservant,

thirty shekels of silver

he shall give to his master, and the ox shall be stoned.

(33)

וְכִֽי־יִפְתַּ֨ח אִ֜ישׁ בּ֗וֹר
א֠וֹ כִּֽי־יִכְרֶ֥ה אִ֛ישׁ בֹּ֖ר
וְלֹ֣א יְכַסֶּ֑נּוּ
וְנָֽפַל־שָׁ֥מָּה שּׁ֖וֹר א֥וֹ חֲמֽוֹר

And if a man shall open a pit,

or if a man shall dig a well

and not cover it,

and an ox fall therein or a donkey,

(34)

בַּ֤עַל הַבּוֹר֙ יְשַׁלֵּ֔ם
כֶּ֖סֶף יָשִׁ֣יב לִבְעָלָ֑יו
וְהַמֵּ֖ת יִֽהְיֶה־לּֽוֹ

The owner of the pit shall repay

he shall give money to its owner,

and the dead one shall be his.

Level Two   שְׁמוֹת ~ כא

(35)

וְכִי-יִגֹּף שׁוֹר-אִישׁ
אֶת-שׁוֹר רֵעֵהוּ וָמֵת

And if one man's ox hurt
* an ox of his neighbor and it dies,

וּמָכְרוּ אֶת-הַשּׁוֹר הַחַי
וְחָצוּ אֶת-כַּסְפּוֹ
וְגַם אֶת-הַמֵּת יֶחֱצוּן

then they shall sell the live * ox,
and they shall divide * the money of it;
and also * the dead they shall divide.

(36)

אוֹ נוֹדַע, כִּי שׁוֹר נַגָּח הוּא
מִתְּמוֹל שִׁלְשֹׁם
וְלֹא יִשְׁמְרֶנּוּ בְּעָלָיו

Or if it is known that the ox was going
heretofore,
and its owner has not kept it,

שַׁלֵּם יְשַׁלֵּם שׁוֹר תַּחַת הַשּׁוֹר
וְהַמֵּת יִהְיֶה-לּוֹ

he shall surely pay ox for ox,
and the dead one shall be his.

Chapter Twenty-Two

More Instructions From YHVH

(1) (21:37)

כִּי יִגְנֹב־אִישׁ

שׁוֹר אוֹ־שֶׂה

וּטְבָחוֹ אוֹ מְכָרוֹ

חֲמִשָּׁה בָקָר

יְשַׁלֵּם תַּחַת הַשּׁוֹר

וְאַרְבַּע־צֹאן תַּחַת הַשֶּׂה

If a man steal an
ox, or a sheep,
and kill it, or sell it,
five oxen
he shall pay for an ox,
and four sheep for a sheep.

(2) (22:1)

אִם־בַּמַּחְתֶּרֶת יִמָּצֵא הַגַּנָּב

וְהֻכָּה וָמֵת

אֵין לוֹ דָּמִים

If a thief be found breaking in,
and he is smitten and he dies,
there shall be no blood for him.

Level Two   שְׁמוֹת ~ כב

(3) (22:2)

אִם־זָרְחָה הַשֶּׁמֶשׁ עָלָיו
דָּמִים לוֹ
שַׁלֵּם יְשַׁלֵּם
אִם־אֵין לוֹ
וְנִמְכַּר בִּגְנֵבָתוֹ

If the sun rose on him,
there shall be blood for him
he shall surely repay;
if he has nothing,
then he shall be sold for his theft.

(4) (22:3)

אִם־הִמָּצֵא תִמָּצֵא
בְיָדוֹ הַגְּנֵבָה
מִשּׁוֹר עַד־חֲמוֹר
עַד־שֶׂה חַיִּים
שְׁנַיִם יְשַׁלֵּם

If it is surely found
in the hand of the theft
from ox unto donkey,
unto flockling alive,
he shall pay double.

(5) (22:4)

כִּי יַבְעֶר־אִישׁ

שָׂדֶה אוֹ־כֶרֶם

וְשִׁלַּח אֶת־בְּעִירֹה

וּבִעֵר בִּשְׂדֵה אַחֵר

If a man cause to be grazed down
a field or a vineyard,
and he lets * his livestock loose,
and it grazes down in the field of another,

מֵיטַב שָׂדֵהוּ

וּמֵיטַב כַּרְמוֹ

יְשַׁלֵּם

of the best of his own field,
and of the best of his own vineyard,
he shall repay.

(6) (22:5)

כִּי־תֵצֵא אֵשׁ

וּמָצְאָה קֹצִים

וְנֶאֱכַל גָּדִישׁ

If fire break out,
and it finds thorns,
and it devours shock,

Level Two — שְׁמוֹת ~ כב

אוֹ הַקָּמָה אוֹ הַשָּׂדֶה

שַׁלֵּם יְשַׁלֵּם

הַמַּבְעִר אֶת־הַבְּעֵרָה

or the standing, or the field,

He shall surely repay -

the one that kindled * the fire.

(7) (22:6)

כִּי־יִתֵּן אִישׁ אֶל־רֵעֵהוּ

כֶּסֶף אוֹ־כֵלִים לִשְׁמֹר

וְגֻנַּב מִבֵּית הָאִישׁ

אִם־יִמָּצֵא הַגַּנָּב

יְשַׁלֵּם שְׁנָיִם

If a man deliver to his neighbor

money or articles to keep,

and it is stolen from the house of the man,

if the thief is found,

he shall pay double.

(8) (22:7)

אִם־לֹא יִמָּצֵא הַגַּנָּב

וְנִקְרַב בַּעַל־הַבַּיִת אֶל־הָאֱלֹהִים

If the thief is not found,

then the master of the house shall come near to Elohim,

אִם־לֹא שָׁלַח יָדוֹ
בִּמְלֶאכֶת רֵעֵהוּ

if he did not put his hand
in his neighbor's business

(9) (22:8)

עַל־כָּל־דְּבַר־פֶּשַׁע
עַל־שׁוֹר עַל־חֲמוֹר
עַל־שֶׂה עַל־שַׂלְמָה
עַל־כָּל־אֲבֵדָה
אֲשֶׁר יֹאמַר כִּי־הוּא זֶה

For every matter of trespass,
over ox, over donkey,
over flockling, over raiment,
over every lost thing
which he says that this is it.

עַד הָאֱלֹהִים יָבֹא דְּבַר־שְׁנֵיהֶם
אֲשֶׁר יַרְשִׁיעֻן אֱלֹהִים
יְשַׁלֵּם שְׁנַיִם לְרֵעֵהוּ

Unto elohim, the matter of the two of them shall come
whomever elohim (they shall condemn)
he shall pay double to his neighbor.

Level Two

שְׁמוֹת ~ כב

(10) (22:9)

כִּי־יִתֵּן אִישׁ אֶל־רֵעֵהוּ
חֲמוֹר אוֹ־שׁוֹר
אוֹ־שֶׂה וְכָל־בְּהֵמָה לִשְׁמֹר
וּמֵת אוֹ־נִשְׁבַּר
אוֹ־נִשְׁבָּה אֵין רֹאֶה

If a man gives to his neighbor
a donkey, or an ox,
or a flockling, or any animal, to keep
and it dies, or it is hurt,
or driven away, nobody seeing it;

(11) (22:10)

שְׁבֻעַת יהוה תִּהְיֶה בֵּין שְׁנֵיהֶם
אִם־לֹא שָׁלַח יָדוֹ
בִּמְלֶאכֶת רֵעֵהוּ
וְלָקַח בְּעָלָיו
וְלֹא יְשַׁלֵּם

the oath of YHVH shall be between them both,
if he has not put his hand
on his neighbor's business;
and the owner accepts,
and he shall not repay.

Exodus ~ 22

(12) (22:11)

וְאִם־גָּנֹב יִגָּנֵב מֵעִמּוֹ
יְשַׁלֵּם לִבְעָלָיו

But if it is surely stolen from him,
he shall repay its owner.

(13) (22:12)

אִם־טָרֹף יִטָּרֵף
יְבִאֵהוּ עֵד
הַטְּרֵפָה לֹא יְשַׁלֵּם

If it is torn in pieces,
let him bring it for a testimony,
that which was torn he shall not repay.

(14) (22:13)

וְכִי־יִשְׁאַל אִישׁ
מֵעִם רֵעֵהוּ
וְנִשְׁבַּר אוֹ־מֵת
בְּעָלָיו אֵין־עִמּוֹ
שַׁלֵּם יְשַׁלֵּם

And if a man borrow
from his neighbor,
and it is broken, or it dies,
the owner of it not with it,
he shall repay.

Level Two   שְׁמוֹת ~ כב

(15) (22:14)

אִם־בְּעָלָיו עִמּוֹ לֹא יְשַׁלֵּם

אִם־שָׂכִיר הוּא

בָּא בִּשְׂכָרוֹ

If the owner of it is with it, he shall not repay;

if it be hired,

it comes in its hire.

(16) (22:15)

וְכִי־יְפַתֶּה אִישׁ בְּתוּלָה

אֲשֶׁר לֹא־אֹרָשָׂה וְשָׁכַב עִמָּהּ

מָהֹר יִמְהָרֶנָּה

לּוֹ לְאִשָּׁה

And if a man entices a virgin

that is not betrothed, and lie with her,

he shall surely pay her bride price

for himself for a wife.

(17) (22:16)

אִם־מָאֵן יְמָאֵן אָבִיהָ לְתִתָּהּ לוֹ

כֶּסֶף יִשְׁקֹל

כְּמֹהַר הַבְּתוּלֹת

If her father utterly refuse to give her to him,

he weigh out money

according to the bride price of virgins.

Exodus ~ 22

(18) (22:17)

מְכַשֵּׁפָה לֹא תְחַיֶּה

An enchantress you shall not let live.

(19) (22:18)

כָּל־שֹׁכֵב עִם־בְּהֵמָה

מוֹת יוּמָת

Every one lying with an animal
shall surely be put to death.

(20) (22:19)

זֹבֵחַ לָאֱלֹהִים יָחֳרָם

בִּלְתִּי לַיהוה לְבַדּוֹ

He that sacrifices to the elohim shall be doomed
unless to YHVH, to Him alone.

(21) (22:20)

וְגֵר לֹא־תוֹנֶה

וְלֹא תִלְחָצֶנּוּ

כִּי־גֵרִים הֱיִיתֶם בְּאֶרֶץ מִצְרָיִם

And a sojourner shall you not tyrannize
and you shall not oppress him;
for you were sojourners in the land of Egypt.

(22) (22:21)

כָּל־אַלְמָנָה וְיָתוֹם

לֹא תְעַנּוּן

Level Two

שְׁמוֹת ~ כב

Any widow or orphan
you shall not humiliate.

(23) (22:22)

אִם-עַנֵּה תְעַנֶּה אֹתוֹ
כִּי אִם-צָעֹק יִצְעַק אֵלַי
שָׁמֹעַ אֶשְׁמַע צַעֲקָתוֹ

If you surely humilitate * him
that if he surely cry to Me,
I will surely hear his cry.

(24) (22:23)

וְחָרָה אַפִּי
וְהָרַגְתִּי אֶתְכֶם בֶּחָרֶב
וְהָיוּ נְשֵׁיכֶם אַלְמָנוֹת
וּבְנֵיכֶם יְתֹמִים

And My wrath shall wax hot,
and I will kill * you with the sword,
and your wives shall be widows,
and your children orphans.

(25) (22:24)

אִם-כֶּסֶף תַּלְוֶה אֶת-עַמִּי
אֶת-הֶעָנִי עִמָּךְ

If you lend money to * My people,
* the poor with you,

Exodus ~ 22

לֹא־תִהְיֶה לוֹ כְּנֹשֶׁה
לֹא־תְשִׂימוּן עָלָיו נֶשֶׁךְ

you shall not be to him as a creditor,
you shall not lay on him interest.

(26) (22:25)

אִם־חָבֹל תַּחְבֹּל
שַׂלְמַת רֵעֶךָ
עַד־בֹּא הַשֶּׁמֶשׁ
תְּשִׁיבֶנּוּ לוֹ

If you surely a pledge
raiment of your neighbor,
by the setting of the sun
you shall restore it to him;

(27) (22:26)

כִּי הִוא כְסוּתֹה לְבַדָּהּ
הִוא שִׂמְלָתוֹ לְעֹרוֹ
בַּמֶּה יִשְׁכָּב

for it is her covering for her alone,
it is his garment for his skin;
What shall he lie down in?

וְהָיָה כִּי־יִצְעַק אֵלַי
וְשָׁמַעְתִּי כִּי־חַנּוּן אָנִי

Level Two   שְׁמוֹת ~ כב

         And it shall be, when he cries to Me,
         that I will hear; for I am gracious.

(28) (22:27)

אֱלֹהִים לֹא תְקַלֵּל
וְנָשִׂיא בְעַמְּךָ לֹא תָאֹר

         You shall not slight Elohim
         nor curse a ruler of your people.

(29) (22:28)

מְלֵאָתְךָ וְדִמְעֲךָ
לֹא תְאַחֵר
בְּכוֹר בָּנֶיךָ
תִּתֶּן-לִי

         Your fullness and your juice
         you shall not delay,
         your firstborn sons
         you shall give to Me.

(30) (22:29)

כֵּן-תַּעֲשֶׂה לְשֹׁרְךָ לְצֹאנֶךָ
שִׁבְעַת יָמִים יִהְיֶה עִם-אִמּוֹ
בַּיּוֹם הַשְּׁמִינִי תִּתְּנוֹ-לִי

         So you shall do to your ox, to your flock;
         seven days it shall be with its mother,
         on the eighth day you shall give it Me.

Exodus ~ 22

(31) (22:30)

וְאַנְשֵׁי־קֹדֶשׁ תִּהְיוּן לִי
וּבָשָׂר בַּשָּׂדֶה טְרֵפָה
לֹא תֹאכֵלוּ
לַכֶּלֶב תַּשְׁלִכוּן אֹתוֹ

And you shall be men of holiness for Me;
and flesh in the field torn to pieces
you shall not eat;
*you shall cast * it to the dogs.*

Chapter Twenty-Three

Some More Instructions From YHVH

(1)

לֹא תִשָּׂא שֵׁמַע שָׁוְא

אַל־תָּשֶׁת יָדְךָ עִם־רָשָׁע

לִהְיֹת עֵד חָמָס

You shall not utter a false report;
You must not your hand with a wicked one
to be an unrighteous witness.

(2)

לֹא־תִהְיֶה אַחֲרֵי־רַבִּים לְרָעֹת

וְלֹא־תַעֲנֶה עַל־רִב

לִנְטֹת אַחֲרֵי רַבִּים לְהַטֹּת

You shall not follow a multitude to do evil;
you shall not testify on a contention
to turn aside after a multitude to pervert justice;

(3)

וְדָל לֹא תֶהְדַּר בְּרִיבוֹ

And a poor man you shall not favor in his cause.

(4)

כִּי תִפְגַּע שׁוֹר אֹיִבְךָ אוֹ חֲמֹרוֹ תֹּעֶה

הָשֵׁב תְּשִׁיבֶנּוּ לוֹ

If you meet your enemy's ox or his donkey going astray,
you shall surely return it to him.

(5)

כִּי־תִרְאֶה חֲמוֹר שֹׂנַאֲךָ

רֹבֵץ תַּחַת מַשָּׂאוֹ

וְחָדַלְתָּ מֵעֲזֹב לוֹ

עָזֹב תַּעֲזֹב עִמּוֹ

If you see the donkey of one that hates you

lying under its burden

you shall forbear to pass by him;

you shall surely release it with him.

(6)

לֹא תַטֶּה מִשְׁפַּט

אֶבְיֹנְךָ בְּרִיבוֹ

You shall not turn aside the judgment

of your poor in his cause.

(7)

מִדְּבַר־שֶׁקֶר תִּרְחָק

וְנָקִי וְצַדִּיק

אַל־תַּהֲרֹג

כִּי לֹא־אַצְדִּיק רָשָׁע

Keep far from a false matter;

and an innocent one and a righteous one

you must not slay;

for I will not justify a wicked one.

Level Two

שְׁמוֹת ~ כג

(8)

וְשֹׁחַד לֹא תִקָּח
כִּי הַשֹּׁחַד יְעַוֵּר פִּקְחִים
וִיסַלֵּף דִּבְרֵי צַדִּיקִים

And you shall not take a bribe;
for the bribe blinds them that have sight,
and perverts the words of the righteous.

(9)

וְגֵר לֹא תִלְחָץ
וְאַתֶּם יְדַעְתֶּם
אֶת-נֶפֶשׁ הַגֵּר
כִּי-גֵרִים הֱיִיתֶם
בְּאֶרֶץ מִצְרָיִם

And a sojourner you shall not oppress;
and * you know
* the soul of a sojourner,
because you were sojourners
in the land of Egypt.

(10)

וְשֵׁשׁ שָׁנִים תִּזְרַע אֶת-אַרְצֶךָ
וְאָסַפְתָּ אֶת-תְּבוּאָתָהּ

And six years you shall sow * your land,
and you shall gather * the increase of it;

(11)

וְהַשְּׁבִיעִת
תִּשְׁמְטֶנָּה וּנְטַשְׁתָּהּ
וְאָכְלוּ אֶבְיֹנֵי עַמֶּךָ

And the seventh
you shall release it and and leave it,
and the poor of your people may eat;

וְיִתְרָם
תֹּאכַל חַיַּת הַשָּׂדֶה
כֵּן־תַּעֲשֶׂה לְכַרְמְךָ
לְזֵיתֶךָ

and what they leave
the animals of the field shall eat.
So you shall do to your vineyard,
and to your oliveyard.

(12)

שֵׁשֶׁת יָמִים תַּעֲשֶׂה מַעֲשֶׂיךָ
וּבַיּוֹם הַשְּׁבִיעִי
תִּשְׁבֹּת
לְמַעַן יָנוּחַ שׁוֹרְךָ וַחֲמֹרֶךָ
וְיִנָּפֵשׁ בֶּן־אֲמָתְךָ
וְהַגֵּר

Level Two שְׁמוֹת ~ כג

Six days you shall do your deeds,
and on the seventh day
you shall rest;
so that your ox may rest and your donkey,
and the son of your handmaid may be refreshed,
and the stranger.

(13)

וּבְכֹל אֲשֶׁר־אָמַרְתִּי אֲלֵיכֶם
תִּשָּׁמֵרוּ
וְשֵׁם אֱלֹהִים אֲחֵרִים
לֹא תַזְכִּירוּ
לֹא יִשָּׁמַע עַל־פִּיךָ

And in all things that I say to you
you should beware;
and the name of other elohim
you shall not mention,
it shall not be heard on your mouth.

(14)

שָׁלֹשׁ רְגָלִים תָּחֹג לִי בַּשָּׁנָה

Three times you keep a feast to Me in the year.

(15)

אֶת־חַג הַמַּצּוֹת תִּשְׁמֹר

The feast of unleavened bread shall you keep;

שִׁבְעַת יָמִים תֹּאכַל מַצּוֹת

כַּאֲשֶׁר צִוִּיתִךָ

לְמוֹעֵד חֹדֶשׁ הָאָבִיב

כִּי־בוֹ יָצָאתָ מִמִּצְרָיִם

וְלֹא־יֵרָאוּ פָנַי רֵיקָם

seven days you shall eat unleavened bread,

as I commanded you,

at the appointed time the month of the abib

for in it you came forth from Egypt;

and none shall appear before Me empty;

(16)

וְחַג הַקָּצִיר

בִּכּוּרֵי מַעֲשֶׂיךָ

אֲשֶׁר תִּזְרַע בַּשָּׂדֶה

וְחַג הָאָסִף

בְּצֵאת הַשָּׁנָה

בְּאָסְפְּךָ אֶת־מַעֲשֶׂיךָ מִן־הַשָּׂדֶה

and the feast of harvest,

the firstfruits of your yields,

which you sow in the field;

and the feast of ingathering,

in the going forth of the year,

in your gathering * your yields from the field.

Level Two ~ שְׁמוֹת כג

(17)

שָׁלֹשׁ פְּעָמִים בַּשָּׁנָה
יֵרָאֶה כָּל־זְכוּרְךָ אֶל־פְּנֵי
הָאָדֹן יהוה

*Three times in the year
all your males shall appear
before the Lord YHVH.*

(18)

לֹא־תִזְבַּח עַל־חָמֵץ
דַּם־זִבְחִי
וְלֹא־יָלִין חֵלֶב־חַגִּי
עַד־בֹּקֶר

*You shall not sacrifice on leaven
the blood of My sacrifice;
And the fat of My feast shall not remain
until morning.*

(19)

רֵאשִׁית בִּכּוּרֵי אַדְמָתְךָ
תָּבִיא בֵּית יהוה אֱלֹהֶיךָ
לֹא־תְבַשֵּׁל גְּדִי בַּחֲלֵב אִמּוֹ

*The beginning of firstfruits of your ground
you shall bring to the house of YHVH your Elohim.
You shall not cook a kid in the milk of his mother.*

Exodus ~ 23

(20)

הִנֵּה אָנֹכִי שֹׁלֵחַ מַלְאָךְ
לְפָנֶיךָ לִשְׁמָרְךָ בַּדָּרֶךְ
וְלַהֲבִיאֲךָ אֶל־הַמָּקוֹם
אֲשֶׁר הֲכִנֹתִי

Behold, I am sending a messenger
before you, to keep you in the way,
and to bring you in the place
which I have prepared.

(21)

הִשָּׁמֶר מִפָּנָיו וּשְׁמַע בְּקֹלוֹ
אַל־תַּמֵּר בּוֹ
כִּי לֹא יִשָּׂא לְפִשְׁעֲכֶם
כִּי שְׁמִי בְּקִרְבּוֹ

Take heed of him, and listen to his voice;
do not be rebellious against him;
for he will not pardon your transgression;
for My name is within him.

(22)

כִּי אִם־שָׁמוֹעַ תִּשְׁמַע בְּקֹלוֹ
וְעָשִׂיתָ כֹּל אֲשֶׁר אֲדַבֵּר

For if you shall indeed hearken to his voice,
and do all that I speak;

Level Two   שְׁמוֹת ~ כג

וְאָיַבְתִּי אֶת-אֹיְבֶיךָ

וְצַרְתִּי אֶת-צֹרְרֶיךָ

then I will be an enemy to * your enemies,

and an adversary to * your adversaries.

(23)

כִּי-יֵלֵךְ מַלְאָכִי לְפָנֶיךָ

וֶהֱבִיאֲךָ אֶל-הָאֱמֹרִי

וְהַחִתִּי וְהַפְּרִזִּי

For My messenger shall go before you,

and bring you to the Amorite,

and the Hittite, and the Perizzite,

וְהַכְּנַעֲנִי הַחִוִּי וְהַיְבוּסִי

וְהִכְחַדְתִּיו

and the Canaanite, the Hivite, and the Jebusite;

and I will cut them off.

(24)

לֹא-תִשְׁתַּחֲוֶה לֵאלֹהֵיהֶם

וְלֹא תָעָבְדֵם וְלֹא תַעֲשֶׂה

כְּמַעֲשֵׂיהֶם

You shall not bow down to their elohim,

and you shall not serve them, and you shall not do

as they do;

189

Exodus ~ 23

כִּי הָרֵס תְּהָרְסֵם
וְשַׁבֵּר תְּשַׁבֵּר מַצֵּבֹתֵיהֶם

because you shall surely demolish them,
and you shall surely break their monuments.

(25)

וַעֲבַדְתֶּם אֵת יהוה אֱלֹהֵיכֶם
וּבֵרַךְ אֶת־לַחְמְךָ וְאֶת־מֵימֶיךָ
וַהֲסִרֹתִי מַחֲלָה מִקִּרְבֶּךָ

And you shall serve * YHVH your Elohim,
and He will bless * your bread, and * your water;
and I will take sickness away from within you.

(26)

לֹא תִהְיֶה מְשַׁכֵּלָה
וַעֲקָרָה בְּאַרְצֶךָ
אֶת־מִסְפַּר יָמֶיךָ אֲמַלֵּא

And there shall not be one miscarrying,
and a barren one in your land;
* the number of your days I will fulfill.

(27)

אֶת־אֵימָתִי אֲשַׁלַּח לְפָנֶיךָ
וְהַמֹּתִי אֶת־כָּל־הָעָם
אֲשֶׁר תָּבֹא בָּהֶם
וְנָתַתִּי אֶת־כָּל־אֹיְבֶיךָ אֵלֶיךָ עֹרֶף

Level Two שְׁמוֹת ~ כג

* My terror I will send before you,
and I will destroy * all the people
to whom you shall come,
and I will give
* all your enemies neck to you.

(28)

וְשָׁלַחְתִּי אֶת־הַצִּרְעָה לְפָנֶיךָ
וְגֵרְשָׁה אֶת־הַחִוִּי
אֶת־הַכְּנַעֲנִי וְאֶת־הַחִתִּי
מִלְּפָנֶיךָ

And I will send * the hornet before you,
and she will drive out * the Hivite,
* the Canaanite, and * the Hittite,
from before you.

(29)

לֹא אֲגָרְשֶׁנּוּ מִפָּנֶיךָ
בְּשָׁנָה אֶחָת
פֶּן־תִּהְיֶה הָאָרֶץ שְׁמָמָה
וְרַבָּה עָלֶיךָ חַיַּת הַשָּׂדֶה

I will not drive them out from before you
in one year,
lest the land become desolate,
and the animal of the field multiply against you.

(30)

מְעַט מְעַט

אֲגָרְשֶׁנּוּ מִפָּנֶיךָ

עַד אֲשֶׁר תִּפְרֶה

וְנָחַלְתָּ אֶת-הָאָרֶץ

Little and little

I will drive them out from before you,

until you increase,

and inherit * the land.

(31)

וְשַׁתִּי אֶת-גְּבֻלְךָ

מִיַּם-סוּף

וְעַד-יָם פְּלִשְׁתִּים

וּמִמִּדְבָּר עַד-הַנָּהָר

And I will set * your border

from the Red Sea

and to the sea of the Philistines,

and from the wilderness to the river;

כִּי אֶתֵּן בְּיֶדְכֶם

אֵת יֹשְׁבֵי הָאָרֶץ

וְגֵרַשְׁתָּמוֹ מִפָּנֶיךָ

Level Two שְׁמוֹת ~ כג

for I will give in your hand
* the inhabitants of the land;
and you shall drive them from before you.

(32)

לֹא־תִכְרֹת לָהֶם
וְלֵאלֹהֵיהֶם בְּרִית

You shall not cut to them
and to their elohim a covenant.

(33)

לֹא יֵשְׁבוּ בְּאַרְצְךָ
פֶּן־יַחֲטִיאוּ אֹתְךָ לִי
כִּי תַעֲבֹד אֶת־אֱלֹהֵיהֶם
כִּי־יִהְיֶה לְךָ לְמוֹקֵשׁ

They shall not dwell in your land
lest they cause * you to sin against Me,
for you will serve their elohim
for it will be for a trap for you.

Chapter Twenty-Four

Ascending The Mountain

(1) וְאֶל-מֹשֶׁה אָמַר *(And to Moses He said)*:

עֲלֵה אֶל-יהוה אַתָּה וְאַהֲרֹן נָדָב וַאֲבִיהוּא
וְשִׁבְעִים מִזִּקְנֵי יִשְׂרָאֵל
וְהִשְׁתַּחֲוִיתֶם מֵרָחֹק

*Ascend to YHVH, * you and Aaron, Nadab, and Abihu,*
and seventy of the elders of Israel;
and bow yourselves down from afar;

(2)

וְנִגַּשׁ מֹשֶׁה לְבַדּוֹ אֶל-יהוה
וְהֵם לֹא יִגָּשׁוּ
וְהָעָם לֹא יַעֲלוּ עִמּוֹ

And Moses shall come close by himself to YHVH
and they shall not come close;
and the people shall not ascend with him.

(3) And מֹשֶׁה came and related לָעָם *(the people)* אֵת כָּל דִּבְרֵי יהוה *(* all the words of YHVH)* וְאֵת כָּל *(* all)* the ordinances; and כָּל-הָעָם *(all the people)* answered with one קוֹל *(voice)* וַיֹּאמְרוּ *(and they said)*:

כָּל-הַדְּבָרִים *(All the words)* אֲשֶׁר-דִּבֶּר יהוה *(which YHVH has spoken)* נַעֲשֶׂה *(we will do)*.

(4) And מֹשֶׁה wrote אֵת כָּל-דִּבְרֵי יהוה *(all the words of YHVH)* and rose early in the morning, and built מִזְבֵּחַ *(an altar)* under הָהָר *(the mountain)* and

Level Two   שְׁמוֹת ~ כד

twelve monuments, for the twelve tribes of יִשְׂרָאֵל

(5) וַיִּשְׁלַח אֶת-נַעֲרֵי בְּנֵי יִשְׂרָאֵל (And he sent * the young men of the children of Israel) who offered burnt-offerings, and sacrificed peace-offerings of oxen לַיהוה

(6) And מֹשֶׁה took half of הַדָּם (the blood) and put it in basins; and half of הַדָּם (the blood) he sprinkled עַל-הַמִּזְבֵּחַ (on the altar).

(7) And he took סֵפֶר הַבְּרִית (the book of the covenant) and read בְּאָזְנֵי הָעָם (in the ears of the people) וַיֹּאמְרוּ (and they said):

כֹּל (All) that דְּבֶר יהוה (YHVH has spoken) נַעֲשֶׂה (we will do) וְנִשְׁמָע (and we will hear/obey)."

(8) And מֹשֶׁה took אֶת-הַדָּם (* the blood) and sprinkled it עַל-הָעָם (on the people) וַיֹּאמֶר (and he said):

"Behold דַּם-הַבְּרִית (the blood of the covenant) which יהוה has cut עִמָּכֶם (with you) עַל כָּל הַדְּבָרִים הָאֵלֶּה (on all these words)."

(9) Then מֹשֶׁה ascended וְאַהֲרֹן נָדָב וַאֲבִיהוּא and seventy of the elders of יִשְׂרָאֵל

(10) וַיִּרְאוּ (And they saw) אֵת אֱלֹהֵי יִשְׂרָאֵל and under רַגְלָיו (His feet) was as a paved work of sapphire, and as the substance of הַשָּׁמַיִם (the sky) for purity.

(11) And on the nobles of בְּנֵי יִשְׂרָאֵל (the children of Israel) לֹא שָׁלַח יָדוֹ (He did not send forth His hand) and they perceived אֶת-הָאֱלֹהִים and they ate and they drank.

(12) וַיֹּאמֶר יהוה אֶל-מֹשֶׁה (And YHVH said to Moses):

עֲלֵה אֵלַי הָהָרָה וֶהְיֵה-שָׁם

Ascend to Me toward the mountain and be there;

Exodus ~ 24

וְאֶתְּנָה לְךָ אֶת-לֻחֹת הָאֶבֶן
וְהַתּוֹרָה וְהַמִּצְוָה
אֲשֶׁר כָּתַבְתִּי לְהוֹרֹתָם

and I will give to you * the tablets of the stone,
and the law and the instruction,
which I have written, to direct them.

(13) And מֹשֶׁה rose וִיהוֹשֻׁעַ his minister; and מֹשֶׁה ascended אֶל-הַר (to the mountain of) הָאֱלֹהִים

(14) And אָמַר (he said) to the elders:

"Tarry here לָנוּ (for us) until we return אֲלֵיכֶם (to you) and, behold, אַהֲרֹן וְחוּר are עִמָּכֶם (with you) whosoever has דְּבָרִים (words/matters) let him come close אֲלֵהֶם (to them)."

(15) And מֹשֶׁה ascended אֶל-הָהָר (to the mountain) and הֶעָנָן (the cloud) covered אֶת-הָהָר (* the mountain).

(16) And כְּבוֹד-יהוה (the glory of YHVH) abode עַל הַר סִינַי (on Mount Sinai) and הֶעָנָן (the cloud) covered it six days וַיִּקְרָא (and He called) אֶל-מֹשֶׁה the seventh day from the midst of הֶעָנָן (the cloud).

(17) And the appearance of כְּבוֹד יהוה (the glory of YHVH) was כְּאֵשׁ אֹכֶלֶת (like devouring fire) בְּרֹאשׁ הָהָר (on the top of the mountain) לְעֵינֵי (to the eyes of) בְּנֵי יִשְׂרָאֵל (the children of Israel).

(18) And מֹשֶׁה entered in the midst of הֶעָנָן (the cloud) and he ascended אֶל-הָהָר (to the mountain) and מֹשֶׁה was בָּהָר (on the mountain) forty days and forty nights.

Chapter Twenty-Five

An Offering For The Tabernacle

(1) וַיְדַבֵּר יהוה אֶל-מֹשֶׁה לֵּאמֹר *(And YHVH spoke to Moses saying)*:

(2)
דַּבֵּר אֶל-בְּנֵי יִשְׂרָאֵל
וְיִקְחוּ-לִי תְּרוּמָה מֵאֵת כָּל-אִישׁ
אֲשֶׁר יִדְּבֶנּוּ לִבּוֹ
תִּקְחוּ אֶת-תְּרוּמָתִי

*Speak to the children of Israel
that they take for Me an offering; from * every man
whose heart makes him willing
you shall take * My offering.*

(3)
וְזֹאת הַתְּרוּמָה
אֲשֶׁר תִּקְחוּ מֵאִתָּם
זָהָב וָכֶסֶף וּנְחֹשֶׁת

*And this is the offering
which you shall take from * them:
gold, and silver, and copper;*

(4)
וּתְכֵלֶת וְאַרְגָּמָן וְתוֹלַעַת שָׁנִי
וְשֵׁשׁ וְעִזִּים

*and blue, and purple, and scarlet,
and fine linen, and goats' hair;*

Exodus ~ 25

(5)

וְעֹרֹת אֵילִם מְאָדָּמִים

וְעֹרֹת תְּחָשִׁים

וַעֲצֵי שִׁטִּים

and rams' skins dyed red,
and [unknown animal] skins,
and acacia-wood;

(6)

שֶׁמֶן לַמָּאֹר

בְּשָׂמִים לְשֶׁמֶן הַמִּשְׁחָה

וְלִקְטֹרֶת הַסַּמִּים

oil for the light,
spices for the anointing oil,
and for the sweet incense;

(7)

אַבְנֵי־שֹׁהַם וְאַבְנֵי מִלֻּאִים

לָאֵפֹד וְלַחֹשֶׁן

stones of onyx, and stones of fillings,
for the ephod, and for the breastplate.

(8)

וְעָשׂוּ לִי מִקְדָּשׁ

וְשָׁכַנְתִּי בְּתוֹכָם

Level Two   שְׁמוֹת ~ כה

And let them make Me a sanctuary,
that I may dwell among them.

(9)

כְּכֹל אֲשֶׁר אֲנִי מַרְאֶה אוֹתְךָ
אֵת תַּבְנִית הַמִּשְׁכָּן
וְאֵת תַּבְנִית כָּל־כֵּלָיו
וְכֵן תַּעֲשׂוּ

*According to all that I show * you,*
* the model of the tabernacle,
and * the model of all its furnishings,
even so shall you make.

The Ark Of The Covenant

(10)

וְעָשׂוּ אֲרוֹן עֲצֵי שִׁטִּים
אַמָּתַיִם וָחֵצִי אָרְכּוֹ
וְאַמָּה וָחֵצִי רָחְבּוֹ
וְאַמָּה וָחֵצִי קֹמָתוֹ

And they shall make an ark of acacia-wood:
two cubits and a half its length,
and a cubit and a half its width
and a cubit and a half its height,

(11)

וְצִפִּיתָ אֹתוֹ זָהָב טָהוֹר

מִבַּיִת וּמִחוּץ תְּצַפֶּנּוּ

וְעָשִׂיתָ עָלָיו

זֵר זָהָב סָבִיב

And you shall overlay it with pure gold,

within and without you shall overlay it,

and shall make on it

a crown of gold round about.

(12)

וְיָצַקְתָּ לּוֹ

אַרְבַּע טַבְּעֹת זָהָב

וְנָתַתָּה עַל אַרְבַּע פַּעֲמֹתָיו

וּשְׁתֵּי טַבָּעֹת

עַל־צַלְעוֹ הָאֶחָת

וּשְׁתֵּי טַבָּעֹת עַל־צַלְעוֹ הַשֵּׁנִית

And you shall cast for it

four rings of gold,

and put them on four of its footings;

and two rings

shall be on the one side of it,

and two rings on the second side of it.

(13)

וְעָשִׂיתָ בַדֵּי עֲצֵי שִׁטִּים

וְצִפִּיתָ אֹתָם זָהָב

And you shall make poles of acacia-wood,
and overlay them with gold.

(14)

וְהֵבֵאתָ אֶת-הַבַּדִּים בַּטַּבָּעֹת

עַל צַלְעֹת הָאָרֹן

לָשֵׂאת אֶת-הָאָרֹן בָּהֶם

And you shall insert * the poles in the rings
on the sides of the ark,
to carry * the ark on them.

(15)

בְּטַבְּעֹת הָאָרֹן יִהְיוּ הַבַּדִּים

לֹא יָסֻרוּ מִמֶּנּוּ

In the rings of the ark the poles shall be;
they shall not be withdrawn from it.

(16)

וְנָתַתָּ אֶל-הָאָרֹן אֵת הָעֵדֻת

אֲשֶׁר אֶתֵּן אֵלֶיךָ

And you shall give to the ark * the testimony
which I shall give to you.

(17)

וְעָשִׂיתָ כַפֹּרֶת
זָהָב טָהוֹר
אַמָּתַיִם וָחֵצִי אָרְכָּהּ
וְאַמָּה וָחֵצִי רָחְבָּהּ

And you shall make a mercy-seat
of pure gold:
two cubits and a half its length,
and a cubit and a half its width.

(18)

וְעָשִׂיתָ שְׁנַיִם כְּרֻבִים זָהָב
מִקְשָׁה תַּעֲשֶׂה אֹתָם
מִשְּׁנֵי קְצוֹת הַכַּפֹּרֶת

And you shall make two cherubim of gold;
of beaten work shall you make them,
from two ends of the mercy-seat.

(19)

וַעֲשֵׂה כְּרוּב אֶחָד מִקָּצָה מִזֶּה
וּכְרוּב־אֶחָד מִקָּצָה מִזֶּה
מִן־הַכַּפֹּרֶת
תַּעֲשׂוּ אֶת־הַכְּרֻבִים
עַל־שְׁנֵי קְצוֹתָיו

Level Two

שְׁמוֹת ~ כה

And make one cherub from this end,
and one cherub from this end;
From the mercy-seat
shall you make * the cherubim
on two ends of it.

(20)

וְהָיוּ הַכְּרֻבִים
פֹּרְשֵׂי כְנָפַיִם לְמַעְלָה
סֹכְכִים בְּכַנְפֵיהֶם עַל־הַכַּפֹּרֶת
וּפְנֵיהֶם אִישׁ אֶל־אָחִיו
אֶל־הַכַּפֹּרֶת יִהְיוּ פְּנֵי הַכְּרֻבִים

And the cherubim shall be
spreading wings upward,
hedging with their wings over the mercy-seat,
with their faces, a man to his brother;
toward the mercy-seat shall be the faces of the cherubim.

(21)

וְנָתַתָּ אֶת־הַכַּפֹּרֶת עַל־הָאָרֹן מִלְמָעְלָה
וְאֶל־הָאָרֹן תִּתֵּן אֶת־הָעֵדֻת
אֲשֶׁר אֶתֵּן אֵלֶיךָ

And you shall put the mercy-seat on the ark from upward;
and to the ark you shall give * the testimony
that I shall give to you.

Exodus ~ 25

(22)

וְנוֹעַדְתִּי לְךָ שָׁם

וְדִבַּרְתִּי אִתְּךָ

מֵעַל הַכַּפֹּרֶת

מִבֵּין שְׁנֵי הַכְּרֻבִים

אֲשֶׁר עַל־אֲרוֹן הָעֵדֻת

אֵת כָּל־אֲשֶׁר אֲצַוֶּה אוֹתְךָ

אֶל־בְּנֵי יִשְׂרָאֵל

And I will meet with you there,

and I will speak with * you

from on the mercy-seat,

from between the two cherubim

which are on the ark of the testimony,

* all that I instruct * you

in regard to the children of Israel.

The Table Of Bread

(23)

וְעָשִׂיתָ שֻׁלְחָן

עֲצֵי שִׁטִּים

אַמָּתַיִם אָרְכּוֹ

וְאַמָּה רָחְבּוֹ

וְאַמָּה וָחֵצִי קֹמָתוֹ

Level Two שְׁמוֹת ~ כה

And you shall make a table
of acacia-wood:
two cubits its length,
and a cubit its width,
and a cubit and a half its height.

(24)

וְצִפִּיתָ אֹתוֹ זָהָב טָהוֹר
וְעָשִׂיתָ לּוֹ זֵר זָהָב סָבִיב

And you shall overlay it with pure gold,
and make for it a crown of gold round about.

(25)

וְעָשִׂיתָ לּוֹ מִסְגֶּרֶת
טֹפַח סָבִיב
וְעָשִׂיתָ זֵר־זָהָב
לְמִסְגַּרְתּוֹ סָבִיב

And you shall make for it a border
a hand-breadth round about,
and you shall make a golden crown
for the border round about.

(26)

וְעָשִׂיתָ לּוֹ
אַרְבַּע טַבְּעֹת זָהָב

And you shall make for it
four rings of gold,

Exodus ~ 25

וְנָתַתָּ אֶת־הַטַּבָּעֹת עַל אַרְבַּע הַפֵּאֹת
אֲשֶׁר לְאַרְבַּע רַגְלָיו

and you shall put * the rings on the four corners
that are on the four feet of it.

(27)

לְעֻמַּת הַמִּסְגֶּרֶת
תִּהְיֶיןָ הַטַּבָּעֹת
לְבָתִּים לְבַדִּים
לָשֵׂאת אֶת־הַשֻּׁלְחָן

Alongside of the border
shall be the rings,
for housings for the poles
for carrying * the table.

(28)

וְעָשִׂיתָ אֶת־הַבַּדִּים
עֲצֵי שִׁטִּים
וְצִפִּיתָ אֹתָם זָהָב
וְנִשָּׂא־בָם אֶת־הַשֻּׁלְחָן

And you shall make * the poles of
acacia-wood,
and overlay * them with gold,
that * the table may be carried on them.

Level Two ~ שְׁמוֹת כה

(29)

וְעָשִׂיתָ קְּעָרֹתָיו וְכַפֹּתָיו

וּקְשׂוֹתָיו וּמְנַקִּיֹּתָיו

אֲשֶׁר יֻסַּךְ בָּהֵן

זָהָב טָהוֹר תַּעֲשֶׂה אֹתָם

And you shall make its dishes, and its pans,

and its jars, and its bowls,

which it is poured out in them;

of pure gold shall you make * them.

(30)

וְנָתַתָּ עַל־הַשֻּׁלְחָן

לֶחֶם פָּנִים

לְפָנַי תָּמִיד

And you shall set on the table

bread of the presence

before Me continually.

(31)

וְעָשִׂיתָ מְנֹרַת

זָהָב טָהוֹר

מִקְשָׁה תֵּעָשֶׂה הַמְּנוֹרָה

And you shall make a candlestick

of pure gold:

of beaten work you shall make the candlestick,

יְרֵכָהּ וְקָנָהּ

גְּבִיעֶיהָ כַּפְתֹּרֶיהָ

וּפְרָחֶיהָ

מִמֶּנָּה יִהְיוּ

its base, and its branch,

its cups, its knops,

and its flowers,

they shall be from it.

(32)

וְשִׁשָּׁה קָנִים

יֹצְאִים מִצִּדֶּיהָ

שְׁלֹשָׁה קְנֵי מְנֹרָה

מִצִּדָּהּ הָאֶחָד

And six branches

coming forth from its sides:

three branches of the candlestick

from the one side of it,

וּשְׁלֹשָׁה קְנֵי מְנֹרָה

מִצִּדָּהּ הַשֵּׁנִי

and three branches of the candlestick

from the second side of it;

Level Two

שְׁמוֹת ~ כה

(33)

שְׁלֹשָׁה גְבִעִים מְשֻׁקָּדִים
בַּקָּנֶה הָאֶחָד
כַּפְתֹּר וָפֶרַח

three cups, almond-shaped
in the one branch,
a knop and a flower;

וּשְׁלֹשָׁה גְבִעִים מְשֻׁקָּדִים
בַּקָּנֶה הָאֶחָד כַּפְתֹּר וָפָרַח
כֵּן לְשֵׁשֶׁת הַקָּנִים
הַיֹּצְאִים מִן־הַמְּנֹרָה

and three cups, almond-shaped
in the one branch, a knop and a flower;
so for six of the branches
coming forth from the candlestick.

(34)

וּבַמְּנֹרָה אַרְבָּעָה גְבִעִים
מְשֻׁקָּדִים
כַּפְתֹּרֶיהָ וּפְרָחֶיהָ

And in the candlestick four cups
almond-shaped,
its knops and its flowers.

209

Exodus ~ 25

(35)

וְכַפְתֹּר תַּחַת שְׁנֵי
הַקָּנִים מִמֶּנָּה
וְכַפְתֹּר תַּחַת שְׁנֵי הַקָּנִים מִמֶּנָּה

And a knop under two of
the branches from it,
and a knop under two of the branches from it,

וְכַפְתֹּר תַּחַת־שְׁנֵי
הַקָּנִים מִמֶּנָּה
לְשֵׁשֶׁת הַקָּנִים
הַיֹּצְאִים מִן־הַמְּנֹרָה

and a knop under two of
the branches from it,
for six of the branches
going forth from the candlestick.

(36)

כַּפְתֹּרֵיהֶם וּקְנֹתָם
מִמֶּנָּה יִהְיוּ
כֻּלָּהּ מִקְשָׁה אַחַת זָהָב טָהוֹר

Their knops and their branches,
they shall be from it;
all of it one beaten work of pure gold.

Level Two — שְׁמוֹת ~ כה

(37)

וְעָשִׂיתָ אֶת־נֵרֹתֶיהָ שִׁבְעָה

וְהֶעֱלָה אֶת־נֵרֹתֶיהָ

וְהֵאִיר עַל־עֵבֶר פָּנֶיהָ

And you shall make seven * lamps of it,

And it sets * lamps of it,

and it gives light over against the faces of it.

(38)

וּמַלְקָחֶיהָ וּמַחְתֹּתֶיהָ זָהָב טָהוֹר

And the tongs of it, and the firepans of it pure gold.

(39)

כִּכָּר זָהָב טָהוֹר

יַעֲשֶׂה אֹתָהּ

אֵת כָּל־הַכֵּלִים הָאֵלֶּה

A talent of pure gold

he shall make * it,

* all these implements.

(40)

וּרְאֵה וַעֲשֵׂה בְּתַבְנִיתָם

אֲשֶׁר־אַתָּה מָרְאֶה בָּהָר

And see that you make them after their model,

which is shown * you on the mountain.

Chapter Twenty-Six

The Curtains

(1)

וְאֶת-הַמִּשְׁכָּן תַּעֲשֶׂה

עֶשֶׂר יְרִיעֹת

שֵׁשׁ מָשְׁזָר

וּתְכֵלֶת וְאַרְגָּמָן וְתֹלַעַת שָׁנִי

כְּרֻבִים מַעֲשֵׂה חֹשֵׁב

תַּעֲשֶׂה אֹתָם

And you shall make * the tabernacle
ten curtains:
fine twined linen,
and blue, and purple, and scarlet,
cherubim the handiwork of the designer
you shall make * them.

(2)

אֹרֶךְ הַיְרִיעָה הָאַחַת

שְׁמֹנֶה וְעֶשְׂרִים בָּאַמָּה

וְרֹחַב אַרְבַּע בָּאַמָּה

The length of the one curtain
eight and twenty in the cubit,
and width, four in the cubit;

Level Two

שְׁמוֹת ~ כו

הַיְרִיעָה הָאֶחָת
מִדָּה אַחַת לְכָל־הַיְרִיעֹת

the one curtain,
one measure for all the curtains.

(3)

חֲמֵשׁ הַיְרִיעֹת
תִּהְיֶיןָ חֹבְרֹת
אִשָּׁה אֶל־אֲחֹתָהּ
וְחָמֵשׁ יְרִיעֹת חֹבְרֹת
אִשָּׁה אֶל־אֲחֹתָהּ

Five of the curtains
shall be joining
a woman to her sister;
and five curtains joining
a woman to her sister.

(4)

וְעָשִׂיתָ לֻלְאֹת תְּכֵלֶת
עַל שְׂפַת הַיְרִיעָה הָאֶחָת
מִקָּצָה בַּחֹבָרֶת

And you shall make loops of blue
on the edge of the one curtain
from the adjoining end;

וְכֵן תַּעֲשֶׂה
בִּשְׂפַת הַיְרִיעָה
הַקִּיצוֹנָה בַּמַּחְבֶּרֶת הַשֵּׁנִית

and you shall make

in the edge of the curtain

the outmost on the adjoining second.

(5)

חֲמִשִּׁים לֻלָאֹת תַּעֲשֶׂה
בַּיְרִיעָה הָאֶחָת
וַחֲמִשִּׁים לֻלָאֹת תַּעֲשֶׂה
בִּקְצֵה הַיְרִיעָה

Fifty loops you shall make

in the one curtain,

and fifty loops you shall make

in the edge of the curtain

אֲשֶׁר בַּמַּחְבֶּרֶת הַשֵּׁנִית
מַקְבִּילֹת הַלֻּלָאֹת
אִשָּׁה אֶל־אֲחֹתָהּ

that is on the adjoining second;

causing the loops to correspond

a woman to her sister.

Level Two   שְׁמוֹת ~ כו

(6)

וְעָשִׂיתָ חֲמִשִּׁים קַרְסֵי זָהָב

וְחִבַּרְתָּ אֶת־הַיְרִיעֹת

אִשָּׁה אֶל־אֲחֹתָהּ

בַּקְּרָסִים

וְהָיָה הַמִּשְׁכָּן אֶחָד

And you shall make fifty hooks of gold,

and join * the curtains

a woman to her sister

with the hooks

that the tabernacle may be one.

(7)

וְעָשִׂיתָ יְרִיעֹת

עִזִּים

לְאֹהֶל עַל־הַמִּשְׁכָּן

עַשְׁתֵּי־עֶשְׂרֵה יְרִיעֹת

תַּעֲשֶׂה אֹתָם

And you shall make curtains

of goats' hair

to tent over the tabernacle;

eleven curtains

you shall make * them.

215

Exodus ~ 26

(8)

אֹרֶךְ הַיְרִיעָה הָאַחַת
שְׁלֹשִׁים בָּאַמָּה
וְרֹחַב אַרְבַּע בָּאַמָּה
הַיְרִיעָה הָאֶחָת
מִדָּה אַחַת לְעַשְׁתֵּי עֶשְׂרֵה יְרִיעֹת

The length of the one curtain
thirty in the cubit,
and width, four in the cubit;
the one curtain,
one measure for eleven curtains.

(9)

וְחִבַּרְתָּ אֶת-חֲמֵשׁ
הַיְרִיעֹת לְבָד
וְאֶת-שֵׁשׁ הַיְרִיעֹת לְבָד
וְכָפַלְתָּ אֶת-הַיְרִיעָה הַשִּׁשִּׁית
אֶל-מוּל פְּנֵי הָאֹהֶל

*And you shall join * five*
curtains by themselves,
*and * six curtains by themselves,*
*and you shall double the sixth * curtain*
to the forefront of the tent.

Level Two שְׁמוֹת ~ כו

(10)

וְעָשִׂיתָ חֲמִשִּׁים לֻלָאֹת
עַל שְׂפַת הַיְרִיעָה הָאֶחָת
הַקִּיצֹנָה בַּחֹבָרֶת
וַחֲמִשִּׁים לֻלָאֹת עַל שְׂפַת
הַיְרִיעָה הַחֹבֶרֶת הַשֵּׁנִית

And you shall make fifty loops
on the edge of the one curtain
the outmost in the adjoining,
and fifty loops on the edge of
the curtain adjoining the second.

(11)

וְעָשִׂיתָ קַרְסֵי נְחֹשֶׁת חֲמִשִּׁים
וְהֵבֵאתָ אֶת־הַקְּרָסִים בַּלֻּלָאֹת
וְחִבַּרְתָּ אֶת־הָאֹהֶל וְהָיָה אֶחָד

And you shall make fifty hooks of copper,
*and put * the hooks in the loops,*
*and you shall join * the tent, that it may be one.*

(12)

וְסֶרַח הָעֹדֵף
בִּירִיעֹת הָאֹהֶל

And as for the overhanging
in the curtains of the tent,

Exodus ~ 26

חֲצִי הַיְרִיעָה הָעֹדֶפֶת
תִּסְרַח עַל אֲחֹרֵי הַמִּשְׁכָּן

the half curtain that is surplus
shall hang over the back of the tabernacle.

(13)

וְהָאַמָּה מִזֶּה וְהָאַמָּה מִזֶּה
בָּעֹדֵף בְּאֹרֶךְ
יְרִיעֹת הָאֹהֶל
יִהְיֶה סָרוּחַ עַל־צִדֵּי הַמִּשְׁכָּן
מִזֶּה וּמִזֶּה לְכַסֹּתוֹ

And the cubit from this, and the cubit from this,
in the surplus in the length of
the curtains of the tent,
shall hang over the sides of the tabernacle
from this and from this to cover it.

(14)

וְעָשִׂיתָ מִכְסֶה לָאֹהֶל
עֹרֹת אֵילִם מְאָדָּמִים

And you shall make a cover for the tent
skins of rams dyed red

וּמִכְסֵה עֹרֹת
תְּחָשִׁים מִלְמָעְלָה

Level Two

שְׁמוֹת ~ כו

and a cover of skins of
[an unknown animal] above.

(15)

וְעָשִׂיתָ אֶת־הַקְּרָשִׁים
לַמִּשְׁכָּן
עֲצֵי שִׁטִּים עֹמְדִים

And you shall make * the boards
for the tabernacle
of standing acacia-wood.

(16)

עֶשֶׂר אַמּוֹת
אֹרֶךְ הַקָּרֶשׁ
וְאַמָּה וַחֲצִי הָאַמָּה
רֹחַב הַקֶּרֶשׁ הָאֶחָד

Ten cubits
shall be the length of a board,
and a cubit and a half
the width of the one board.

(17)

שְׁתֵּי יָדוֹת לַקֶּרֶשׁ הָאֶחָד
מְשֻׁלָּבֹת אִשָּׁה אֶל־אֲחֹתָהּ

Two tenons for the one board,
joining a woman to her sister;

כֵּן תַּעֲשֶׂה לְכֹל

קַרְשֵׁי הַמִּשְׁכָּן

so you shall make for all

the boards of the tabernacle.

(18)

וְעָשִׂיתָ אֶת־הַקְּרָשִׁים

לַמִּשְׁכָּן

עֶשְׂרִים קֶרֶשׁ

לִפְאַת נֶגְבָּה תֵימָנָה

And you shall make * the boards

for the tabernacle,

twenty boards

for the edge toward Negev southward:

(19)

וְאַרְבָּעִים אַדְנֵי־כֶסֶף

תַּעֲשֶׂה תַּחַת עֶשְׂרִים הַקָּרֶשׁ

And forty pedestals of silver

you shall make under the twenty boards:

שְׁנֵי אֲדָנִים

תַּחַת־הַקֶּרֶשׁ הָאֶחָד

לִשְׁתֵּי יְדֹתָיו

Level Two

שְׁמוֹת ~ כו

two pedestals
under the one board
for two of its tenons,

וּשְׁנֵי אֲדָנִים
תַּחַת־הַקֶּרֶשׁ הָאֶחָד
לִשְׁתֵּי יְדֹתָיו

and two pedestals
under the one board
for two of its tenons;

(20)

וּלְצֶלַע הַמִּשְׁכָּן הַשֵּׁנִית
לִפְאַת צָפוֹן
עֶשְׂרִים קָרֶשׁ

and for the second side of the tabernacle,
for the north side,
twenty boards.

(21)

וְאַרְבָּעִים אַדְנֵיהֶם כָּסֶף
שְׁנֵי אֲדָנִים תַּחַת הַקֶּרֶשׁ הָאֶחָד
וּשְׁנֵי אֲדָנִים תַּחַת הַקֶּרֶשׁ הָאֶחָד

And their forty pedestals of silver:
two pedestals under the one board,
and two pedestals under the one board.

Exodus ~ 26

(22)

וּלְיַרְכְּתֵי הַמִּשְׁכָּן

יָמָּה תַּעֲשֶׂה

שִׁשָּׁה קְרָשִׁים

And for the hinder part of the tabernacle
seaward you shall make
six boards.

(23)

וּשְׁנֵי קְרָשִׁים תַּעֲשֶׂה

לִמְקֻצְעֹת הַמִּשְׁכָּן

בַּיַּרְכָתָיִם

And two boards you shall make
for the corners of the tabernacle
in the hinder part.

(24)

וְיִהְיוּ תֹאֲמִם מִלְּמַטָּה

וְיַחְדָּו יִהְיוּ תַמִּים עַל־רֹאשׁוֹ

אֶל־הַטַּבַּעַת הָאֶחָת

And they shall be joined from below,
and together they shall be joined top of it
to the one ring;

כֵּן יִהְיֶה לִשְׁנֵיהֶם

לִשְׁנֵי הַמִּקְצֹעֹת יִהְיוּ

Level Two שְׁמוֹת ~ כו

so shall it be for them both;
they shall be for the two corners.

(25)

וְהָיוּ שְׁמֹנָה קְרָשִׁים
וְאַדְנֵיהֶם כֶּסֶף
שִׁשָּׁה עָשָׂר אֲדָנִים

And there shall be eight boards,
and their pedestals of silver,
sixteen pedestals:

שְׁנֵי אֲדָנִים
תַּחַת הַקֶּרֶשׁ הָאֶחָד
וּשְׁנֵי אֲדָנִים
תַּחַת הַקֶּרֶשׁ הָאֶחָד

two pedestals
under the one board,
and two pedestals
under the one board.

The Bars

(26)

וְעָשִׂיתָ בְרִיחִם
עֲצֵי שִׁטִּים

And you shall make bars
of acacia-wood:

חֲמִשָּׁה לְקַרְשֵׁי
צֶלַע־הַמִּשְׁכָּן הָאֶחָד

five for the boards of
the one side of the tabernacle,

(27)

וַחֲמִשָּׁה בְרִיחִם לְקַרְשֵׁי
צֶלַע־הַמִּשְׁכָּן הַשֵּׁנִית
וַחֲמִשָּׁה בְרִיחִם
לְקַרְשֵׁי צֶלַע הַמִּשְׁכָּן
לַיַּרְכָתַיִם יָמָּה

and five bars for the boards of
the second side of the tabernacle,
and five bars
for the boards of the side of the tabernacle,
for the hinder part seaward;

(28)

וְהַבְּרִיחַ הַתִּיכֹן
בְּתוֹךְ הַקְּרָשִׁים
מַבְרִחַ מִן־הַקָּצֶה אֶל־הַקָּצֶה

and the middle bar
in the midst of the boards,
going through from end to end.

Level Two

שְׁמוֹת ~ כו

(29)

וְאֶת־הַקְּרָשִׁים תְּצַפֶּה זָהָב
וְאֶת־טַבְּעֹתֵיהֶם תַּעֲשֶׂה זָהָב
בָּתִּים לַבְּרִיחִם
וְצִפִּיתָ אֶת־הַבְּרִיחִם זָהָב

And you shall overlay * the boards with gold,
and make * their rings of gold
housings for the bars;
and you shall overlay * the bars with gold.

(30)

וַהֲקֵמֹתָ אֶת־הַמִּשְׁכָּן
כְּמִשְׁפָּטוֹ אֲשֶׁר
הָרְאֵיתָ בָּהָר

And you shall set up * the tabernacle
according to the fashion which
you are shown on the mount.

The Veil

(31)

וְעָשִׂיתָ פָרֹכֶת תְּכֵלֶת
וְאַרְגָּמָן וְתוֹלַעַת שָׁנִי

And you shall make a veil of blue,
and purple, and scarlet,

Exodus ~ 26

וְשֵׁשׁ מָשְׁזָר
מַעֲשֵׂה חֹשֵׁב
יַעֲשֶׂה אֹתָהּ כְּרֻבִים

and fine twined linen;
the handiwork of the designer
*he shall make * it cherubim.*

(32)

וּנְתַתָּה אֹתָהּ
עַל־אַרְבָּעָה עַמּוּדֵי שִׁטִּים
מְצֻפִּים זָהָב
וָוֵיהֶם זָהָב
עַל־אַרְבָּעָה אַדְנֵי־כָסֶף

*And you shall hang * it*
on four pillars of acacia
overlaid with gold,
and their hooks being of gold,
on four pedestals of silver.

(33)

וְנָתַתָּה אֶת־הַפָּרֹכֶת
תַּחַת הַקְּרָסִים
וְהֵבֵאתָ שָׁמָּה מִבֵּית לַפָּרֹכֶת
אֵת אֲרוֹן הָעֵדוּת

Level Two

שְׁמוֹת ~ כו

And you shall hang up * the veil
under the clasps,
and you shall bring thither within the veil
* the ark of the testimony;

וְהִבְדִּילָה הַפָּרֹכֶת לָכֶם
בֵּין הַקֹּדֶשׁ
וּבֵין קֹדֶשׁ הַקֳּדָשִׁים

and the veil shall divide to you
between the holy
and between the holy of holies.

(34)

וְנָתַתָּ אֶת־הַכַּפֹּרֶת
עַל אֲרוֹן הָעֵדֻת
בְּקֹדֶשׁ הַקֳּדָשִׁים

And you shall put * the mercy-seat
on the ark of the testimony
in the holy of holies.

(35)

וְשַׂמְתָּ אֶת־הַשֻּׁלְחָן
מִחוּץ לַפָּרֹכֶת

And you shall set * the table
without the veil,

Exodus ~ 26

וְאֶת־הַמְּנֹרָה
נֹכַח הַשֻּׁלְחָן

and * the candlestick
opposite the table

עַל צֶלַע הַמִּשְׁכָּן תֵּימָנָה
וְהַשֻּׁלְחָן תִּתֵּן
עַל־צֶלַע צָפוֹן

on the side of the tabernacle toward the south;
and you shall put the table
on the north side.

(36)

וְעָשִׂיתָ מָסָךְ
לְפֶתַח הָאֹהֶל
תְּכֵלֶת וְאַרְגָּמָן וְתוֹלַעַת שָׁנִי

And you shall make a screen
for the door of the tent,
blue, and purple, and scarlet,

וְשֵׁשׁ מָשְׁזָר
מַעֲשֵׂה רֹקֵם

and fine twined linen,
the handiwork of embroidering.

(37)

וְעָשִׂ֣יתָ לַמָּסָ֗ךְ
חֲמִשָּׁה֙ עַמּוּדֵ֣י שִׁטִּ֔ים
וְצִפִּיתָ֥ אֹתָ֖ם זָהָ֑ב

And you shall make for the screen
five pillars of acacia,
and overlay * them with gold;

וָוֵיהֶ֖ם זָהָ֑ב
וְיָצַקְתָּ֣ לָהֶ֔ם
חֲמִשָּׁ֖ה אַדְנֵ֥י נְחֹֽשֶׁת

their hooks shall be of gold;
and you shall cast for them
five pedestals of copper.

Chapter Twenty-Seven

The Altar

(1)

וְעָשִׂיתָ אֶת־הַמִּזְבֵּחַ עֲצֵי שִׁטִּים

חָמֵשׁ אַמּוֹת אֹרֶךְ

וְחָמֵשׁ אַמּוֹת רֹחַב

רָבוּעַ יִהְיֶה הַמִּזְבֵּחַ

וְשָׁלֹשׁ אַמּוֹת קֹמָתוֹ

And you shall make * the altar of acacia-wood,

five cubits long,

and five cubits width;

the altar shall be square;

and three cubits its height.

(2)

וְעָשִׂיתָ קַרְנֹתָיו

עַל אַרְבַּע פִּנֹּתָיו

מִמֶּנּוּ תִּהְיֶיןָ קַרְנֹתָיו

וְצִפִּיתָ אֹתוֹ נְחֹשֶׁת

And you shall make its horns

on its four corners;

the horns shall be from it;

and you shall overlay * it with copper.

Level Two

שְׁמוֹת ~ כז

(3)

וְעָשִׂיתָ סִּירֹתָיו לְדַשְּׁנוֹ

וְיָעָיו וּמִזְרְקֹתָיו

וּמִזְלְגֹתָיו וּמַחְתֹּתָיו

לְכָל־כֵּלָיו

תַּעֲשֶׂה נְחֹשֶׁת

And you shall make its pots to take remove its ashes,

and its shovels, and its basins,

and its flesh-hooks, and its fire-pans;

for all the implements

you shall make of copper.

(4)

וְעָשִׂיתָ לּוֹ מִכְבָּר

מַעֲשֵׂה רֶשֶׁת נְחֹשֶׁת

וְעָשִׂיתָ עַל־הָרֶשֶׁת

אַרְבַּע טַבְּעֹת נְחֹשֶׁת

עַל אַרְבַּע קְצוֹתָיו

And you shall make for it a grate

handiwork of a net of copper;

and you shall make on the net

four rings of copper

on the four corners of it.

231

Exodus ~ 27

(5)

וְנָתַתָּה אֹתָהּ תַּחַת

כַּרְכֹּב הַמִּזְבֵּחַ מִלְּמָטָּה

וְהָיְתָה הָרֶשֶׁת

עַד חֲצִי הַמִּזְבֵּחַ

And you shall put * it under

the ledge round the altar from below,

that the net may be

halfway up the altar.

(6)

וְעָשִׂיתָ בַדִּים לַמִּזְבֵּחַ

בַּדֵּי עֲצֵי שִׁטִּים

וְצִפִּיתָ אֹתָם נְחֹשֶׁת

And you shall make poles for the altar,

poles of acacia-wood,

and you shall overlay * them with copper.

(7)

וְהוּבָא אֶת־בַּדָּיו בַּטַּבָּעֹת

וְהָיוּ הַבַּדִּים

עַל־שְׁתֵּי צַלְעֹת הַמִּזְבֵּחַ

בִּשְׂאֵת אֹתוֹ

Level Two

שְׁמוֹת ~ כז

And * the poles of it shall be put in the rings,

and the poles shall be

on the two sides of the altar,

in carrying it.

(8)

נְבוּב לֻחֹת תַּעֲשֶׂה אֹתוֹ

כַּאֲשֶׁר הֶרְאָה אֹתְךָ בָּהָר

כֵּן יַעֲשׂוּ

Hollow with planks you shall make * it;

as it has been shown * you on the mountain,

so they shall do.

The Court

(9)

וְעָשִׂיתָ אֵת חֲצַר הַמִּשְׁכָּן

לִפְאַת נֶגֶב-תֵּימָנָה

קְלָעִים לֶחָצֵר שֵׁשׁ מָשְׁזָר

מֵאָה בָאַמָּה אֹרֶךְ

לַפֵּאָה הָאֶחָת

And you shall make * the court of the tabernacle:

for the Negev southward

hangings for the court of fine twined linen

a hundred cubits long

for the one edge.

Exodus ~ 27

(10)

וְעַמֻּדָיו עֶשְׂרִים
וְאַדְנֵיהֶם עֶשְׂרִים נְחֹשֶׁת
וָוֵי הָעַמֻּדִים
וַחֲשֻׁקֵיהֶם כָּסֶף

And its pillars - twenty,
and their pedestals - twenty, of copper;
the hooks of the pillars
and their connections shall be silver.

(11)

וְכֵן לִפְאַת צָפוֹן בָּאֹרֶךְ
קְלָעִים מֵאָה אֹרֶךְ

And so for the north edge in length
hangings a hundred cubits long,

וְעַמֻּדָו עֶשְׂרִים
וְאַדְנֵיהֶם עֶשְׂרִים נְחֹשֶׁת
וָוֵי הָעַמֻּדִים
וַחֲשֻׁקֵיהֶם כָּסֶף

and the pillars of it, twenty,
and their pedestals twenty, of copper;
the hooks of the pillars
and their connections of silver.

Level Two   שְׁמוֹת ~ כז

(12)

וְרֹחַב הֶחָצֵר לִפְאַת־יָם

קְלָעִים חֲמִשִּׁים אַמָּה

עַמֻּדֵיהֶם עֲשָׂרָה

וְאַדְנֵיהֶם עֲשָׂרָה

And the width of the court for the sea edge

hangings of fifty cubits:

their pillars - ten,

and their pedestals - ten.

(13)

וְרֹחַב הֶחָצֵר

לִפְאַת קֵדְמָה מִזְרָחָה

חֲמִשִּׁים אַמָּה

And the width of the court

for the edge eastward, towards the sunrise

fifty cubits.

(14)

וַחֲמֵשׁ עֶשְׂרֵה אַמָּה קְלָעִים לַכָּתֵף

עַמֻּדֵיהֶם שְׁלֹשָׁה

וְאַדְנֵיהֶם שְׁלֹשָׁה

And fifteen cubits hangings for the flank:

their pillars - three,

and their pedestals - three.

Exodus ~ 27

(15)

וּלְכָּתֵף הַשֵּׁנִית
חֲמֵשׁ עֶשְׂרֵה קְלָעִים
עַמֻּדֵיהֶם שְׁלֹשָׁה
וְאַדְנֵיהֶם שְׁלֹשָׁה

And for the second flank
hangings of fifteen:
their pillars - three,
and their pedestals - three.

(16)

וּלְשַׁעַר הֶחָצֵר
מָסָךְ עֶשְׂרִים אַמָּה

And for the gate of the court
a screen of twenty cubits,

תְּכֵלֶת וְאַרְגָּמָן וְתוֹלַעַת שָׁנִי
וְשֵׁשׁ מָשְׁזָר

of blue, and purple, and scarlet,
and fine twined linen,

מַעֲשֵׂה רֹקֵם
עַמֻּדֵיהֶם אַרְבָּעָה
וְאַדְנֵיהֶם אַרְבָּעָה

Level Two

שְׁמוֹת ~ כז

handiwork of embroidering:
their pillars - four,
and their pedestals - four.

(17)

כָּל־עַמּוּדֵי הֶחָצֵר סָבִיב

מְחֻשָּׁקִים כֶּסֶף

וָוֵיהֶם כָּסֶף

וְאַדְנֵיהֶם נְחֹשֶׁת

All the pillars of the court round about
shall be connected with silver;
and their hooks of silver,
and their pedestals of copper.

(18)

אֹרֶךְ הֶחָצֵר

מֵאָה בָאַמָּה

וְרֹחַב חֲמִשִּׁים בַּחֲמִשִּׁים

וְקֹמָה חָמֵשׁ אַמּוֹת

שֵׁשׁ מָשְׁזָר וְאַדְנֵיהֶם נְחֹשֶׁת

The length of the court –
a hundred cubits,
and width - fifty in the fifty,
and height five cubits,
of fine twined linen, and their pedestals of copper.

Exodus ~ 27

(19)

לְכֹל כְּלֵי הַמִּשְׁכָּן

בְּכֹל עֲבֹדָתוֹ וְכָל־יְתֵדֹתָיו

וְכָל־יִתְדֹת הֶחָצֵר נְחֹשֶׁת

All the implements of the tabernacle
in all the service of it, and all the pegs of it,
and all the pegs of the court, copper.

(20)

וְאַתָּה תְּצַוֶּה אֶת־בְּנֵי יִשְׂרָאֵל

וְיִקְחוּ אֵלֶיךָ שֶׁמֶן זַיִת זָךְ

כָּתִית לַמָּאוֹר

לְהַעֲלֹת נֵר תָּמִיד

*And * you shall command*
* the children of Israel
that they bring to you pure olive oil
beaten for the light,
to cause a lamp to burn continually.

(21)

בְּאֹהֶל מוֹעֵד

מִחוּץ לַפָּרֹכֶת

אֲשֶׁר עַל־הָעֵדֻת

יַעֲרֹךְ אֹתוֹ אַהֲרֹן וּבָנָיו

מֵעֶרֶב עַד־בֹּקֶר לִפְנֵי יהוה

Level Two   שְׁמוֹת ~ כז

> In the tent of appointment,
> from outside the veil
> which is over the testimony,
> Aaron shall arrange * it and his sons,
> from evening to morning before YHVH

> חֻקַּת עוֹלָם לְדֹרֹתָם
> מֵאֵת בְּנֵי יִשְׂרָאֵל

> a statute forever for their generations
> from * the children of Israel.

Chapter Twenty-Eight

The Priesthood

(1)

וְאַתָּה הַקְרֵב אֵלֶיךָ אֶת-אַהֲרֹן אָחִיךָ

וְאֶת-בָּנָיו אִתּוֹ

מִתּוֹךְ בְּנֵי יִשְׂרָאֵל

And * you, bring near to you * Aaron your brother,
and * his sons with * him,
from among the children of Israel,

לְכַהֲנוֹ-לִי

אַהֲרֹן נָדָב וַאֲבִיהוּא

אֶלְעָזָר וְאִיתָמָר בְּנֵי אַהֲרֹן

to serve as its priest for Me,
Aaron, Nadab and Abihu,
Eleazar and Ithamar, sons of Aaron.

(2)

וְעָשִׂיתָ בִגְדֵי-קֹדֶשׁ

לְאַהֲרֹן אָחִיךָ

לְכָבוֹד וּלְתִפְאָרֶת

And you shall make holy garments
for Aaron your brother,
for splendor and for beauty.

Level Two

שְׁמוֹת ~ כח

(3)

וְאַתָּה תְּדַבֵּר
אֶל־כָּל־חַכְמֵי־לֵב
אֲשֶׁר מִלֵּאתִיו רוּחַ חָכְמָה

*And * you shall speak*
to all wise ones of heart,
whom I have filled with the spirit of wisdom,

וְעָשׂוּ אֶת־בִּגְדֵי אַהֲרֹן
לְקַדְּשׁוֹ
לְכַהֲנוֹ־לִי

*that they make * garments of Aaron*
to sanctify him,
to serve as its priest for Me.

The Priestly Garments

(4)

וְאֵלֶּה הַבְּגָדִים אֲשֶׁר יַעֲשׂוּ
חֹשֶׁן וְאֵפוֹד וּמְעִיל
וּכְתֹנֶת תַּשְׁבֵּץ מִצְנֶפֶת וְאַבְנֵט

And these garments which they shall make:
a breastplate, and an ephod, and a robe,
and a embroidered tunic, a turban, and a sash;

Exodus ~ 28

וְעָשׂוּ בִגְדֵי-קֹדֶשׁ
לְאַהֲרֹן אָחִיךָ וּלְבָנָיו
לְכַהֲנוֹ-לִי

and they shall make holy garments
for Aaron your brother, and his sons,
to serve as its priest for Me.

(5)

וְהֵם יִקְחוּ אֶת-הַזָּהָב
וְאֶת-הַתְּכֵלֶת וְאֶת-הָאַרְגָּמָן
וְאֶת-תּוֹלַעַת הַשָּׁנִי וְאֶת-הַשֵּׁשׁ

And they shall take * the gold,
and * the blue, and * the purple,
and * the scarlet, and * the fine linen.

The Ephod

(6)

וְעָשׂוּ אֶת-הָאֵפֹד
זָהָב תְּכֵלֶת וְאַרְגָּמָן תּוֹלַעַת שָׁנִי
וְשֵׁשׁ מָשְׁזָר מַעֲשֵׂה חֹשֵׁב

And they shall make * the ephod
gold, of blue, and purple, scarlet,
and fine twined linen, the handiwork of a designer.

Level Two   שְׁמוֹת ~ כח

(7)

שְׁתֵּי כְתֵפֹת חֹבְרֹת
יִהְיֶה־לּוֹ
אֶל־שְׁנֵי קְצוֹתָיו וְחֻבָּר

Two adjoining shoulder-pieces

it shall be for it

to two ends of it, and it is joined.

(8)

וְחֵשֶׁב אֲפֻדָּתוֹ אֲשֶׁר עָלָיו
כְּמַעֲשֵׂהוּ מִמֶּנּוּ יִהְיֶה
זָהָב תְּכֵלֶת וְאַרְגָּמָן
וְתוֹלַעַת שָׁנִי וְשֵׁשׁ מָשְׁזָר

And its skillfully woven band, which is on it,

as handiwork from it shall be

gold, blue, and purple,

and scarlet, and fine twined linen.

(9)

וְלָקַחְתָּ אֶת־שְׁתֵּי אַבְנֵי־שֹׁהַם
וּפִתַּחְתָּ עֲלֵיהֶם
שְׁמוֹת בְּנֵי יִשְׂרָאֵל

And you shall take * two onyx stones,

and engrave on them

the names of the children of Israel:

(10)

שִׁשָּׁה מִשְּׁמֹתָם עַל הָאֶבֶן הָאֶחָת

וְאֶת־שְׁמוֹת הַשִּׁשָּׁה הַנּוֹתָרִים

עַל־הָאֶבֶן הַשֵּׁנִית

כְּתוֹלְדֹתָם

six of their names on the one stone,
and * the names of the six that remain
on the second stone,
according to their genealogy.

(11)

מַעֲשֵׂה חָרַשׁ אֶבֶן

פִּתּוּחֵי חֹתָם

Handiwork of an artificer of stone,
like the engravings of a signet,

תְּפַתַּח אֶת־שְׁתֵּי הָאֲבָנִים

עַל־שְׁמֹת בְּנֵי יִשְׂרָאֵל

you shall engrave the * two stones,
on the names of the children of Israel;

מֻסַבֹּת

מִשְׁבְּצוֹת זָהָב

תַּעֲשֶׂה אֹתָם

Settings round about
of mountings of gold
you shall make * them.

(12)

וְשַׂמְתָּ אֶת־שְׁתֵּי הָאֲבָנִים
עַל כִּתְפֹת הָאֵפֹד
אַבְנֵי זִכָּרֹן לִבְנֵי יִשְׂרָאֵל

And you shall put the * two stones
on the shoulder-pieces of the ephod,
stones of memorial for the children of Israel;

נָשָׂא אַהֲרֹן אֶת־שְׁמוֹתָם לִפְנֵי יהוה
עַל־שְׁתֵּי כְתֵפָיו לְזִכָּרֹן

and Aaron shall bear * their names before YHVH
on his two shoulders for a memorial.

(13)

וְעָשִׂיתָ מִשְׁבְּצֹת זָהָב

And you shall make settings of gold;

(14)

וּשְׁתֵּי שַׁרְשְׁרֹת זָהָב טָהוֹר
מִגְבָּלֹת תַּעֲשֶׂה אֹתָם

and two chains of pure gold;
you shall make * them twisted,

Exodus ~ 28

מַעֲשֵׂה עֲבֹת
וְנָתַתָּה אֶת-שַׁרְשְׁרֹת הָעֲבֹתֹת
עַל-הַמִּשְׁבְּצֹת

handiwork of rope;
and you shall put * the chains of the ropes
on the mountings.

The Breastplate

(15)

וְעָשִׂיתָ חֹשֶׁן מִשְׁפָּט
מַעֲשֵׂה חֹשֵׁב
כְּמַעֲשֵׂה אֵפֹד תַּעֲשֶׂנּוּ

And you shall make a breastplate of judgment,
the handiwork of a designer;
like the handiwork of the ephod you shall make it:

זָהָב תְּכֵלֶת וְאַרְגָּמָן
וְתוֹלַעַת שָׁנִי וְשֵׁשׁ מָשְׁזָר
תַּעֲשֶׂה אֹתוֹ

gold, blue, and purple,
and scarlet, and fine twined linen,
you shall make * it.

(16)

רָבוּעַ יִהְיֶה כָּפוּל

זֶרֶת אָרְכּוֹ

וְזֶרֶת רָחְבּוֹ

Squared, it shall be double:

a span shall be its length,

and a span its width.

(17)

וּמִלֵּאתָ בוֹ מִלֻּאַת אֶבֶן

אַרְבָּעָה טוּרִים אָבֶן

And you shall set in it settings of stone,

four rows of stones:

טוּר אֹדֶם

פִּטְדָה וּבָרֶקֶת

הַטּוּר הָאֶחָד

a row of [a red gem – perhaps a ruby],

topaz, and emerald

shall be the first row;

(18)

וְהַטּוּר הַשֵּׁנִי

and the second row

נֹ֥פֶךְ

סַפִּ֖יר

וְיָהֲלֹֽם׃

[a glistening gem – perhaps a garnet],

a sapphire,

and [a hard gem - perhaps a diamond];

(19)

וְהַטּ֖וּר הַשְּׁלִישִׁ֑י

לֶ֥שֶׁם שְׁב֖וֹ וְאַחְלָֽמָה׃

and the third row

a jacinth, an agate, and an amethyst;

(20)

וְהַטּוּר֙ הָֽרְבִיעִ֔י

תַּרְשִׁ֥ישׁ

וְשֹׁ֖הַם וְיָשְׁפֵ֑ה

מְשֻׁבָּצִ֥ים זָהָ֛ב יִהְי֖וּ

בְּמִלּוּאֹתָֽם׃

and the fourth row

[a yellow gem – perhaps a chrysolite],

and an onyx, and a jasper;

they shall be mounted in gold

in their settings.

Level Two

שְׁמוֹת ~ כח

(21)

וְהָאֲבָנִים תִּהְיֶיןָ
עַל־שְׁמֹת בְּנֵי־יִשְׂרָאֵל
שְׁתֵּים עֶשְׂרֵה עַל־שְׁמֹתָם
פִּתּוּחֵי חוֹתָם
אִישׁ עַל־שְׁמוֹ
תִּהְיֶיןָ לִשְׁנֵי עָשָׂר שָׁבֶט

And the stones shall be
according to the names of the children of Israel,
twelve, according to their names;
engravings of a signet,
a man by his name,
they shall be for the twelve tribes.

(22)

וְעָשִׂיתָ עַל־הַחֹשֶׁן
שַׁרְשֹׁת גַּבְלֻת
מַעֲשֵׂה עֲבֹת
זָהָב טָהוֹר

And you shall make on the breastplate
chains of a twisting
handiwork of a rope
pure gold.

(23)

וְעָשִׂיתָ עַל-הַחֹשֶׁן
שְׁתֵּי טַבְּעוֹת זָהָב
וְנָתַתָּ אֶת-שְׁתֵּי הַטַּבָּעוֹת
עַל-שְׁנֵי קְצוֹת הַחֹשֶׁן

And you shall make on the breastplate

two rings of gold,

and shall put the * two rings

on the two ends of the breastplate.

(24)

וְנָתַתָּה אֶת-שְׁתֵּי
עֲבֹתֹת הַזָּהָב
עַל-שְׁתֵּי הַטַּבָּעֹת
אֶל-קְצוֹת הַחֹשֶׁן

And you shall put the * two

ropes of gold

on the two rings

at the ends of the breastplate.

(25)

וְאֵת שְׁתֵּי קְצוֹת שְׁתֵּי הָעֲבֹתֹת
תִּתֵּן עַל-שְׁתֵּי הַמִּשְׁבְּצוֹת
וְנָתַתָּה עַל-כִּתְפוֹת הָאֵפֹד
אֶל-מוּל פָּנָיו

Level Two   שְׁמוֹת ~ כח

And the * two ends of the two ropes

you shall put on the two mountings,

and put on the shoulder-pieces of the ephod,

to the forepart of it.

(26)

וְעָשִׂיתָ שְׁתֵּי טַבְּעוֹת זָהָב

וְשַׂמְתָּ אֹתָם

עַל־שְׁנֵי קְצוֹת הַחֹשֶׁן עַל־שְׂפָתוֹ

אֲשֶׁר אֶל־עֵבֶר הָאֵפֹד בָּיְתָה

And you shall make two rings of gold,

and you shall put * them

on the two ends of the breastplate, on the edge thereof,

which is toward the side of the ephod inward.

(27)

וְעָשִׂיתָ שְׁתֵּי טַבְּעוֹת זָהָב

וְנָתַתָּה אֹתָם עַל־שְׁתֵּי

כִתְפוֹת הָאֵפוֹד

מִלְּמַטָּה מִמּוּל פָּנָיו

And you shall make two rings of gold,

and shall put * them on the two

shoulder-pieces of the ephod

underneath, in the forepart thereof,

Exodus ~ 28

לְעֻמַּת מַחְבַּרְתּוֹ
מִמַּעַל לְחֵשֶׁב הָאֵפוֹד

close by the coupling thereof,
above the skillfully woven band of the ephod.

(28)

וְיִרְכְּסוּ אֶת-הַחֹשֶׁן
מִטַּבְּעֹתָו אֶל-טַבְּעֹת הָאֵפוֹד
בִּפְתִיל תְּכֵלֶת

And they shall bind * the breastplate
by the rings thereof to the rings of the ephod
with a thread of blue,

לִהְיוֹת עַל-חֵשֶׁב הָאֵפוֹד
וְלֹא-יִזַּח הַחֹשֶׁן מֵעַל הָאֵפוֹד

to be on the skillfully woven band of the ephod,
and that the breastplate not be displaced from on the ephod.

(29)

וְנָשָׂא אַהֲרֹן
אֶת-שְׁמוֹת בְּנֵי-יִשְׂרָאֵל
בְּחֹשֶׁן הַמִּשְׁפָּט עַל-לִבּוֹ

And Aaron shall bear
* the names of the children of Israel
in the breastplate of judgment on his heart,

Level Two

שְׁמוֹת ~ כח

בְּבֹאוֹ אֶל־הַקֹּדֶשׁ
לְזִכָּרֹן לִפְנֵי־יהוה תָּמִיד

when he goes in to the holy place,
for a memorial before YHVH continually.

Urim And Thummin

(30)

וְנָתַתָּ אֶל־חֹשֶׁן הַמִּשְׁפָּט
אֶת־הָאוּרִים וְאֶת־הַתֻּמִּים
וְהָיוּ עַל־לֵב אַהֲרֹן
בְּבֹאוֹ לִפְנֵי יהוה

And you shall put in the breastplate of judgment
* the Urim and * the Thummim;
and they shall be on the heart of Aaron,
when he goes in before YHVH

וְנָשָׂא אַהֲרֹן אֶת־מִשְׁפַּט
בְּנֵי־יִשְׂרָאֵל עַל־לִבּוֹ
לִפְנֵי יהוה תָּמִיד

and Aaron shall bear * the judgment
of the children of Israel on his heart
before YHVH continually.

Exodus ~ 28

The Priest's Robe

(31)

וְעָשִׂיתָ
אֶת־מְעִיל הָאֵפוֹד
כְּלִיל תְּכֵלֶת

And you shall make
* the robe of the ephod
wholly of blue.

(32)

וְהָיָה פִי־רֹאשׁוֹ בְּתוֹכוֹ
שָׂפָה יִהְיֶה לְפִיו סָבִיב
מַעֲשֵׂה אֹרֵג
כְּפִי תַחְרָא יִהְיֶה־לּוֹ
לֹא יִקָּרֵעַ

And it shall have a hole for the head in the midst thereof;
it shall have a hem round about the hole of it
handiwork of weaving
as it were the hole of a coat of mail
it shall not be torn.

(33)

וְעָשִׂיתָ עַל־שׁוּלָיו
רִמֹּנֵי תְּכֵלֶת וְאַרְגָּמָן
וְתוֹלַעַת שָׁנִי

Level Two שְׁמוֹת ~ כח

And you shall make on his skirts
pomegranates of blue, and of purple,
and of scarlet,

עַל־שׁוּלָיו סָבִיב

וּפַעֲמֹנֵי זָהָב בְּתוֹכָם סָבִיב

on his skirts round about;
and bells of gold in the midst of them round about:

(34)

פַּעֲמֹן זָהָב וְרִמּוֹן

פַּעֲמֹן זָהָב וְרִמּוֹן

עַל־שׁוּלֵי הַמְּעִיל סָבִיב

a golden bell and a pomegranate,
a golden bell and a pomegranate,
on the skirts of the robe round about.

(35)

וְהָיָה עַל־אַהֲרֹן לְשָׁרֵת

וְנִשְׁמַע קוֹלוֹ

בְּבֹאוֹ אֶל־הַקֹּדֶשׁ לִפְנֵי יהוה

וּבְצֵאתוֹ וְלֹא יָמוּת

And it shall be on Aaron to minister;
and the sound of it shall be heard
when he goes in to the holy place before YHVH
and when he comes out, that he doesn't die.

Exodus ~ 28

Priest's Headcovering

(36)

וְעָשִׂיתָ צִּיץ זָהָב טָהוֹר
וּפִתַּחְתָּ עָלָיו פִּתּוּחֵי חֹתָם
קֹדֶשׁ לַיהוה

And you shall make a plate of pure gold,
and engrave on it the engravings of a signet:
HOLY TO YHVH.

(37)

וְשַׂמְתָּ אֹתוֹ עַל־פְּתִיל תְּכֵלֶת
וְהָיָה עַל־הַמִּצְנָפֶת
אֶל־מוּל פְּנֵי־הַמִּצְנֶפֶת יִהְיֶה

And you shall put * it on a thread of blue,
and it shall be on the turban;
it shall be on the forefront of the turban.

(38)

וְהָיָה עַל־מֵצַח אַהֲרֹן
וְנָשָׂא אַהֲרֹן
אֶת־עֲוֹן הַקֳּדָשִׁים
אֲשֶׁר יַקְדִּישׁוּ בְּנֵי יִשְׂרָאֵל
לְכָל־מַתְּנֹת קָדְשֵׁיהֶם

And it shall be on Aaron's forehead,
and Aaron shall bear
* the iniquity of the holy things,
which the children of Israel shall hallow,
for all their holy gifts;

וְהָיָה עַל־מִצְחוֹ תָּמִיד
לְרָצוֹן לָהֶם לִפְנֵי יהוה

and it shall be on his forehead continually,
that they may be accepted before YHVH

(39)

וְשִׁבַּצְתָּ הַכְּתֹנֶת שֵׁשׁ
וְעָשִׂיתָ מִצְנֶפֶת שֵׁשׁ
וְאַבְנֵט תַּעֲשֶׂה
מַעֲשֵׂה רֹקֵם

And you shall weave the tunic of fine linen,
and you shall make a turban of fine linen,
and you shall make a sash,
handiwork of embroidering.

(40)

וְלִבְנֵי אַהֲרֹן תַּעֲשֶׂה כֻתֳּנֹת
וְעָשִׂיתָ לָהֶם אַבְנֵטִים

And for the sons of Aaron, you shall make tunics,
and you shall make for them sashes,

Exodus ~ 28

וּמִגְבָּעוֹת תַּעֲשֶׂה לָהֶם
לְכָבוֹד וּלְתִפְאָרֶת

and you shall make head-gear for them,
for splendor and for beauty.

(41)

וְהִלְבַּשְׁתָּ אֹתָם
אֶת־אַהֲרֹן אָחִיךָ וְאֶת־בָּנָיו אִתּוֹ
וּמָשַׁחְתָּ אֹתָם
וּמִלֵּאתָ אֶת־יָדָם
וְקִדַּשְׁתָּ אֹתָם
וְכִהֲנוּ לִי

*And you shall put * them on*
* Aaron your brother, and * his sons with * him;
and shall anoint * them,
and you shall fill * their hand,
and sanctify * them,
and they shall serve as priests for Me.

Priest's Breeches

(42)

וַעֲשֵׂה לָהֶם מִכְנְסֵי־בָד
לְכַסּוֹת בְּשַׂר עֶרְוָה
מִמָּתְנַיִם וְעַד־יְרֵכַיִם יִהְיוּ

Level Two   שְׁמוֹת ~ כח

And you shall make them linen breeches
to cover the flesh of their nakedness;
they shall be from waists and to thighs.

(43)

וְהָיוּ עַל־אַהֲרֹן וְעַל־בָּנָיו
בְּבֹאָם אֶל־אֹהֶל מוֹעֵד
אוֹ בְגִשְׁתָּם אֶל־הַמִּזְבֵּחַ
לְשָׁרֵת בַּקֹּדֶשׁ

And they shall be on Aaron, and on his sons,
when they go in to the tent of appointment,
or when they come near to the altar
to minister in the holy place;

וְלֹא־יִשְׂאוּ עָוֹן וָמֵתוּ
חֻקַּת עוֹלָם לוֹ
וּלְזַרְעוֹ אַחֲרָיו

that they don't bear iniquity, and die;
it shall be a statute forever for him
and for his seed after him.

Chapter Twenty-Nine

Concecrating The Priests

(1)

וְזֶה הַדָּבָר
אֲשֶׁר-תַּעֲשֶׂה לָהֶם לְקַדֵּשׁ אֹתָם
לְכַהֵן לִי
לְקַח פַּר אֶחָד בֶּן-בָּקָר
וְאֵילִם שְׁנַיִם תְּמִימִם

And this is the thing
that you shall do to them to hallow * them,
to be priests for Me:
take one young bull, son of a herd
and two rams, flawless ones

(2)

וְלֶחֶם מַצּוֹת
וְחַלֹּת מַצֹּת בְּלוּלֹת בַּשֶּׁמֶן
וּרְקִיקֵי מַצּוֹת מְשֻׁחִים בַּשָּׁמֶן
סֹלֶת חִטִּים תַּעֲשֶׂה אֹתָם

and unleavened bread,
and cakes unleavened mingled with oil,
and unleavened wafers anointed with oil;
you shall make * them of fine wheat flour.

Level Two ~ שְׁמוֹת ~ כט

(3)

וְנָתַתָּ אוֹתָם עַל-סַל אֶחָד
וְהִקְרַבְתָּ אֹתָם בַּסָּל
וְאֶת-הַפָּר וְאֵת שְׁנֵי הָאֵילִם

And you shall put * them in one basket,
and bring * them in the basket,
and * the bullock and * the two rams.

(4)

וְאֶת-אַהֲרֹן וְאֶת-בָּנָיו תַּקְרִיב
אֶל-פֶּתַח אֹהֶל מוֹעֵד
וְרָחַצְתָּ אֹתָם בַּמָּיִם

And you shall bring * Aaron and * his sons
to the door of the tent of appointment,
and shall wash * them with water.

(5)

וְלָקַחְתָּ אֶת-הַבְּגָדִים
וְהִלְבַּשְׁתָּ אֶת-אַהֲרֹן אֶת-הַכֻּתֹּנֶת
וְאֵת מְעִיל הָאֵפֹד
וְאֶת-הָאֵפֹד וְאֶת-הַחֹשֶׁן

And you shall take * the garments,
and put * the tunic on * Aaron,
and * the robe of the ephod,
and * the ephod, and * the breastplate,

Exodus ~ 29

וְאָפַדְתָּ לוֹ
בְּחֵשֶׁב הָאֵפֹד

and you shall gird for him
the skillfully woven band of the ephod.

(6)

וְשַׂמְתָּ הַמִּצְנֶפֶת עַל־רֹאשׁוֹ
וְנָתַתָּ אֶת־נֵזֶר הַקֹּדֶשׁ עַל־הַמִּצְנָפֶת

And you shall set the turban on his head,
*and put * the insignia of holiness on the turban.*

(7)

וְלָקַחְתָּ אֶת־שֶׁמֶן הַמִּשְׁחָה
וְיָצַקְתָּ עַל־רֹאשׁוֹ וּמָשַׁחְתָּ אֹתוֹ

*Then shall you take * the oil of the anointing,*
*and pour it on his head, and anoint * him.*

(8)

וְאֶת־בָּנָיו תַּקְרִיב
וְהִלְבַּשְׁתָּם כֻּתֳּנֹת

*And you shall bring * his sons,*
and put tunics on them.

(9)

וְחָגַרְתָּ אֹתָם אַבְנֵט
אַהֲרֹן וּבָנָיו
וְחָבַשְׁתָּ לָהֶם מִגְבָּעֹת

Level Two

שְׁמוֹת ~ כט

And you shall gird * them with a sash

Aaron and his sons,

and bind head-gear for them;

וְהָיְתָה לָהֶם כְּהֻנָּה

לְחֻקַּת עוֹלָם

וּמִלֵּאתָ יַד־אַהֲרֹן וְיַד־בָּנָיו

and it shall be a priesthood to them

for a statute forever;

and you shall fill the hand of Aaron and the hand of his sons.

(10)

וְהִקְרַבְתָּ אֶת־הַפָּר

לִפְנֵי אֹהֶל מוֹעֵד

וְסָמַךְ אַהֲרֹן וּבָנָיו אֶת־יְדֵיהֶם

עַל־רֹאשׁ הַפָּר

And you shall bring * the bullock

before the tent of appointment;

and Aaron and his sons shall lay * their hands

on the head of the bullock.

(11)

וְשָׁחַטְתָּ אֶת־הַפָּר לִפְנֵי יהוה

פֶּתַח אֹהֶל מוֹעֵד

And you shall kill * the bullock before YHVH

at the door of the tent of appointment.

(12)

וְלָקַחְתָּ מִדַּם הַפָּר
וְנָתַתָּה עַל־קַרְנֹת הַמִּזְבֵּחַ בְּאֶצְבָּעֶךָ
וְאֶת־כָּל־הַדָּם
תִּשְׁפֹּךְ אֶל־יְסוֹד הַמִּזְבֵּחַ

And you shall take from the blood of the bullock,
and put it on the horns of the altarwith your finger;
and * all the blood
you shall pour out at the base of the altar.

(13)

וְלָקַחְתָּ אֶת־כָּל־הַחֵלֶב
הַמְכַסֶּה אֶת־הַקֶּרֶב

And you shall take * all the fat
the covering of * the inwards,

וְאֵת הַיֹּתֶרֶת עַל־הַכָּבֵד
וְאֵת שְׁתֵּי הַכְּלָיֹת
וְאֶת־הַחֵלֶב אֲשֶׁר עֲלֵיהֶן
וְהִקְטַרְתָּ הַמִּזְבֵּחָה

and * the lobe above the liver,
and * the two kidneys,
and * the fat that is on them,
and make them smoke on the altar.

Level Two   שְׁמוֹת ~ כט

(14)

וְאֶת־בְּשַׂר הַפָּר
וְאֶת־עֹרוֹ וְאֶת־פִּרְשׁוֹ
תִּשְׂרֹף בָּאֵשׁ
מִחוּץ לַמַּחֲנֶה
חַטָּאת הוּא

And * the flesh of the bullock,
and * its skin, and * its dung,
shall you burn with fire
outside the camp;
it is a sin-offering.

(15)

וְאֶת־הָאַיִל הָאֶחָד תִּקָּח
וְסָמְכוּ אַהֲרֹן וּבָנָיו
אֶת־יְדֵיהֶם עַל־רֹאשׁ הָאָיִל

You shall also take the one * ram;
and Aaron and his sons shall lay
* their hands on the head of the ram.

(16)

וְשָׁחַטְתָּ אֶת־הָאָיִל
וְלָקַחְתָּ אֶת־דָּמוֹ

And you shall slay * the ram,
and you shall take * its blood,

265

Exodus ~ 29

וְזָרַקְתָּ
עַל-הַמִּזְבֵּחַ סָבִיב

and you shall sprinkle it
on the alter round about.

(17)

וְאֶת-הָאַיִל תְּנַתֵּחַ לִנְתָחָיו
וְרָחַצְתָּ קִרְבּוֹ וּכְרָעָיו
וְנָתַתָּ עַל-נְתָחָיו
וְעַל-רֹאשׁוֹ

And you shall cut * the ram in its pieces,
and wash its inwards, and its legs,
and put them with its pieces,
and with its head.

(18)

וְהִקְטַרְתָּ אֶת-כָּל-הָאַיִל הַמִּזְבֵּחָה
עֹלָה הוּא לַיהוה
רֵיחַ נִיחוֹחַ
אִשֶּׁה לַיהוה הוּא

And you shall make * the whole ram to smoke on the altar;
it is a burnt-offering to YHVH
a sweet savor,
it is an offering made by fire to YHVH.

Level Two ~ שְׁמוֹת ~ כט

(19)

וְלָקַחְתָּ אֵת הָאַיִל הַשֵּׁנִי
וְסָמַךְ אַהֲרֹן וּבָנָיו אֶת־יְדֵיהֶם
עַל־רֹאשׁ הָאָיִל

*And you shall take the second * ram;
and Aaron shall lay and his sons * their hands
on the head of the ram.*

(20)

וְשָׁחַטְתָּ אֶת־הָאַיִל
וְלָקַחְתָּ מִדָּמוֹ
וְנָתַתָּה עַל־תְּנוּךְ אֹזֶן אַהֲרֹן
וְעַל־תְּנוּךְ אֹזֶן בָּנָיו
הַיְמָנִית

*Then shall you slay * the ram,
and you shall take from its blood,
and put it on the lobe of ear of Aaron,
and on the lobe of the ear of his sons,
the right;*

וְעַל־בֹּהֶן יָדָם הַיְמָנִית
וְעַל־בֹּהֶן רַגְלָם הַיְמָנִית

*and on the thumb of their right hand,
and on the big toe of their right foot,*

Exodus ~ 29

וְזָרַקְתָּ אֶת־הַדָּם
עַל־הַמִּזְבֵּחַ סָבִיב

and you shall sprinkle * the blood
on the altar round about.

(21)

וְלָקַחְתָּ מִן־הַדָּם
אֲשֶׁר עַל־הַמִּזְבֵּחַ
וּמִשֶּׁמֶן הַמִּשְׁחָה
וְהִזֵּיתָ עַל־אַהֲרֹן
וְעַל־בְּגָדָיו וְעַל־בָּנָיו

And you shall take from the blood
that is on the altar,
and of the anointing oil,
and sprinkle it on Aaron,
and on his garments, and on his sons,

וְעַל־בִּגְדֵי בָנָיו אִתּוֹ
וְקָדַשׁ הוּא וּבְגָדָיו
וּבָנָיו וּבִגְדֵי בָנָיו אִתּוֹ

and on the garments of his sons with * him;
and he and his garments shall be hallowed,
and his sons and his sons' garments with * him.

Level Two   שְׁמוֹת ~ כט

(22)

וְלָקַחְתָּ מִן־הָאַיִל
הַחֵלֶב וְהָאַלְיָה
וְאֶת־הַחֵלֶב הַמְכַסֶּה אֶת־הַקֶּרֶב

And you shall take from the ram,
the fat and the fat tail,
and * the fat that covers * the inwards,

וְאֵת יֹתֶרֶת הַכָּבֵד
וְאֵת שְׁתֵּי הַכְּלָיֹת
וְאֶת־הַחֵלֶב אֲשֶׁר עֲלֵיהֶן
וְאֵת שׁוֹק הַיָּמִין
כִּי אֵיל מִלֻּאִים הוּא

and * the lobe of the liver,
and * the two kidneys,
and * the fat that is on them,
and * the leg, the right;
for it is a ram of installation;

(23)

וְכִכַּר לֶחֶם אַחַת
וְחַלַּת לֶחֶם שֶׁמֶן אַחַת וְרָקִיק אֶחָד

and one loaf of bread,
and one cake of oiled bread, and one wafer,

Exodus ~ 29

מִסַּל הַמַּצּוֹת
אֲשֶׁר לִפְנֵי יהוה

from the basket of the unleavened bread
that is before YHVH.

(24)

וְשַׂמְתָּ הַכֹּל
עַל כַּפֵּי אַהֲרֹן
וְעַל כַּפֵּי בָנָיו
וְהֵנַפְתָּ אֹתָם תְּנוּפָה
לִפְנֵי יהוה

And you shall put everything
on the palms of Aaron,
and on the palms of his sons;
*and shall wave * them for a wave- offering*
before YHVH.

(25)

וְלָקַחְתָּ אֹתָם מִיָּדָם
וְהִקְטַרְתָּ הַמִּזְבֵּחָה
עַל־הָעֹלָה
לְרֵיחַ נִיחוֹחַ לִפְנֵי יהוה
אִשֶּׁה הוּא לַיהוה

Level Two שְׁמוֹת ~ כט

And you shall take * them from their hand,
and cause smoke on the altar,
on the burnt-offering,
for a sweet savor before YHVH
it is an offering made by fire to YHVH.

(26)

וְלָקַחְתָּ אֶת-הֶחָזֶה
מֵאֵיל הַמִּלֻּאִים אֲשֶׁר לְאַהֲרֹן
וְהֵנַפְתָּ אֹתוֹ תְּנוּפָה לִפְנֵי יהוה
וְהָיָה לְךָ לְמָנָה

And you shall take * the chest
from the ram of the consecration for Aaron,
and wave * it for a wave-offering before YHVH
and it shall be for your portion.

(27)

וְקִדַּשְׁתָּ אֵת חֲזֵה
הַתְּנוּפָה
וְאֵת שׁוֹק הַתְּרוּמָה
אֲשֶׁר הוּנַף וַאֲשֶׁר הוּרָם

And you shall sanctify * the breast of
the wave-offering,
and * the leg of the heave-offering,
which is waved, and which is heaved up,

מֵאֵיל הַמִּלֻּאִים

מֵאֲשֶׁר לְאַהֲרֹן

וּמֵאֲשֶׁר לְבָנָיו

from the ram of the consecration,

from which is for Aaron,

and from which is for his sons.

(28)

וְהָיָה לְאַהֲרֹן וּלְבָנָיו

לְחָק־עוֹלָם

מֵאֵת בְּנֵי יִשְׂרָאֵל כִּי תְרוּמָה הוּא

And it shall be for Aaron and for his sons

for a statute forever

from * the children of Israel; for it is a heave-offering;

וּתְרוּמָה יִהְיֶה

מֵאֵת בְּנֵי־יִשְׂרָאֵל

מִזִּבְחֵי שַׁלְמֵיהֶם

תְּרוּמָתָם לַיהוה

and it shall be a heave-offering

from * the children of Israel

from their sacrifices of peace-offerings,

their heave-offering to YHVH.

Level Two

שְׁמוֹת ~ כט

(29)

וּבִגְדֵי הַקֹּדֶשׁ אֲשֶׁר לְאַהֲרֹן

יִהְיוּ לְבָנָיו אַחֲרָיו

לְמָשְׁחָה בָהֶם

וּלְמַלֵּא־בָם אֶת־יָדָם

And the holy garments which are for Aaron,

they shall be for his sons after him,

to be anointed in them,

and to fill in them * their hand.

(30)

שִׁבְעַת יָמִים יִלְבָּשָׁם

הַכֹּהֵן תַּחְתָּיו מִבָּנָיו

אֲשֶׁר יָבֹא אֶל־אֹהֶל מוֹעֵד

לְשָׁרֵת בַּקֹּדֶשׁ

Seven days he shall put them on,

the priest in his stead from his sons,

he who comes in the tent of appointment

to minister in the holy place.

(31)

וְאֵת אֵיל הַמִּלֻּאִים תִּקָּח

וּבִשַּׁלְתָּ אֶת־בְּשָׂרוֹ בְּמָקֹם קָדֹשׁ

And you shall take * the ram of the consecration,

and you shall cook * its flesh in a holy place.

Exodus ~ 29

(32)

וְאָכַל אַהֲרֹן וּבָנָיו
אֶת־בְּשַׂר הָאַיִל
וְאֶת־הַלֶּחֶם אֲשֶׁר בַּסָּל
פֶּתַח אֹהֶל מוֹעֵד

And Aaron shall eat, and his sons,
* the flesh of the ram,
and * the bread that is in the basket,
at the door of the tent of appointment.

(33)

וְאָכְלוּ אֹתָם
אֲשֶׁר כֻּפַּר בָּהֶם
לְמַלֵּא אֶת־יָדָם
לְקַדֵּשׁ אֹתָם
וְזָר לֹא־יֹאכַל
כִּי־קֹדֶשׁ הֵם

And they shall eat * them
in which atonement was made,
to fill * their hand,
to sanctify * them;
but a stranger shall not eat thereof,
because they are holy.

Level Two שְׁמוֹת ~ כט

(34)

וְאִם־יִוָּתֵר מִבְּשַׂר הַמִּלֻּאִים

וּמִן־הַלֶּחֶם עַד־הַבֹּקֶר

וְשָׂרַפְתָּ אֶת־הַנּוֹתָר בָּאֵשׁ

לֹא יֵאָכֵל

כִּי־קֹדֶשׁ הוּא

And if aught of the flesh of the consecration,

or of the bread, remain to the morning,

then you shall burn * the remainder with fire;

it shall not be eaten,

because it is holy.

(35)

וְעָשִׂיתָ לְאַהֲרֹן וּלְבָנָיו

כָּכָה כְּכֹל אֲשֶׁר־צִוִּיתִי אֹתָכָה

שִׁבְעַת יָמִים תְּמַלֵּא יָדָם

And thus shall you do for Aaron, and for his sons,

according to all that I have commanded * you;

seven days you shall fill their hand.

(36)

וּפַר חַטָּאת תַּעֲשֶׂה

לַיּוֹם עַל־הַכִּפֻּרִים

And you shall offer the bullock of sin-offering

daily for the atonements,

וְחִטֵּאתָ עַל־הַמִּזְבֵּחַ

בְּכַפֶּרְךָ עָלָיו

וּמָשַׁחְתָּ אֹתוֹ לְקַדְּשׁוֹ

and you shall make a sin-offering on the altar

when you make atonement for it;

and you shall anoint * it, to sanctify it.

(37)

שִׁבְעַת יָמִים

תְּכַפֵּר עַל־הַמִּזְבֵּחַ

וְקִדַּשְׁתָּ אֹתוֹ

וְהָיָה הַמִּזְבֵּחַ קֹדֶשׁ קָדָשִׁים

כָּל־הַנֹּגֵעַ בַּמִּזְבֵּחַ יִקְדָּשׁ

Seven days

you shall make atonement on the altar,

and sanctify * it;

and the altar shall be most holy;

whatsoever touches the altar he shall be holy.

(38)

וְזֶה אֲשֶׁר תַּעֲשֶׂה עַל־הַמִּזְבֵּחַ

כְּבָשִׂים בְּנֵי־שָׁנָה שְׁנַיִם לַיּוֹם תָּמִיד

Now this is that which you shall make on the altar:

two lambs of the first year daily continually.

Level Two ~ שְׁמוֹת ~ כט

(39)

אֶת־הַכֶּבֶשׂ הָאֶחָד
תַּעֲשֶׂה בַבֹּקֶר
וְאֵת הַכֶּבֶשׂ הַשֵּׁנִי
תַּעֲשֶׂה בֵּין הָעַרְבָּיִם

The one * he-lamb

you shall make in the morning;

and the second* he- lamb

you shall make between the evenings.

(40)

וְעִשָּׂרֹן סֹלֶת בָּלוּל
בְּשֶׁמֶן כָּתִית רֶבַע הַהִין
וְנֵסֶךְ רְבִיעִת הַהִין יָיִן
לַכֶּבֶשׂ הָאֶחָד

And a tenth part of fine flour mingled with

the fourth part of the hin of beaten oil

and libation, the fourth part of the hin of wine

for the one he-lamb.

(41)

וְאֵת הַכֶּבֶשׂ הַשֵּׁנִי
תַּעֲשֶׂה בֵּין הָעַרְבָּיִם

And the second * he-lamb

you shall make between the evenings,

Exodus ~ 28

כְּמִנְחַת הַבֹּקֶר וּכְנִסְכָּהּ
תַּעֲשֶׂה־לָּהּ לְרֵיחַ נִיחֹחַ
אִשֶּׁה לַיהוה

as the offering of the morning, and as its libation,
You shall make for it for a sweet savor,
an offering made by fire to YHVH.

(42)

עֹלַת תָּמִיד לְדֹרֹתֵיכֶם
פֶּתַח אֹהֶל־מוֹעֵד לִפְנֵי יהוה
אֲשֶׁר אִוָּעֵד לָכֶם שָׁמָּה
לְדַבֵּר אֵלֶיךָ שָׁם

A burnt-offering continually for your generations
at the door of the tent of appointment before YHVH
where I will keep appointment for you there,
to speak to you there.

(43)

וְנֹעַדְתִּי שָׁמָּה לִבְנֵי יִשְׂרָאֵל
וְנִקְדַּשׁ בִּכְבֹדִי

And I will keep appointment there for the children of Israel
and it is holy by My glory.

(44)

וְקִדַּשְׁתִּי אֶת־אֹהֶל מוֹעֵד וְאֶת־הַמִּזְבֵּחַ

And I will sanctify * the tent of appointment, and * the altar;

Level Two　　　　　　　　　　　　　　　שְׁמוֹת ~ כח

וְאֶת־אַהֲרֹן וְאֶת־בָּנָיו
אֲקַדֵּשׁ לְכַהֵן לִי

and * Aaron and * his sons
I will sanctify to be priests for Me.

(45)

וְשָׁכַנְתִּי בְּתוֹךְ בְּנֵי יִשְׂרָאֵל
וְהָיִיתִי לָהֶם לֵאלֹהִים

And I will dwell among the children of Israel
and I will be to them for Elohim.

(46)

וְיָדְעוּ כִּי אֲנִי יהוה אֱלֹהֵיהֶם
אֲשֶׁר הוֹצֵאתִי אֹתָם
מֵאֶרֶץ מִצְרַיִם
לְשָׁכְנִי בְתוֹכָם
אֲנִי יהוה אֱלֹהֵיהֶם

And they shall know that I am YHVH their Elohim,
that brought * them forth
from the land of Egypt,
for My tabernacling among them.
I am YHVH their Elohim.

Chapter Thirty

Altar Of Incense

(1)

וְעָשִׂיתָ מִזְבֵּחַ מִקְטַר קְטֹרֶת

עֲצֵי שִׁטִּים תַּעֲשֶׂה אֹתוֹ

And you shall make an altar to burn incense on;
of acacia-wood shall you make * it.

(2)

אַמָּה אָרְכּוֹ וְאַמָּה רָחְבּוֹ

רָבוּעַ יִהְיֶה

וְאַמָּתַיִם קֹמָתוֹ

מִמֶּנּוּ קַרְנֹתָיו

A cubit, its length, and a cubit, its width;
it shall be square;
and two cubits, its height;
its horns shall be from it.

(3)

וְצִפִּיתָ אֹתוֹ זָהָב טָהוֹר

אֶת-גַּגּוֹ וְאֶת-קִירֹתָיו סָבִיב

וְאֶת-קַרְנֹתָיו

And you shall overlay * it with pure gold,
* the top of it, and * the sides of it round about,
and * the horns of it;

Level Two   שְׁמוֹת ~ ל

וְעָשִׂיתָ לּוֹ
זֵר זָהָב סָבִיב

and you shall make for it
a border of gold round about.

(4)

וּשְׁתֵּי טַבְּעֹת זָהָב תַּעֲשֶׂה-לּוֹ
מִתַּחַת לְזֵרוֹ
עַל שְׁתֵּי צַלְעֹתָיו
תַּעֲשֶׂה עַל-שְׁנֵי צִדָּיו
וְהָיָה לְבָתִּים לְבַדִּים
לָשֵׂאת אֹתוֹ בָּהֵמָּה

And you shall make for it two golden rings
under the border of it,
on the two ribs of it,
you shall make on the two sides of it;
and they shall be for housings
for poles for carrying * it in them.

(5)

וְעָשִׂיתָ אֶת-הַבַּדִּים עֲצֵי שִׁטִּים
וְצִפִּיתָ אֹתָם זָהָב

And you shall make * the poles of acacia-wood,
and overlay them with gold.

281

Exodus ~ 30

(6)

וְנָתַתָּה אֹתוֹ לִפְנֵי הַפָּרֹכֶת

אֲשֶׁר עַל־אֲרֹן הָעֵדֻת

לִפְנֵי הַכַּפֹּרֶת

אֲשֶׁר עַל־הָעֵדֻת

אֲשֶׁר אִוָּעֵד לְךָ שָׁמָּה

And you shall put * it before the veil
that is by the ark of the testimony,
before the mercy-seat
that is over the testimony,
where I will keep an appointment for you there.

(7)

וְהִקְטִיר עָלָיו אַהֲרֹן

קְטֹרֶת סַמִּים

בַּבֹּקֶר בַּבֹּקֶר

בְּהֵיטִיבוֹ אֶת־הַנֵּרֹת

יַקְטִירֶנָּה

And Aaron shall burn thereon
incense of sweet spices;
every morning,
when he dresses * the lamps,
he shall burn it.

Level Two   שְׁמוֹת ~ ל

(8)

וּבְהַעֲלֹת אַהֲרֹן אֶת־הַנֵּרֹת

בֵּין הָעַרְבַּיִם

יַקְטִירֶנָּה

קְטֹרֶת תָּמִיד לִפְנֵי יהוה

לְדֹרֹתֵיכֶם

And when Aaron lights * the lamps

between the evenings,

he shall burn it,

a perpetual incense before YHVH

for your generations.

(9)

לֹא־תַעֲלוּ עָלָיו קְטֹרֶת זָרָה

וְעֹלָה וּמִנְחָה

וְנֵסֶךְ לֹא תִסְּכוּ עָלָיו

You shall offer no strange incense thereon,

nor burnt-offering, nor meal-offering;

and you shall pour no drink-offering thereon.

(10)

וְכִפֶּר אַהֲרֹן

עַל־קַרְנֹתָיו אַחַת בַּשָּׁנָה

And Aaron shall make atonement

on the horns of it once in the year;

283

Exodus ~ 30

מִדַּם חַטַּאת הַכִּפֻּרִים
אַחַת בַּשָּׁנָה יְכַפֵּר עָלָיו
לְדֹרֹתֵיכֶם קֹדֶשׁ-קָדָשִׁים הוּא לַיהוה

with the blood of the sin-offering of atonement
once in the year he shall make atonement for it
for your generations; it is most holy to YHVH.

Taking A Census

(11) וַיְדַבֵּר יהוה אֶל-מֹשֶׁה לֵּאמֹר (And YHVH spoke to Moses saying):

(12)

כִּי תִשָּׂא אֶת-רֹאשׁ בְּנֵי-יִשְׂרָאֵל
לִפְקֻדֵיהֶם
וְנָתְנוּ אִישׁ כֹּפֶר נַפְשׁוֹ לַיהוה
בִּפְקֹד אֹתָם
וְלֹא-יִהְיֶה בָהֶם נֶגֶף
בִּפְקֹד אֹתָם

*When you take * the sum of the children of Israel*
according to their number,
and they give a man a ransom for his soul to YHVH
*when you number * them;*
that there be no plague among them,
*when you number * them.*

284

Level Two   שְׁמוֹת ~ ל

(13)

זֶה יִתְּנוּ כָּל־הָעֹבֵר
עַל־הַפְּקֻדִים
מַחֲצִית הַשֶּׁקֶל
בְּשֶׁקֶל הַקֹּדֶשׁ

This they shall give, everyone that passes

among them that are numbered,

half a shekel

after the shekel of the sanctuary,

עֶשְׂרִים גֵּרָה הַשֶּׁקֶל
מַחֲצִית הַשֶּׁקֶל
תְּרוּמָה לַיהוה

the shekel is twenty gerahs,

half a shekel

an offering to YHVH.

(14)

כֹּל הָעֹבֵר עַל־הַפְּקֻדִים
מִבֶּן עֶשְׂרִים

Every one that passes among them that are numbered,

from the son of twenty

שָׁנָה וָמָעְלָה

יִתֵּן תְּרוּמַת יהוה

years old and upward,

he shall give the offering of YHVH.

(15)

הֶעָשִׁיר לֹא־יַרְבֶּה

וְהַדַּל לֹא יַמְעִיט

מִמַּחֲצִית הַשָּׁקֶל

לָתֵת אֶת־תְּרוּמַת יהוה

לְכַפֵּר עַל־נַפְשֹׁתֵיכֶם

The rich shall not increase,

and the poor shall not decrease,

from the half shekel,

when they give * the offering of YHVH

to make atonement over your souls.

(16)

וְלָקַחְתָּ אֶת־כֶּסֶף

הַכִּפֻּרִים

מֵאֵת בְּנֵי יִשְׂרָאֵל

And you shall take * money

of the atonement

from * the children of Israel

Level Two

שְׁמוֹת ~ ל

וְנָתַתָּ אֹתוֹ עַל־עֲבֹדַת
אֹהֶל מוֹעֵד
וְהָיָה לִבְנֵי יִשְׂרָאֵל
לְזִכָּרוֹן לִפְנֵי יהוה
לְכַפֵּר עַל־נַפְשֹׁתֵיכֶם

and shall appoint * it on the work of

the tent of appointment,

and it shall be for the children of Israel

for a memorial before YHVH

to make atonement for your souls.

The Laver

(17) וַיְדַבֵּר יהוה אֶל־מֹשֶׁה לֵּאמֹר (And YHVH spoke to Moses saying):

(18)

וְעָשִׂיתָ כִּיּוֹר נְחֹשֶׁת
וְכַנּוֹ נְחֹשֶׁת לְרָחְצָה
וְנָתַתָּ אֹתוֹ
בֵּין־אֹהֶל מוֹעֵד וּבֵין הַמִּזְבֵּחַ
וְנָתַתָּ שָׁמָּה מָיִם

You shall make a laver of copper,

and the base thereof of copper, for washing;

and you shall put * it

between the tent of appointment and the altar,

and you shall put therein water.

Exodus ~ 30

(19)

וְרָחֲצוּ אַהֲרֹן וּבָנָיו מִמֶּנּוּ

אֶת־יְדֵיהֶם וְאֶת־רַגְלֵיהֶם

And Aaron and his sons shall wash from it
* their hands and * their feet;

(20)

בְּבֹאָם אֶל־אֹהֶל מוֹעֵד

יִרְחֲצוּ־מַיִם

וְלֹא יָמֻתוּ

אוֹ בְגִשְׁתָּם אֶל־הַמִּזְבֵּחַ לְשָׁרֵת

לְהַקְטִיר אִשֶּׁה לַיהוה

when they go in to the tent of appointment,
they shall wash with water,
that they don't die;
or when they come near to the altar to minister,
to cause an offering made by fire to smoke to YHVH.

(21)

וְרָחֲצוּ יְדֵיהֶם

וְרַגְלֵיהֶם

וְלֹא יָמֻתוּ

וְהָיְתָה לָהֶם חָק־עוֹלָם

לוֹ וּלְזַרְעוֹ לְדֹרֹתָם

Level Two   שְׁמוֹת ~ ל

> And they shall wash their hands
> and their feet,
> that they don't die;
> and it shall be to them a statute forever,
> to him and to his seed for their generations.

The Anointing Oil

(22) וַיְדַבֵּר יהוה אֶל-מֹשֶׁה לֵּאמֹר (And YHVH spoke to Moses saying):

(23)

> וְאַתָּה קַח-לְךָ בְּשָׂמִים רֹאשׁ
> מָר-דְּרוֹר חֲמֵשׁ מֵאוֹת
> וְקִנְּמָן-בֶּשֶׂם מַחֲצִיתוֹ
> חֲמִשִּׁים וּמָאתָיִם
> וּקְנֵה-בֹשֶׂם חֲמִשִּׁים וּמָאתָיִם

> And * you, take for you the chief spices,
> of flowing myrrh five hundred shekels,
> and of sweet cinnamon half so much,
> two hundred and fifty,
> and of sweet calamus, two hundred and fifty,

(24)

> וְקִדָּה חֲמֵשׁ מֵאוֹת
> בְּשֶׁקֶל הַקֹּדֶשׁ וְשֶׁמֶן זַיִת הִין

> and of cassia five hundred,
> after the shekel of the sanctuary, and of olive oil a hin.

Exodus ~ 30

(25)

וְעָשִׂיתָ אֹתוֹ שֶׁמֶן מִשְׁחַת־קֹדֶשׁ
רֹקַח מִרְקַחַת

And you shall make * it a holy anointing oil,
a compound ointment,

מַעֲשֵׂה רֹקֵחַ
שֶׁמֶן מִשְׁחַת־קֹדֶשׁ יִהְיֶה

handiwork of a compounder;
it shall be a holy anointing oil.

(26)

וּמָשַׁחְתָּ בוֹ
אֶת־אֹהֶל מוֹעֵד
וְאֵת אֲרוֹן הָעֵדֻת

And you shall anoint with it
* the tent of appointment,
and * the ark of the testimony,

(27)

וְאֶת־הַשֻּׁלְחָן וְאֶת־כָּל־כֵּלָיו
וְאֶת־הַמְּנֹרָה
וְאֶת־כֵּלֶיהָ
וְאֵת מִזְבַּח הַקְּטֹרֶת

Level Two   שְׁמוֹת ~ ל

and * the table and * all the implements of it,

and * the candlestick

and * the implements of it,

and * the altar of incense,

(28)

וְאֶת־מִזְבַּח הָעֹלָה

וְאֶת־כָּל־כֵּלָיו

וְאֶת־הַכִּיֹּר וְאֶת־כַּנּוֹ

and * the altar of burnt-offering

and * all the implements of it,

and * the laver and * the base of it.

(29)

וְקִדַּשְׁתָּ אֹתָם

וְהָיוּ קֹדֶשׁ קָדָשִׁים

כָּל־הַנֹּגֵעַ בָּהֶם יִקְדָּשׁ

And you shall sanctify * them,

and they may be most holy;

whatsoever touches them shall be holy.

(30)

וְאֶת־אַהֲרֹן וְאֶת־בָּנָיו תִּמְשָׁח

וְקִדַּשְׁתָּ אֹתָם לְכַהֵן לִי

And * Aaron and * his sons you shall anoint,

and sanctify * them, to be priest for Me.

Exodus ~ 30

(31)

וְאֶל־בְּנֵי יִשְׂרָאֵל
תְּדַבֵּר לֵאמֹר
שֶׁמֶן מִשְׁחַת־קֹדֶשׁ יִהְיֶה זֶה לִי
לְדֹרֹתֵיכֶם

And to the children of Israel
you shall speak saying:
This shall be a holy anointing oil to Me
for your generations.

(32)

עַל־בְּשַׂר אָדָם לֹא יִיסָךְ
וּבְמַתְכֻּנְתּוֹ לֹא תַעֲשׂוּ כָּמֹהוּ
קֹדֶשׁ הוּא קֹדֶשׁ יִהְיֶה לָכֶם

On the flesh of human it shall not be poured,
neither shall you make any recipe like it,
it is holy, and it shall be holy to you.

(33)

אִישׁ אֲשֶׁר יִרְקַח כָּמֹהוּ
וַאֲשֶׁר יִתֵּן מִמֶּנּוּ עַל־זָר
וְנִכְרַת מֵעַמָּיו

A man who compounds like it,
or whosoever puts from it on a stranger,
he shall be cut off from his people.

Level Two   שְׁמוֹת ~ ל

The Incense

(34) וַיֹּאמֶר יהוה אֶל־מֹשֶׁה (And YHVH said to Moses):

קַח־לְךָ סַמִּים נָטָף
וּשְׁחֵלֶת וְחֶלְבְּנָה
סַמִּים וּלְבֹנָה זַכָּה
בַּד בְּבַד יִהְיֶה

Take to you sweet spices, stacte,
and onycha, and galbanum;
sweet spices and pure frankincense;
they shall be part for part.

(35)

וְעָשִׂיתָ אֹתָהּ קְטֹרֶת
רֹקַח מַעֲשֵׂה רוֹקֵחַ
מְמֻלָּח טָהוֹר קֹדֶשׁ

*And you shall make of * it incense,*
a compound, handiwork of a compounder
being salt, pure and holy.

(36)

וְשָׁחַקְתָּ מִמֶּנָּה הָדֵק
וְנָתַתָּה מִמֶּנָּה לִפְנֵי הָעֵדֻת

And you shall beat some of it to powder,
and put of it before the testimony

בְּאֹהֶל מוֹעֵד
אֲשֶׁר אִוָּעֵד לְךָ שָׁמָּה
קֹדֶשׁ קָדָשִׁים תִּהְיֶה לָכֶם

in the tent of appointment,

where I will keep an appointment for you there;

it shall be to you most holy.

(37)

וְהַקְּטֹרֶת אֲשֶׁר תַּעֲשֶׂה
בְּמַתְכֻּנְתָּהּ לֹא תַעֲשׂוּ לָכֶם
קֹדֶשׁ תִּהְיֶה לְךָ לַיהוה

And the incense which you shall make,

in its recipe you shall not make for yourselves;

it shall be holy to you for YHVH.

(38)

אִישׁ אֲשֶׁר־יַעֲשֶׂה כָמוֹהָ
לְהָרִיחַ בָּהּ
וְנִכְרַת מֵעַמָּיו

A man who makes like it

to smell thereof,

he shall be cut off from his people.

Chapter Thirty-One

Bezalel

(1) וַיְדַבֵּר יהוה אֶל-מֹשֶׁה לֵּאמֹר *(And YHVH spoke to Moses saying):*

(2)
רְאֵה קָרָאתִי בְשֵׁם בְּצַלְאֵל
בֶּן-אוּרִי בֶן-חוּר לְמַטֵּה יְהוּדָה

*See, I have called by name Bezalel
the son of Uri, the son of Hur, of the tribe of Judah;*

(3)
וָאֲמַלֵּא אֹתוֹ רוּחַ אֱלֹהִים
בְּחָכְמָה וּבִתְבוּנָה
וּבְדַעַת וּבְכָל-מְלָאכָה

*and I have filled * him with the spirit of Elohim,
in wisdom, and in understanding,
and in knowledge, and in all workmanship,*

(4)
לַחְשֹׁב מַחֲשָׁבֹת
לַעֲשׂוֹת בַּזָּהָב וּבַכֶּסֶף וּבַנְּחֹשֶׁת

*For designing designs,
to work in gold, and in silver, and in copper,*

(5)
וּבַחֲרֹשֶׁת אֶבֶן לְמַלֹּאת

and in cutting of stones for setting,

Exodus ~ 31

וּבַחֲרֹשֶׁת עֵץ
לַעֲשׂוֹת בְּכָל־מְלָאכָה

and in carving of wood,
to work in all workmanship.

(6)

וַאֲנִי הִנֵּה נָתַתִּי אִתּוֹ
אֵת אָהֳלִיאָב בֶּן־אֲחִיסָמָךְ לְמַטֵּה־דָן

And I, behold, I have appointed with * him
* Oholiab, the son of Ahisamach, of the tribe of Dan;

וּבְלֵב כָּל־חֲכַם־לֵב
נָתַתִּי חָכְמָה
וְעָשׂוּ אֵת כָּל־אֲשֶׁר
צִוִּיתִךָ

and in the hearts of all that are wise-hearted
I have put wisdom,
and they shall make * all that
I have commanded you:

(7)

אֵת אֹהֶל מוֹעֵד
וְאֶת־הָאָרֹן לָעֵדֻת
וְאֶת־הַכַּפֹּרֶת אֲשֶׁר עָלָיו
וְאֵת כָּל־כְּלֵי הָאֹהֶל

Level Two   שְׁמוֹת ~ לא

* the tent of appointment,

and * the ark of the testimony,

and * the mercy-seat that is on it,

and * all the implements of the tent;

(8)

וְאֶת־הַשֻּׁלְחָן וְאֶת־כֵּלָיו

וְאֶת־הַמְּנֹרָה הַטְּהֹרָה וְאֶת־כָּל־כֵּלֶיהָ

וְאֵת מִזְבַּח הַקְּטֹרֶת

and * the table and * implements of it,

and the pure * candlestick and * all its implements,

and * the altar of incense;

(9)

וְאֶת־מִזְבַּח הָעֹלָה וְאֶת־כָּל־כֵּלָיו

וְאֶת־הַכִּיּוֹר וְאֶת־כַּנּוֹ

and * the altar of burnt-offering and * all its implements,

and * the laver and * base of it;

(10)

וְאֵת בִּגְדֵי הַשְּׂרָד

וְאֶת־בִּגְדֵי הַקֹּדֶשׁ

לְאַהֲרֹן הַכֹּהֵן וְאֶת־בִּגְדֵי בָנָיו לְכַהֵן

and * the garments of tapestry,

and * the garments of holiness

for Aaron the priest, and * the garments of his sons, for being priest;

Exodus ~ 31

(11)

וְאֵת שֶׁמֶן הַמִּשְׁחָה
וְאֶת־קְטֹרֶת הַסַּמִּים לַקֹּדֶשׁ
כְּכֹל אֲשֶׁר־צִוִּיתִךָ יַעֲשׂוּ

and * the oil of the anointing,
and * the incense of sweet spices for the holy place;
as all that I have commanded you, they shall do.

Keep The Sabbath

(12) וַיֹּאמֶר יהוה אֶל־מֹשֶׁה לֵּאמֹר (And YHVH said to Moses saying):

(13)

וְאַתָּה דַּבֵּר אֶל־בְּנֵי יִשְׂרָאֵל לֵאמֹר
אַךְ אֶת־שַׁבְּתֹתַי תִּשְׁמֹרוּ
כִּי אוֹת הִוא בֵּינִי וּבֵינֵיכֶם

And * you, speak to the children of Israel saying:
Verily you shall keep * the Sabbaths of Me,
for it is a sign between Me and you

לְדֹרֹתֵיכֶם
לָדַעַת כִּי אֲנִי יהוה
מְקַדִּשְׁכֶם

throughout your generations,
that you may know that I am YHVH
Who sanctifies you.

Level Two   שְׁמוֹת ~ לֹא

(14)

וּשְׁמַרְתֶּם אֶת־הַשַּׁבָּת

כִּי קֹדֶשׁ הִוא לָכֶם

מְחַלְלֶיהָ מוֹת יוּמָת

כִּי כָּל־הָעֹשֶׂה בָהּ מְלָאכָה

וְנִכְרְתָה הַנֶּפֶשׁ הַהִוא

מִקֶּרֶב עַמֶּיהָ

You shall keep * the Sabbath,

for it is holy to you;

Ones profaning it shall surely be put to death;

for every one doing any work on it,

that soul shall be cut off

from among his people.

(15)

שֵׁשֶׁת יָמִים יֵעָשֶׂה מְלָאכָה וּבַיּוֹם הַשְּׁבִיעִי

שַׁבַּת שַׁבָּתוֹן קֹדֶשׁ לַיהוה

כָּל־הָעֹשֶׂה מְלָאכָה בְּיוֹם הַשַּׁבָּת

מוֹת יוּמָת

Six days shall work be done; and on the seventh day

is a Sabbath of solemn rest, holy to YHVH

all doing work on the Sabbath day,

he shall surely be put to death.

Exodus ~ 31

(16)

וְשָׁמְרוּ בְנֵי-יִשְׂרָאֵל אֶת-הַשַּׁבָּת
לַעֲשׂוֹת אֶת-הַשַּׁבָּת לְדֹרֹתָם
בְּרִית עוֹלָם

And the children of Israel shall keep * the Sabbath,

to make * the Sabbath for their generations,

a covenant forever.

(17)

בֵּינִי וּבֵין בְּנֵי יִשְׂרָאֵל
אוֹת הִוא לְעֹלָם

Between Me and the children of Israel,

it is a sign forever;

כִּי-שֵׁשֶׁת יָמִים
עָשָׂה יהוה אֶת-הַשָּׁמַיִם וְאֶת-הָאָרֶץ
וּבַיּוֹם הַשְּׁבִיעִי שָׁבַת וַיִּנָּפַשׁ

for in six days

YHVH made * sky and * the land,

and on the seventh day He ceased and was refreshed.

(18) And He gave אֶל-מֹשֶׁה when He had made an end of לְדַבֵּר אִתּוֹ (speaking with * him) בְּהַר סִינַי (on Mount Sinai) the two לֻחֹת הָעֵדֻת (tablets of the testimony) לֻחֹת אֶבֶן (tablets of stone) written בְּאֶצְבַּע אֱלֹהִים (with the finger of Elohim).

Chapter Thirty-Two

The Molten Calf

(1) וַיַּרְא הָעָם (And the people saw) that מֹשֶׁה delayed to come down מִן־הָהָר (from the mountain) הָעָם (the people) gathered themselves together עַל־אַהֲרֹן (on Aaron) וַיֹּאמְרוּ אֵלָיו (and they said to him):

"Rise, make לָנוּ (for us) אֱלֹהִים who shall יֵלְכוּ (go) before us; for as for this מֹשֶׁה הָאִישׁ (Moses the man) that brought us up מֵאֶרֶץ מִצְרַיִם (from the land of Egypt) we do not know what has become לוֹ (of him)."

(2) וַיֹּאמֶר אֲלֵהֶם אַהֲרֹן (And Aaron said to them):

"Break off the golden rings, which are בְּאָזְנֵי נְשֵׁיכֶם (in the ears of your wives) בְּנֵיכֶם (of your sons) וּבְנֹתֵיכֶם (and of your daughters) and bring them אֵלָי (to me)."

(3) And כָּל־הָעָם (all the people) broke off אֵת the rings of gold which were בְּאָזְנֵיהֶם (in their ears) and brought them אֶל־אַהֲרֹן

(4) And מִיָּדָם (from their hand) he received אֹתוֹ and fashioned it with a graving tool, and made it a molten calf; וַיֹּאמְרוּ (and they said):

"These are אֱלֹהֶיךָ יִשְׂרָאֵל which brought you up מֵאֶרֶץ מִצְרָיִם (from the land of Egypt)."

(5) וַיַּרְא אַהֲרֹן (And Aaron saw) and he built מִזְבֵּחַ (an altar) לְפָנָיו (before it) וַיִּקְרָא אַהֲרֹן וַיֹּאמַר (and Aaron called and said):

"Tomorrow shall be a feast לַיהוה

(6) And they rose up early on the morrow, and offered burnt-offerings, and brought שְׁלָמִים (peace-offerings) and הָעָם (the people) sat down to eat and to drink, and rose up to make merry.

Exodus ~ 32

YHVH Gets Mad At The People

(7) וַיְדַבֵּר יהוה אֶל-מֹשֶׁה *(And YHVH spoke to Moses):*

לֶךְ-רֵד כִּי שִׁחֵת עַמְּךָ
אֲשֶׁר הֶעֱלֵיתָ מֵאֶרֶץ מִצְרָיִם

Go, descend; for your people, have corrupted;
that you brought up from the land of Egypt,

(8)

סָרוּ מַהֵר
מִן-הַדֶּרֶךְ אֲשֶׁר צִוִּיתִם
עָשׂוּ לָהֶם עֵגֶל מַסֵּכָה
וַיִּשְׁתַּחֲווּ-לוֹ
וַיִּזְבְּחוּ-לוֹ וַיֹּאמְרוּ

they have turned aside quickly
from the way which I commanded them;
they have made for them a molten calf,
and have bowed down to it,
and have sacrificed to it, and said:

אֵלֶּה אֱלֹהֶיךָ יִשְׂרָאֵל
אֲשֶׁר הֶעֱלוּךָ מֵאֶרֶץ מִצְרָיִם

These are your elohim, O Israel,
which brought you up from the land of Egypt.

Level Two   שְׁמוֹת ~ לב

(9) וַיֹּאמֶר יהוה אֶל-מֹשֶׁה *(And YHVH said to Moses)*:

רָאִיתִי אֶת-הָעָם הַזֶּה

וְהִנֵּה עַם-קְשֵׁה-עֹרֶף הוּא

I have seen this * people,

and, behold, it is a stiffnecked people.

(10)

וְעַתָּה הַנִּיחָה לִי

וְיִחַר-אַפִּי בָהֶם

וַאֲכַלֵּם

וְאֶעֱשֶׂה אוֹתְךָ לְגוֹי גָּדוֹל

Now therefore leave Me,

that My wrath may wax hot against them,

and that I may consume them;

and I will make * you a great nation.

Moses Intercedes For The People

(11) And מֹשֶׁה besought וַיֹּאמֶר אֱלֹהָיו יהוה פְּנֵי-אֶת *(* the face of YHVH his Elohim, and said)*:

יהוה *why does Your wrath wax hot* בְּעַמֶּךָ *(on Your people) that You have brought forth* מֵאֶרֶץ מִצְרַיִם *(from the land of Egypt) with great power* וּבְיָד חֲזָקָה *(and with a mighty hand)?"*

(12)

"Why יֹאמְרוּ מִצְרַיִם לֵאמֹר *(should Egypt speak, saying)*:

Exodus ~ 32   The Progressive To רה

'For evil He brought אֹתָם forth, to slay them בֶּהָרִים (in the mountains) and to consume them מֵעַל פְּנֵי הָאֲדָמָה (from the face of the ground)?'

"Turn from Your fierce wrath, and repent עַל (over) this evil לְעַמֶּךָ (for Your people)."

(13) זְכֹר לְאַבְרָהָם לְיִצְחָק וּלְיִשְׂרָאֵל עֲבָדֶיךָ (Remember for Abraham, for Isaac, and for Israel, Your servants) to whom You swore לָהֶם בָּךְ (to them in Yourself) וַתְּדַבֵּר אֲלֵהֶם (and You spoke to them):

אַרְבֶּה אֶת־זַרְעֲכֶם
כְּכוֹכְבֵי הַשָּׁמָיִם
וְכָל־הָאָרֶץ הַזֹּאת אֲשֶׁר אָמַרְתִּי
אֶתֵּן לְזַרְעֲכֶם וְנָחֲלוּ לְעֹלָם

I will multiply * your seed

as the stars of sky,

and all this land that I have said

will I give to your seed, and they shall inherit it forever.

(14) And יהוה repented עַל (over) the evil which דִּבֶּר (He spoke) He would do לְעַמּוֹ (to His people).

Moses Descends From The Mountain

(15) And מֹשֶׁה turned, and descended מִן־הָהָר (from the mountain) with the two לֻחֹת הָעֵדֻת (tablets of the testimony) בְּיָדוֹ (in his hand) לֻחֹת (tablets) that

304

Level Two   שְׁמוֹת ~ לב

were written on both their sides; on the one side and on the other הֵם (they) were written.

(16) וְהַלֻּחֹת (And the tablets) הֵמָּה (they) were the handiwork of אֱלֹהִים and the writing הוּא (it) was the writing of אֱלֹהִים engraved עַל הַלֻּחֹת (on the tablets).

(17) וַיִּשְׁמַע יְהוֹשֻׁעַ אֶת-קוֹל הָעָם (And Joshua heard * the voice of the people) as they shouted וַיֹּאמֶר אֶל-מֹשֶׁה (and he said to Moses):

"There is קוֹל (a voice of) war in the camp."

(18) וַיֹּאמֶר (And he said):

"It is not קוֹל (a voice) that shouts for mastery, neither is it קוֹל (a voice) that cries for being overcome קוֹל (a voice of) singing אָנֹכִי שֹׁמֵעַ (I hear)."

(19) And it was, as he came near אֶל-הַמַּחֲנֶה (to the camp) וַיַּרְא (he saw) אֶת the calf and the dancing; and the anger of מֹשֶׁה waxed hot וַיַּשְׁלֵךְ מִיָּדָו (and he cast from his hands) אֶת-הַלֻּחֹת (* the tablets) and broke אֹתָם beneath הָהָר (the mountain).

(20) And he took אֶת the calf which they had made, and burnt it בָּאֵשׁ (with fire) and ground it to powder, and strewed it עַל פְּנֵי הַמַּיִם (on the face of the water) and made אֶת בְּנֵי יִשְׂרָאֵל (* the children of Israel) drink it.

(21) וַיֹּאמֶר מֹשֶׁה אֶל-אַהֲרֹן (And Moses said to Aaron):

"What did הָעָם הַזֶּה (this people) do לְךָ (to you) that you brought עָלָיו (on it) a great sin?"

(22) וַיֹּאמֶר אַהֲרֹן (And Aaron said):

"Let not the anger of אֲדֹנִי wax hot; אַתָּה know אֶת-הָעָם (the people) that הוּא (it) is set on evil."

Exodus ~ 32

(23) וַיֹּאמְרוּ לִי (And they said to me):

'Make לָנוּ (for us) אֱלֹהִים which יֵלְכוּ (they shall go) before us; for as for this מֹשֶׁה הָאִישׁ (Moses the man) that brought us up מֵאֶרֶץ מִצְרַיִם (from the land of Egypt) we do not know what has happened לוֹ (to him).'

(24) וָאֹמַר לָהֶם (And I said to them):

'Whosoever has any זָהָב (gold), let them break it off; and they gave it לִי (to me) וָאַשְׁלִכֵהוּ (and I cast it) בָאֵשׁ (in the fire), and there came out this calf."

Consequences For The Molten Calf

(25) וַיַּרְא מֹשֶׁה אֶת־הָעָם (And Moses saw * the people) were broken loose - for אַהֲרֹן had let them loose for a derision among their enemies -

(26) then מֹשֶׁה stood in the gate of הַמַּחֲנֶה (the camp) וַיֹּאמֶר (and he said):

'Whoso is לַיהוה let him come אֵלַי (to me)."

And כָּל־בְּנֵי לֵוִי (all the sons of Levi) gathered themselves together אֵלָיו (to him).

(27) וַיֹּאמֶר לָהֶם (And he said to them):

"Thus אָמַר יהוה אֱלֹהֵי יִשְׂרָאֵל (says YHVH the Elohim of Israel):

שִׂימוּ אִישׁ־חַרְבּוֹ עַל־יְרֵכוֹ

Put a man his sword on his thigh,

Level Two   שְׁמוֹת ~ לב

עִבְרוּ וָשׁוּבוּ מִשַּׁעַר לָשַׁעַר בַּמַּחֲנֶה
וְהִרְגוּ אִישׁ-אֶת-אָחִיו
וְאִישׁ אֶת-רֵעֵהוּ
וְאִישׁ אֶת-קְרֹבוֹ

and pass from gate to gate in the camp,
and slay * a man his brother,
and * a man his companion,
and * a man his neighbor.

(28) And בְנֵי-לֵוִי (the sons of Levi) did כִּדְבַר מֹשֶׁה (according to the word of Moses) and there fell מִן-הָעָם (from the people) that day about three thousands of אִישׁ (man).

(29) וַיֹּאמֶר מֹשֶׁה (And Moses said):

"Fill יֶדְכֶם (your hand) today לַיהוה for אִישׁ בִּבְנוֹ וּבְאָחִיו (a man on his son and on his brother) to put עֲלֵיכֶם (on you) a blessing today."

(30) And it was on the morrow וַיֹּאמֶר מֹשֶׁה אֶל-הָעָם (and Moses said to the people):

אַתֶּם have sinned a great sin; and now I will ascend אֶל-יהוה peradventure I shall make atonement for your sin."

Moses Returns To YHVH

(31) And מֹשֶׁה returned אֶל-יהוה (to YHVH) וַיֹּאמַר (and he said):

"Oh הָעָם הַזֶּה (this people) have sinned a great sin, and have made

Exodus ~ 32

אֱלֹהֵי זָהָב (elohim of old)." לָהֶם (for them)

(32)

"Yet now, if You will forgive their sin; and if not, blot me, I pray You, from Your book which You have written."

(33) וַיֹּאמֶר יהוה אֶל-מֹשֶׁה (And YHVH said to Moses):

מִי אֲשֶׁר חָטָא-לִי
אֶמְחֶנּוּ מִסִּפְרִי

Whosoever has sinned against Me,
I will blot him from My book.

(34)

וְעַתָּה לֵךְ נְחֵה אֶת-הָעָם
אֶל אֲשֶׁר-דִּבַּרְתִּי לָךְ
הִנֵּה מַלְאָכִי יֵלֵךְ לְפָנֶיךָ
וּבְיוֹם פָּקְדִי
וּפָקַדְתִּי עֲלֵהֶם חַטָּאתָם

And now go, lead * the people
to where I have spoken to you;
behold, My messenger shall go before you;
and in the day when I visit,
then I will visit their sin on them.

(35) And יהוה smote אֶת-הָעָם (* the people) עַל (over) what because they made אֶת the calf, which אַהֲרֹן made.

Chapter Thirty-Three

YHVH Sends A Messenger

(1) וַיְדַבֵּר יְהוָה אֶל-מֹשֶׁה (And YHVH spoke to Moses):

לֵךְ עֲלֵה מִזֶּה אַתָּה וְהָעָם

אֲשֶׁר הֶעֱלִיתָ מֵאֶרֶץ מִצְרָיִם

אֶל-הָאָרֶץ אֲשֶׁר נִשְׁבַּעְתִּי לְאַבְרָהָם

לְיִצְחָק וּלְיַעֲקֹב לֵאמֹר

לְזַרְעֲךָ אֶתְּנֶנָּה

* You and the people go and ascend from this,

that you have brought up from the land of Egypt,

to the land of which I swore to Abraham,

to Isaac, and to Jacob, saying:

To your seed will I give it -

(2)

וְשָׁלַחְתִּי לְפָנֶיךָ מַלְאָךְ

וְגֵרַשְׁתִּי אֶת-הַכְּנַעֲנִי

הָאֱמֹרִי וְהַחִתִּי וְהַפְּרִזִּי

הַחִוִּי וְהַיְבוּסִי

and I will send an messenger before you;

and I will drive out * the Canaanite,

the Amorite, and the Hittite, and the Perizzite,

the Hivite, and the Jebusite,

Exodus ~ 33

(3)
אֶל־אֶרֶץ זָבַת חָלָב וּדְבָשׁ
כִּי לֹא אֶעֱלֶה בְּקִרְבְּךָ
כִּי עַם־קְשֵׁה־עֹרֶף אַתָּה
פֶּן־אֲכֶלְךָ בַּדָּרֶךְ

to a land flowing with milk and honey;
for I will not go up in the midst of you;
for * you are a stiffnecked people;
lest I consume you in the way.

(4) וַיִּשְׁמַע הָעָם (And the people heard) אֶת־הַדָּבָר הָרָע הַזֶּה (this evil * word) they mourned; and no אִישׁ (man) put his ornaments עָלָיו (on himself).

(5) וַיֹּאמֶר יהוה אֶל־מֹשֶׁה (And YHVH said to Moses):

אֱמֹר אֶל־בְּנֵי־יִשְׂרָאֵל
אַתֶּם עַם־קְשֵׁה־עֹרֶף
רֶגַע אֶחָד אֶעֱלֶה
בְקִרְבְּךָ
וְכִלִּיתִיךָ

Say to the children of Israel:
* You are a stiffnecked people;
if for one moment I go up
in the midst of you,
and I shall consume you.

310

Level Two
שְׁמוֹת ~ לג

וְעַתָּה הוֹרֵד עֶדְיְךָ מֵעָלֶיךָ
וְאֵדְעָה מָה אֶעֱשֶׂה־לָּךְ

*And now take off your ornaments from on you,
that I may know what to do to you.*

(6) And בְּנֵי יִשְׂרָאֵל (the children of Israel) stripped themselves of אֶת their ornaments מֵהַר חוֹרֵב (from Mount Horeb).

(7) Now מֹשֶׁה took אֶת־הָאֹהֶל (* the tent) and pitched it לוֹ (for him) outside לַמַּחֲנֶה (to the camp), afar off מִן הַמַּחֲנֶה (from the camp) וְקָרָא לוֹ (and he called for it) אֹהֶל מוֹעֵד (the tent of appointment). And it was, that כָּל (every) one that sought יהוה went out אֶל־אֹהֶל מוֹעֵד (to the tent of appointment), which was outside לַמַּחֲנֶה (to the camp).

(8) And it was, when מֹשֶׁה went out אֶל־הָאֹהֶל (to the tent), that כָּל הָעָם (all the people) rose up, and stood אִישׁ (a man) at the door of אָהֳלוֹ (his tent), and looked after מֹשֶׁה until he entered הָאֹהֱלָה (to the tent).

(9) And it was, as מֹשֶׁה entered in הָאֹהֱלָה (to the tent) עַמּוּד הֶעָנָן (the pillar of the cloud) descended, and stood at the door of הָאֹהֶל (the tent) וְדִבֶּר עִם מֹשֶׁה (and He spoke with Moses).

(10) וְרָאָה כָל־הָעָם (And all the people saw) אֶת עַמּוּד הֶעָנָן (* the pillar of the cloud) stand at the door of הָאֹהֶל (the tent), and כָּל־הָעָם (all the people) rose up and bowed themselves down אִישׁ (a man) at the door of אָהֳלוֹ (his tent).

(11) וְדִבֶּר יהוה אֶל־מֹשֶׁה פָּנִים אֶל־פָּנִים (And YHVH spoke to Moses face to face) as יְדַבֵּר אִישׁ (a man speaks) to his friend. And he would return אֶל־הַמַּחֲנֶה (to the camp); but his minister יְהוֹשֻׁעַ בִּן־נוּן (Joshua, the son of Nun) נַעַר (a young man) did not depart from the midst of הָאֹהֶל (the tent).

Exodus ~ 33

(12) וַיֹּאמֶר מֹשֶׁה אֶל-יהוה (And Moses said to YHVH):

רְאֵה אַתָּה אֹמֵר אֵלַי (See, * You say to me):

הַעַל אֶת-הָעָם הַזֶּה

Bring up this * people;

וְאַתָּה have not let me know אֵת whom עִמִּי תִּשְׁלַח (You will send with me) וְאַתָּה אָמַרְתָּ (And * You, You said):

יְדַעְתִּיךָ בְשֵׁם

וְגַם-מָצָאתָ חֵן בְּעֵינָי

I know you by name,
and also you have found grace in My eyes.

(13)

"Now therefore, I pray You, if I have found grace בְּעֵינֶיךָ (in Your eyes) Please, let me know אֶת-דְּרָכֶךָ (* Your ways) that I may know You, so that I may find grace בְּעֵינֶיךָ (in Your eyes) וּרְאֵה (and see) that this nation is עַמֶּךָ (Your people)."

(14) וַיֹּאמַר (And He said):

פָּנַי יֵלֵכוּ וַהֲנִחֹתִי לָךְ

My presence shall go with you, and I will give you rest.

(15) וַיֹּאמֶר אֵלָיו (And he said to Him):

"If Your presence does not הֹלְכִים (go) with me, do not carry us up מִזֶּה (from this)."

Level Two   שְׁמוֹת ~ לג

(16)
"For wherein now shall it be known that I have found grace בְּעֵינֶיךָ (in Your eyes) אֲנִי וְעַמֶּךָ בְּלֶכְתְּךָ עִמָּנוּ (I and Your people)? Is it not (in Your going with us) so that we are distinguished, אֲנִי וְעַמֶּךָ (I and Your people) מִכָּל־הָעָם עַל־פְּנֵי (from all the people) that are הָאֲדָמָה (on the face of the ground)?"

(17) וַיֹּאמֶר יהוה אֶל־מֹשֶׁה (And YHVH said to Moses):

גַּם אֶת־הַדָּבָר הַזֶּה
אֲשֶׁר דִּבַּרְתָּ אֶעֱשֶׂה
כִּי־מָצָאתָ חֵן בְּעֵינַי
וָאֵדָעֲךָ בְּשֵׁם

This * thing also
that you have spoken, I will do
for you have found grace in My eyes,
and I know you by name.

(18) וַיֹּאמַר (And he said):

הַרְאֵנִי נָא אֶת־כְּבֹדֶךָ (Show me, I pray, * Your glory)."

(19) וַיֹּאמֶר (And He said):

אֲנִי אַעֲבִיר כָּל־טוּבִי עַל־פָּנֶיךָ
וְקָרָאתִי בְשֵׁם יהוה לְפָנֶיךָ

I will make all My goodness pass on your faces,
and will proclaim the name of YHVH before you;

Exodus ~ 33

וְחַנֹּתִי אֶת-אֲשֶׁר אָחֹן
וְרִחַמְתִּי אֶת-אֲשֶׁר אֲרַחֵם

and I will be gracious to * whom I will be gracious,
and will show mercy on * whom I will show mercy.

(20) וַיֹּאמֶר (And He said):

לֹא תוּכַל לִרְאֹת אֶת-פָּנָי
כִּי לֹא-יִרְאַנִי הָאָדָם וָחָי

You are not able to see * My faces,
for the human shall not see Me and live.

(21) וַיֹּאמֶר יהוה (And YHVH said):

הִנֵּה מָקוֹם אִתִּי
וְנִצַּבְתָּ עַל-הַצּוּר

Behold, there is a place with * Me,
and you shall stand on the rock.

(22)

וְהָיָה בַּעֲבֹר כְּבֹדִי
וְשַׂמְתִּיךָ
בְּנִקְרַת הַצּוּר
וְשַׂכֹּתִי כַפִּי עָלֶיךָ
עַד-עָבְרִי

Level Two   שְׁמוֹת ~ לג

And it shall be, while My glory passes by,

that I will put you

in a cleft of the rock,

and will cover you with My palm

until I have passed by.

(23)

וַהֲסִרֹתִי אֶת־כַּפִּי

וְרָאִיתָ אֶת־אֲחֹרָי

וּפָנַי לֹא יֵרָאוּ

And I will take away * My palm,

and you shall see * My back;

and My faces, they shall not be seen.

Chapter Thirty-Four

Second Set Of Tablets

(1) וַיֹּאמֶר יהוה אֶל־מֹשֶׁה *(And YHVH said to Moses)*:

פְּסָל־לְךָ שְׁנֵי־לֻחֹת אֲבָנִים
כָּרִאשֹׁנִים
וְכָתַבְתִּי עַל־הַלֻּחֹת אֶת־הַדְּבָרִים
אֲשֶׁר הָיוּ עַל־הַלֻּחֹת הָרִאשֹׁנִים
אֲשֶׁר שִׁבַּרְתָּ

Carve for you two tablets of stones
like the first ones;
*and I will write on the tablets * the words*
that were on the first tablets,
which you broke.

(2)

וֶהְיֵה נָכוֹן לַבֹּקֶר
וְעָלִיתָ בַבֹּקֶר אֶל־הַר סִינַי
וְנִצַּבְתָּ לִי שָׁם
עַל־רֹאשׁ הָהָר

And be ready for the morning,
and ascend in the morning to Mount Sinai,
and station yourself there for Me
on the top of the mountain.

(3)

וְאִישׁ לֹא־יַעֲלֶה עִמָּךְ
וְגַם־אִישׁ אַל־יֵרָא בְּכָל־הָהָר
גַּם־הַצֹּאן וְהַבָּקָר אַל־יִרְעוּ
אֶל־מוּל הָהָר הַהוּא

*And no man shall ascend with you,
neither shall a man be seen in all the mountain;
neither let the flocks nor herds feed
before that mountain.*

(4) And he carved two לֻחֹת אֲבָנִים (tablets of stone) like to the first; and מֹשֶׁה rose up early in the morning, and went up אֶל־הַר סִינַי (to Mount Sinai) as יהוה had commanded אֹתוֹ and took בְּיָדוֹ (in his hand) two לֻחֹת אֲבָנִים (tablets of stone).

(5) And יהוה descended בֶּעָנָן (in the cloud) and he stood עִמּוֹ (with Him) there וַיִּקְרָא בְשֵׁם יהוה (and he called on the name of YHVH).

YHVH Passes Before Moses

(6) And יהוה passed עַל־פָּנָיו (on before him) וַיִּקְרָא (and he called):

אֵל -- יהוה יהוה merciful and gracious, long suffering and abundant in goodness and truth;"

(7) "Keeping mercy to the thousands, forgiving iniquity and transgression and sin; and that will by no means clear the guilty; visiting the iniquity of אָבוֹת עַל־בָּנִים וְעַל־בְּנֵי בָנִים (the fathers on the children, and on the children's children)

Exodus ~ 34

עַל (on) the third וְעַל (and on) the fourth generation."

(8) And מֹשֶׁה made haste, and bowed his head אַרְצָה (toward the land) and worshipped.

(9) וַיֹּאמֶר (And he said):

"If now I have found grace בְּעֵינֶיךָ אֲדֹנָי (in Your eyes, my Lord) יֵלֶךְ-נָא אֲדֹנָי (let my Lord, I pray, go) in the midst of us; for it is עַם-קְשֵׁה-עֹרֶף (a people stiffnecked) and pardon our iniquity and our sin, and take us for Your inheritance."

(10) וַיֹּאמֶר (And He said):

הִנֵּה אָנֹכִי כֹּרֵת בְּרִית
נֶגֶד כָּל-עַמְּךָ
אֶעֱשֶׂה נִפְלָאֹת
אֲשֶׁר לֹא-נִבְרְאוּ
בְכָל-הָאָרֶץ וּבְכָל-הַגּוֹיִם

Behold, I make a covenant;
before all your people
I will do marvels,
such as have not been created
in all the land, nor in any nation;

וְרָאָה כָל-הָעָם
אֲשֶׁר-אַתָּה בְקִרְבּוֹ
אֶת-מַעֲשֵׂה יהוה

Level Two   שְׁמוֹת ~ לד

and all the people shall see
among which * you are
* the handiwork of YHVH

כִּי-נוֹרָא הוּא
אֲשֶׁר אֲנִי עֹשֶׂה עִמָּךְ

because it is fearful
that which I am doing with you.

(11)

שְׁמָר-לְךָ--אֵת אֲשֶׁר אָנֹכִי
אָנֹכִי מְצַוְּךָ הַיּוֹם

Observe for you * that which
I am commanding you today;

הִנְנִי גֹרֵשׁ מִפָּנֶיךָ
אֶת-הָאֱמֹרִי וְהַכְּנַעֲנִי
וְהַחִתִּי וְהַפְּרִזִּי
וְהַחִוִּי וְהַיְבוּסִי

behold, I am driving out before you
* the Amorite, and the Canaanite,
and the Hittite, and the Perizzite,
and the Hivite, and the Jebusite.

Exodus ~ 34

Makeing Other Covenants

(12)

הִשָּׁמֶר לְךָ

פֶּן-תִּכְרֹת בְּרִית

לְיוֹשֵׁב הָאָרֶץ

אֲשֶׁר אַתָּה בָּא עָלֶיהָ

פֶּן-יִהְיֶה לְמוֹקֵשׁ בְּקִרְבֶּךָ

Guard for yourself,
lest you make a covenant
for the inhabitants of the land
where * you enter on it,
lest they be for a snare in the midst of you.

(13)

כִּי אֶת-מִזְבְּחֹתָם תִּתֹּצוּן

וְאֶת-מַצֵּבֹתָם תְּשַׁבֵּרוּן

וְאֶת-אֲשֵׁרָיו תִּכְרֹתוּן

Because you shall break down * their altars,
and dash in pieces * their pillars,
and you shall cut down * their Asherim.

(14)

כִּי לֹא תִשְׁתַּחֲוֶה לְאֵל אַחֵר

For you shall not bow down to another el;

Level Two שְׁמוֹת ~ לד

כִּי יהוה קַנָּא שְׁמוֹ
אֵל קַנָּא הוּא

for YHVH whose name is Jealous,
He is a jealous El;

(15)

פֶּן־תִּכְרֹת בְּרִית
לְיוֹשֵׁב הָאָרֶץ

lest you make a covenant
for the inhabitants of the land,

וְזָנוּ אַחֲרֵי אֱלֹהֵיהֶם
וְזָבְחוּ לֵאלֹהֵיהֶם
וְקָרָא לְךָ
וְאָכַלְתָּ מִזִּבְחוֹ

and they prostitute after their elohim,
and sacrifice to their elohim,
and he call for you,
and you eat from his sacrifice;

(16)

וְלָקַחְתָּ מִבְּנֹתָיו לְבָנֶיךָ
וְזָנוּ בְנֹתָיו אַחֲרֵי אֱלֹהֵיהֶן

and you take from their daughters for your sons,
and his daughters prostitute after their elohim,

Exodus ~ 34

וְהִזְנוּ אֶת־בָּנֶיךָ
אַחֲרֵי אֱלֹהֵיהֶן

and make * your sons prostitute
after their elohim.

Commandments Reiterated

(17)

אֱלֹהֵי מַסֵּכָה לֹא תַעֲשֶׂה־לָּךְ

You shall make for yourself any molten elohim.

(18)

אֶת־חַג הַמַּצּוֹת תִּשְׁמֹר
שִׁבְעַת יָמִים תֹּאכַל מַצּוֹת
אֲשֶׁר צִוִּיתִךָ
לְמוֹעֵד חֹדֶשׁ הָאָבִיב
כִּי בְּחֹדֶשׁ הָאָבִיב
יָצָאתָ מִמִּצְרָיִם

* The feast of unleavened bread shall you keep.
Seven days you shall eat unleavened bread,
which I commanded you,
for the appointed time in the month Abib,
for in the month Abib
you came forth from Egypt.

Level Two שְׁמוֹת ~ לד

(19)

כָּל־פֶּטֶר רֶחֶם לִי
וְכָל־מִקְנְךָ תִּזָּכָר
פֶּטֶר שׁוֹר וָשֶׂה

All that opens the womb is Mine;
and of all your male cattle,
the firstlings of ox and sheep.

(20)

וּפֶטֶר חֲמוֹר
תִּפְדֶּה בְשֶׂה
וְאִם־לֹא תִפְדֶּה
וַעֲרַפְתּוֹ

And the firstling donkey
you shall redeem with a lamb;
and if you will not redeem it,
then you shall break its neck.

כֹּל בְּכוֹר בָּנֶיךָ תִּפְדֶּה
וְלֹא־יֵרָאוּ
פָנַי רֵיקָם

all the firstborn of your sons you shall redeem.
and they shall not appear
before Me empty.

(21)

שֵׁ֤שֶׁת יָמִים֙ תַּֽעֲבֹ֔ד

וּבַיּ֥וֹם הַשְּׁבִיעִ֖י תִּשְׁבֹּ֑ת

בֶּחָרִ֥ישׁ וּבַקָּצִ֖יר תִּשְׁבֹּֽת

Six days you shall work,

and on the seventh day you shall rest;

in plowing and in harvest you shall rest.

(22)

וְחַ֤ג שָׁבֻעֹת֙ תַּעֲשֶׂ֣ה לְךָ֔

בִּכּוּרֵ֖י קְצִ֣יר חִטִּ֑ים

וְחַג֙ הָ֣אָסִ֔יף

תְּקוּפַ֖ת הַשָּׁנָֽה

And you shall observe the feast of weeks for you,

the first-fruits of wheat harvest,

and the feast of ingathering

the turn of the year.

(23)

שָׁלֹ֥שׁ פְּעָמִ֖ים בַּשָּׁנָ֑ה

יֵרָאֶה֙ כָּל־זְכ֣וּרְךָ֔

אֶת־פְּנֵ֛י הָאָדֹ֥ן ׀ יְהוָ֖ה אֱלֹהֵ֥י יִשְׂרָאֵֽל

Three times in the year

shall all your males appear

* before the Lord YHVH the Elohim of Israel.

Level Two שְׁמוֹת ~ לד

(24)

כִּי-אוֹרִישׁ גּוֹיִם מִפָּנֶיךָ

וְהִרְחַבְתִּי אֶת-גְּבֻלֶךָ

וְלֹא-יַחְמֹד אִישׁ אֶת-אַרְצְךָ

בַּעֲלֹתְךָ לֵרָאוֹת

אֶת-פְּנֵי יהוה אֱלֹהֶיךָ

For I will cast out nations from your faces,

And I will enlarge * your borders;

neither shall any man covet * your land,

in your ascending to appear

* before YHVH your Elohim

three times in the year.

(25)

לֹא-תִשְׁחַט עַל-חָמֵץ

דַּם-זִבְחִי

וְלֹא-יָלִין לַבֹּקֶר

זֶבַח

חַג הַפָּסַח

You shall not offer with leavened bread

the blood of My sacrifice;

and it shall not be left to the morning

the sacrifice

of the feast of the Passover.

325

Exodus ~ 34

(26)

רֵאשִׁית בִּכּוּרֵי אַדְמָתְךָ
תָּבִיא בֵּית יהוה אֱלֹהֶיךָ
לֹא-תְבַשֵּׁל גְּדִי בַּחֲלֵב אִמּוֹ

The choicest first-fruits of your ground
bring to the house of YHVH your Elohim
You shall not seethe a kid in its mother's milk.

(27) וַיֹּאמֶר יהוה אֶל-מֹשֶׁה *(And YHVH said to Moses):*

כְּתָב-לְךָ אֶת-הַדְּבָרִים הָאֵלֶּה
כִּי עַל-פִּי הַדְּבָרִים הָאֵלֶּה
כָּרַתִּי אִתְּךָ בְּרִית וְאֶת-יִשְׂרָאֵל

*Write for yourself these * words,*
for after the tenor of these words
*I have made a covenant with * you and with * Israel.*

Moses' Face Glows

(28) And he was there with יהוה forty days and forty nights; he ate no לֶחֶם (bread) and he drank no וּמַיִם (water). And he wrote עַל-הַלֻּחֹת (on the tablets) אֵת דִּבְרֵי הַבְּרִית (* the words of the covenant) the ten of הַדְּבָרִים (the words).

(29) And it was, when מֹשֶׁה came down מֵהַר סִינַי with the two לֻחֹת הָעֵדֻת (tablets of the testimony) בְּיַד-מֹשֶׁה (in the hand of Moses) when he came down מִן-הָהָר (from the mountain) וּמֹשֶׁה did not know that עוֹר פָּנָיו (the skin of his face) sent forth beams בְּדַבְּרוֹ אִתּוֹ (in His speaking with * him).

(30) וַיַּרְא אַהֲרֹן (And Aaron saw) וְכָל-בְּנֵי יִשְׂרָאֵל (and all the children of

326

Level Two   שְׁמוֹת ~ לד

Israel) אֶת-מֹשֶׁה behold עוֹר פָּנָיו *(the skin of his face)* send forth beams; and they were afraid to come close אֵלָיו *(to him)*.

(31) וְכָל *(Aaron)* אַהֲרֹן and *(And Moses called to them)* וַיִּקְרָא אֲלֵהֶם מֹשֶׁה *(and all)* the rulers of בָּעֵדָה *(the congregation)* returned אֵלָיו *(to him)* וַיְדַבֵּר מֹשֶׁה אֲלֵהֶם *(and Moses spoke to them)*.

(32) And afterward all וְכָל-בְּנֵי יִשְׂרָאֵל *(and all the children of Israel)* came near, and he instructed them אֵת כָּל *(* all)* that דִּבֶּר יהוה אִתּוֹ *(YHVH had spoken with him)* בְּהַר סִינָי

(33) And when מֹשֶׁה was done מִדַּבֵּר אִתָּם *(from speaking with them)* he put עַל-פָּנָיו מַסְוֶה *(on his face, a veil)*.

(34) But when מֹשֶׁה went in לִפְנֵי יהוה *(before YHVH)* לְדַבֵּר אִתּוֹ *(to speak with * Him)* he took אֶת-הַמַּסְוֶה *(* the veil)* off, until he came out; and he came out וְדִבֶּר אֶל-בְּנֵי יִשְׂרָאֵל *(and he spoke to the children of Israel)* אֵת that which he was commanded.

(35) וְרָאוּ בְנֵי יִשְׂרָאֵל *(And the children of Israel saw)* אֶת-פְּנֵי מֹשֶׁה *(* the face of Moses)* that עוֹר פְּנֵי מֹשֶׁה *(the skin of the face of Moses)* sent forth beams; and מֹשֶׁה put אֶת-הַמַּסְוֶה עַל-פָּנָיו *(* the veil on his face)* until he went in לְדַבֵּר אִתּוֹ *(to speak with * Him)*.

Chapter Thirty-Five

An Offering For The Tabernacle

(1) And מֹשֶׁה assembled אֵת כָּל עֲדַת בְּנֵי יִשְׂרָאֵל (* all the congregation of the children of Israel) וַיֹּאמֶר אֲלֵהֶם (and said to them):

"These are הַדְּבָרִים (the words) which יהוה has commanded, that you should do אֹתָם

(2)

"Six days shall work be done, but on the seventh day there shall be a holy day לָכֶם (for you) שַׁבַּת (a Sabbath) of solemn rest לַיהוה (to YHVH) כָּל (every) one doing work בוֹ (on it) shall be put to death."

(3)

"You shall not kindle אֵשׁ (a fire) בְּכֹל (in all) your habitations on הַשַּׁבָּת (the Sabbath) day."

(4) וַיֹּאמֶר מֹשֶׁה (And Moses spoke) אֶל-כָּל-עֲדַת בְּנֵי-יִשְׂרָאֵל (to all the congregation of the children of Israel) לֵאמֹר (saying):

"This is הַדָּבָר (the word) which יהוה commanded לֵאמֹר (saying):

(5)

קְחוּ מֵאִתְּכֶם תְּרוּמָה לַיהוה
כֹּל נְדִיב לִבּוֹ

*Take from among * you an offering for YHVH
whosoever is of a willing heart,*

Level Two

שְׁמוֹת ~ לה

יְבִיאֶהָ אֵת תְּרוּמַת יהוה
זָהָב וָכֶסֶף וּנְחֹשֶׁת

let him bring YHVH * an offering:
gold, and silver, and copper;

(6)

וּתְכֵלֶת וְאַרְגָּמָן וְתוֹלַעַת שָׁנִי
וְשֵׁשׁ וְעִזִּים

and blue, and purple, and scarlet,
and fine linen, and goats' hair;

(7)

וְעֹרֹת אֵילִם מְאָדָּמִים
וְעֹרֹת תְּחָשִׁים
וַעֲצֵי שִׁטִּים

and rams' skins dyed red,
and [unknown animal] skins,
and acacia-wood;

(8)

וְשֶׁמֶן לַמָּאוֹר
וּבְשָׂמִים לְשֶׁמֶן הַמִּשְׁחָה
וְלִקְטֹרֶת הַסַּמִּים

and oil for the light,
and spices for the anointing oil,
and for the sweet incense;

329

(9)

וְאַבְנֵי-שֹׁהַם וְאַבְנֵי מִלֻּאִים
לָאֵפוֹד וְלַחֹשֶׁן

and onyx stones, and stones to be set,

for the ephod, and for the breastplate.

(10)

וְכָל-חֲכַם-לֵב בָּכֶם

יָבֹאוּ וְיַעֲשׂוּ

אֵת כָּל-אֲשֶׁר צִוָּה יהוה

And all wise-hearted among you

they shall come, and they shall make

* all that YHVH has commanded:

(11)

אֶת-הַמִּשְׁכָּן אֶת-אָהֳלוֹ וְאֶת-מִכְסֵהוּ
אֶת-קְרָסָיו וְאֶת-קְרָשָׁיו אֶת-בְּרִיחָו
אֶת-עַמֻּדָיו וְאֶת-אֲדָנָיו

* the tabernacle, * its tent, and * its covering,

* its clasps, and * its boards, * its bars,

* its pillars, and * its pedestals;

(12)

אֶת-הָאָרֹן וְאֶת-בַּדָּיו
אֶת-הַכַּפֹּרֶת וְאֵת פָּרֹכֶת הַמָּסָךְ

Level Two   שְׁמוֹת ~ לה

* the ark, and * its poles,

* the mercy-seat, and * the veil of the screen;

(13)

אֶת־הַשֻּׁלְחָן וְאֶת־בַּדָּיו

וְאֶת־כָּל־כֵּלָיו וְאֵת לֶחֶם הַפָּנִים

* the table, and * its poles,

and * all its implements, and * the shewbread;

(14)

וְאֶת־מְנֹרַת הַמָּאוֹר

וְאֶת־כֵּלֶיהָ וְאֶת־נֵרֹתֶיהָ

וְאֵת שֶׁמֶן הַמָּאוֹר

* the candlestick for the light,

and * its implements, and * its lamps,

and * the oil for the light;

(15)

וְאֶת־מִזְבַּח הַקְּטֹרֶת וְאֶת־בַּדָּיו

וְאֵת שֶׁמֶן הַמִּשְׁחָה

וְאֶת קְטֹרֶת הַסַּמִּים

and * the altar of incense, and * its poles,

and * the oil of the anointing,

and * the incense of the spices,

וְאֶת־מָסַךְ הַפֶּתַח
לְפֶתַח הַמִּשְׁכָּן

and *the screen for the door,
at the door of the tabernacle;

(16)

אֵת מִזְבַּח הָעֹלָה
וְאֶת־מִכְבַּר הַנְּחֹשֶׁת
אֲשֶׁר־לוֹ
אֶת־בַּדָּיו וְאֶת־כָּל־כֵּלָיו
אֶת־הַכִּיֹּר וְאֶת־כַּנּוֹ

* the altar of burnt-offering,
And * the grate of copper
which is for it,
* its poles, and * all its implements,
* the laver and * its base;

(17)

אֵת קַלְעֵי הֶחָצֵר אֶת־עַמֻּדָיו
וְאֶת־אֲדָנֶיהָ
וְאֵת מָסַךְ שַׁעַר הֶחָצֵר

* the hangings of the court, * its pillars,
and * their pedestals,
and * the screen for the gate of the court;

Level Two   שְׁמוֹת ~ לה

(18)

אֶת־יִתְדֹת הַמִּשְׁכָּן

וְאֶת־יִתְדֹת הֶחָצֵר

וְאֶת־מֵיתְרֵיהֶם

the pins of the tabernacle,

*and * the pins of the court,*

*and * their cords;*

(19)

אֵת־בִּגְדֵי הַשְּׂרָד

לְשָׁרֵת בַּקֹּדֶשׁ

אֶת־בִּגְדֵי הַקֹּדֶשׁ לְאַהֲרֹן הַכֹּהֵן

וְאֶת־בִּגְדֵי בָנָיו לְכַהֵן

the garments of tapestry,

for ministering in the holy place,

* the holy garments for Aaron the priest,

*and * the garments of his sons, to be priest.*

(20) And כָּל־עֲדַת בְּנֵי־יִשְׂרָאֵל (all the congregation of the children of Israel) departed מִלִּפְנֵי (from before) מֹשֶׁה.

(21) And they came כָּל־אִישׁ (every man) who is stirred up by לִבּוֹ (his heart) and everyone whom רוּחוֹ (his spirit) makes אֹתוֹ willing, and brought אֵת offering of יהוה for the work of אֹהֶל מוֹעֵד (the tent of appointment) וּלְכָל־עֲבֹדָתוֹ (and for all its service) and for the holy garments.

(22) And הָאֲנָשִׁים עַל־הַנָּשִׁים (the men over the women) came כֹּל (all) willing

Exodus ~ 35

of לֵב (heart) and brought nose-rings, and ear-rings, and signet-rings, and girdles כָּל כְּלִי זָהָב (all implements of gold) וְכָל אִישׁ (and every man) who brought an offering of זָהָב (gold) לַיהוה

(23) וְכָל-אִישׁ (And every man) with whom was found תְּכֵלֶת (blue) וְאַרְגָּמָן (and purple) וְתוֹלַעַת שָׁנִי (and scarlet) וְשֵׁשׁ וְעִזִּים (and fine linen) and goats' hair, and rams' skins הַמְאָדָּמִים (dyed red) and [unknown animal] skins, brought them.

(24) כָּל (Every) one raising up אֵת an offering of כֶּסֶף (silver) וּנְחֹשֶׁת (and copper) brought יהוה offering וְכֹל (and all) was found אִתּוֹ acacia-wood לְכָל (for any work of) הָעֲבֹדָה (the service) brought it.

(25) וְכָל-אִשָּׁה (And every woman) that was wise of לֵב (heart) spun בְּיָדֶיהָ (with her hands) and brought that which they had spun אֵת הַתְּכֵלֶת (* the blue) וְאֶת-הָאַרְגָּמָן (and * the purple) אֵת תּוֹלַעַת הַשָּׁנִי (* the scarlet) וְאֶת-הַשֵּׁשׁ (and * the fine linen).

(26) וְכָל-הַנָּשִׁים (And all the women) who He prompted אֹתָנָה (them) לִבָּן (their heart) in wisdom spun אֵת the goats' hair.

(27) And the rulers brought אֵת אַבְנֵי (* stones) of the onyx וְאֵת אַבְנֵי (and * the stones) to be set לָאֵפוֹד (for the ephod) וְלַחֹשֶׁן (and for the breastplate);

(28) וְאֵת the spice וְאֵת the oil, for the light, and for the anointing oil, and for the sweet incense.

(29) כָּל-אִישׁ וְאִשָּׁה (Every man and woman) who He made אֹתָם willing לִבָּם (their heart) to bring לְכָל (for all) the work which יהוה had commanded to be made בְּיַד-מֹשֶׁה (by the hand of Moses) בְּנֵי יִשְׂרָאֵל (the children of Israel) brought a freewill-offering לַיהוה

Level Two   שְׁמוֹת ~ לה

Skillful Men

(30) רְאוּ (See) קָרָא יהוה בְּשֵׁם בְּצַלְאֵל בֶּן אוּרִי בֶן-חוּר לְמַטֵּה יְהוּדָה וַיֹּאמֶר מֹשֶׁה אֶל-בְּנֵי יִשְׂרָאֵל (And Moses said to the children of Israel): (YHVH has called by name Bezalel the son of Uri, the son of Hur of the tribe of Judah).

(31) "And He has filled אֹתוֹ with רוּחַ אֱלֹהִים in wisdom, in understanding, and in knowledge וּבְכָל (and in all) manner of workmanship."

(32) "And to design skillful works, to work בַּזָּהָב (in gold) וּבַכֶּסֶף (and in silver) וּבַנְּחֹשֶׁת (and in copper),"

(33) "And in cutting of אֶבֶן (stone) for setting, and in carving of wood, to work בְּכָל (in all) manner of skillful workmanship."

(34) "And He has put בְּלִבּוֹ (in his heart) that הוּא (he) may teach וְאָהֳלִיאָב בֶּן-אֲחִיסָמָךְ לְמַטֵּה דָן (and Aholiab, the son of Ahisamach of the tribe of Dan).

(35) "He has filled אֹתָם with wisdom of לֵב (heart) to work כָּל (all) manner of workmanship, of the craftsman, and of the skillful workman, and of embroidering בַּתְּכֵלֶת (in blue) וּבָאַרְגָּמָן (and in purple) בְּתוֹלַעַת הַשָּׁנִי (in scarlet) וּבַשֵּׁשׁ (and in fine linen) and of the weavers doing כָּל (all) work, and designers of skillful works."

Chapter Thirty-Six

Making The Tabernacle

(1)

"And בְּצַלְאֵל וְאָהֳלִיאָב shall work וְכֹל אִישׁ (and every man) wise of לֵב (heart) in whom יהוה has put wisdom and understanding בָּהֵמָּה (in them) to know how to do אֶת כָּל (* all) the work for עֲבֹדַת (the service of) הַקֹּדֶשׁ (the sanctuary) according לְכֹל (to all) that יהוה has commanded."

(2) וַיִּקְרָא מֹשֶׁה אֶל-בְּצַלְאֵל וְאֶל-אָהֳלִיאָב (And Moses called to Bezalel and to Aholiab) וְאֶל כָּל-אִישׁ (and every man) wise of לֵב (heart) who יהוה had put wisdom בְּלִבּוֹ (in his heart) כֹּל (all) who He prompted לִבּוֹ (his heart) to come to the work to do אֹתָהּ

(3) And they received מִלִּפְנֵי מֹשֶׁה (from before Moses) אֶת כָּל (* all) the offering, which בְּנֵי יִשְׂרָאֵל (the children of Israel) had brought for the work of עֲבֹדַת (the service of) הַקֹּדֶשׁ (the sanctuary) wherewith to make אֹתָהּ (* it) וְהֵם (And they) still brought אֵלָיו (to him) freewill-offerings every morning.

(4) And כָּל (all) the wise ones, that were doing אֶת כָּל (* all) the work of הַקֹּדֶשׁ (the sanctuary) came אִישׁ-אִישׁ (every man) from his work which הֵמָּה (they) were doing.

(5) וַיֹּאמְרוּ אֶל-מֹשֶׁה לֵּאמֹר (And they spoke to Moses saying):

הָעָם (The people) bring much more than enough for the work of הָעֲבֹדָה (the service) which יהוה commanded to make אֹתָהּ

(6) And מֹשֶׁה gave commandment, and they caused it to קוֹל (voice) בַּמַּחֲנֶה (in the camp) לֵאמֹר (saying):

Level Two   שְׁמוֹת ~ לו

"Let neither אִישׁ וְאִשָּׁה (man and woman) make any more work for the offering of הַקֹּדֶשׁ (the sanctuary)."

So הָעָם (the people) were restrained from bringing.

(7) For the stuff they had was sufficient לְכָל (for all) the work to make אֹתָהּ and have reserve.

(8) And כָל (all) wise of לֵב (heart) among them that did the work made אֶת- הַמִּשְׁכָּן (* the tabernacle) with ten curtains: of שֵׁשׁ מָשְׁזָר (fine twined linen) וּתְכֵלֶת (and blue) וְאַרְגָּמָן (and purple) וְתוֹלַעַת שָׁנִי (and scarlet) with כְּרֻבִים (cherubim) the work of the skillful workman he made אֹתָם

(9) The length of each curtain was eight and twenty cubits, and the width of each curtain four cubits לְכָל (for all) the curtains had one measure.

(10) And he coupled אֶת five curtains one to another; and the other five curtains he coupled one to another.

(11) And he made loops of תְּכֵלֶת (blue) עַל (on) the edge of the one curtain that was outmost in the first set; likewise, he made in the edge of the curtain that was outmost in the second set.

(12) He made fifty loops in the one curtain, and he made fifty loops in the edge of the curtain that was in the second set; the loops were opposite one to another.

(13) And he made fifty clasps of זָהָב (gold) and coupled אֶת the curtains one to another with the clasps; so הַמִּשְׁכָּן (the tabernacle) was one.

(14) And he made curtains of goats' hair לְאֹהֶל עַל הַמִּשְׁכָּן (for a tent over the tabernacle); eleven curtains he made אֹתָם

(15) The length of each curtain was thirty cubits, and four cubits the width of each curtain; the eleven curtains had one measure.

(16) And he coupled אֶת five curtains by themselves וְאֶת six curtains by themselves.

337

(17) And he made fifty loops עַל (on) the edge of the curtain that was outmost in the first set, and he made fifty loops עַל (on) the edge of the curtain which was outmost in the second set.

(18) And he made fifty clasps of נְחֹשֶׁת (copper) to couple אֶת הָאֹהֶל (* the tent) together, that it might be one.

(19) And he made a covering לָאֹהֶל (for the tent) of rams' skins הַמְאָדָּמִים (dyed red) and a covering of [unknown animal] skins above.

(20) And he made אֵת the boards לַמִּשְׁכָּן (for the tabernacle) of acacia-wood, standing up.

(21) Ten cubits was the length of a board, and a cubit and a half the width of each board.

(22) Each board had two tenons, joined one to another. Thus he made לְכֹל (for all) the boards of הַמִּשְׁכָּן (the tabernacle).

(23) And he made אֵת the boards לַמִּשְׁכָּן (for the tabernacle) twenty boards for the edge נֶגֶב תֵּימָנָה (Negev southward).

(24) And he made forty pedestals of כֶּסֶף (silver) under the twenty boards: two pedestals under one board for its two tenons, and two pedestals under another board for its two tenons.

(25) And for the second side of הַמִּשְׁכָּן (the tabernacle) on the צָפוֹן (north) edge, he made twenty boards,

(26) and their forty pedestals of כֶּסֶף (silver): two pedestals under one board, and two pedestals under another board.

(27) And for the hinder part of הַמִּשְׁכָּן (the tabernacle) יָמָּה (seaward/westward) he made six boards.

(28) And he made two boards for the corners of הַמִּשְׁכָּן (the tabernacle) in the hinder part;

Level Two שְׁמוֹת ~ לו

(29) that they might be double beneath, and in like manner they should be complete אֶל-רֹאשׁוֹ (to its top) to the first ring. Thus, he did to both of them in the two corners.

(30) And there were eight boards, and their pedestals of כֶּסֶף (silver), sixteen pedestals: under every board two pedestals.

(31) And he made bars of acacia-wood: five for the boards of the one side of הַמִּשְׁכָּן (the tabernacle)

(32) and five bars for the boards of the other side of הַמִּשְׁכָּן (the tabernacle) and five bars for the boards of הַמִּשְׁכָּן (the tabernacle) for the hinder part יָמָּה (seaward/westward).

(33) And he made the middle אֵת bar to pass through in the midst of the boards מִן (from) the one end to the other.

(34) וְאֵת the boards he overlaid זָהָב (gold) וְאֵת the rings of them he made of זָהָב בָּתִּים (gold houses) for the bars, and overlaid אֵת the bars with זָהָב (gold).

(35) And he made אֶת-הַפָּרֹכֶת (* the veil) תְּכֵלֶת (blue) וְאַרְגָּמָן (and purple) וְתוֹלַעַת שָׁנִי (and scarlet) וְשֵׁשׁ מָשְׁזָר (and fine twined linen); with כְּרֻבִים (cherubim) the work of the skillful workman he made אֹתָהּ

(36) And he made לָהּ (for it) four pillars of acacia, and overlaid them with זָהָב (gold), their hooks being of זָהָב (gold); and he cast לָהֶם (for them) four pedestals of כֶּסֶף (silver).

(37) And he made a screen for the door of הָאֹהֶל (the tent) תְּכֵלֶת (blue) וְאַרְגָּמָן (and purple) וְתוֹלַעַת שָׁנִי (and scarlet) וְשֵׁשׁ מָשְׁזָר (and fine twined linen), the handiwork of embroidering;

(38) וְאֵת the pillars of it – five - וְאֵת their hooks; and he overlaid רָאשֵׁיהֶם (their heads) and their connections with זָהָב (gold); and their five pedestals were of נְחֹשֶׁת (copper).

Chapter Thirty-Seven

Making The Ark Of The Testimony

(1) And בְּצַלְאֵל made הָאָרֹן-אֶת (* the ark) of acacia-wood: two cubits and a half was the length of it, and a cubit and a half the width of it, and a cubit and a half the height of it.

(2) And he overlaid it with זָהָב טָהוֹר (pure gold) within and without, and made a crown of זָהָב (gold) לוֹ (for it) round about.

(3) And he cast four rings of זָהָב (gold) לוֹ (for it) עַל (on) the four footings thereof: and two rings עַל (on) the one side of it, and two rings עַל (on) the second side of it.

(4) And he made poles of acacia-wood, and overlaid אֹתָם with זָהָב (gold).

(5) And he put אֵת the poles in the rings עַל (on) the sides of הָאָרֹן (the ark) to carry הָאָרֹן-אֶת (* the ark).

(6) And he made כַּפֹּרֶת (the mercy-seat of) זָהָב טָהוֹר (pure gold): two cubits and a half was the length thereof, and a cubit and a half the width thereof.

(7) And he made two כְּרֻבִים זָהָב (cherubim of gold): of beaten work he made אֹתָם at the two ends of כַּפֹּרֶת (the mercy-seat):

(8) one כְּרוּב (cherub) מִזֶּה (from this) end וּכְרוּב (and a cherub) one מִזֶּה (from that) end; מִן-הַכַּפֹּרֶת (from the mercy-seat) he made הַכְּרֻבִים-אֶת (* the cherubim) at the two ends thereof.

(9) And הַכְּרֻבִים (the cherubim) spread out their wings on high, covering with their wings עַל-הַכַּפֹּרֶת (over the mercy seat) וּפְנֵיהֶם (and their faces) one to another אֶל-הַכַּפֹּרֶת (to the mercy-seat) were פְּנֵי הַכְּרֻבִים (the faces of the cherubim).

(10) And he made הַשֻּׁלְחָן-אֶת (* the table) of acacia-wood: two cubits was the length thereof, and a cubit the width thereof, and a cubit and a half the height thereof.

Level Two   שְׁמוֹת ~ לז

(11) And he overlaid אֹתוֹ with זָהָב טָהוֹר (pure gold), and made a crown of זָהָב (gold) לוֹ (for it) round about.

(12) And he made a border לוֹ (for it) of a handwidth round about, and made a crown of זָהָב (gold) to the border thereof round about.

(13) And he cast four rings of זָהָב (gold) לוֹ (for it) and put אֶת the rings in the four corners that were עַל (on) the four רַגְלָיו (feet of it).

(14) Close by the border were the rings בָּתִּים (the housings) for the poles to carry אֶת-הַשֻּׁלְחָן (* the table).

(15) And he made אֶת the poles of acacia-wood, and overlaid אֹתָם with זָהָב (gold), to carry אֶת-הַשֻּׁלְחָן (* the table).

(16) And he made אֶת-הַכֵּלִים (* the vessels) which were עַל-הַשֻּׁלְחָן (on the table) אֶת the dishes thereof וְאֶת the pans thereof וְאֶת the bowls thereof וְאֶת the jars thereof בָּהֵן (in them) to pour out, of זָהָב טָהוֹר (pure gold).

Making The Candlestick

(17) And he made אֶת-הַמְּנֹרָה זָהָב טָהוֹר (* the candlestick of pure gold): of beaten work he made אֶת הַמְּנֹרָה (* the candlestick) even its base, and its shaft; its cups, its knops, and its flowers, were of one piece with it.

(18) And there were six branches going out of the sides thereof: three branches of מְנֹרָה (a candlestick) out of the one side thereof, and three branches of מְנֹרָה (a candlestick) out of the second side thereof;

(19) three cups made like almond-blossoms in one branch, a knop and a flower; and three cups made like almond-blossoms in the other branch, a knop and a flower. So for the six branches coming מִן-הַמְּנֹרָה (from the candlestick).

(20) וּבַמְּנֹרָה (And in the candlestick) were four cups made like almond-blossoms, the knops thereof, and the flowers thereof;

(21) and a knop under two branches of one piece with it, and a knop under two branches of one piece with it, and a knop under two branches of one piece with it, for the six branches going out of it.

(22) Their knops and their branches were of one piece with it כֻּלָּהּ (all) of it was one beaten work of זָהָב טָהוֹר (pure gold).

(23) And he made אֶת-נֵרֹתֶיהָ (* the lamps of it) seven, and the tongs thereof, and the snuff-dishes thereof, of זָהָב טָהוֹר (pure gold).

(24) Of a talent of זָהָב טָהוֹר (pure gold) he made אֹתָהּ וְאֵת כָּל כֵּלֶיהָ (* it and * all the implements of it).

Making The Alter Of Incense

(25) And he made אֶת-מִזְבַּח הַקְּטֹרֶת (* the altar of incense) of acacia-wood: a cubit was the length thereof, and a cubit the width thereof, four-square; and two cubits was the height thereof; the horns thereof were of one piece with it.

(26) And he overlaid אֹתוֹ with זָהָב טָהוֹר (pure gold) אֵת the top thereof וְאֶת the sides thereof round about וְאֶת the horns of it; and he made a crown of זָהָב (gold) לוֹ (for it) round about.

(27) And he made two rings of זָהָב (gold) לוֹ (for it) under the crown thereof עַל (on) the two ribs thereof עַל (on) the two sides of it, לְבָתִּים (for housings) for poles wherewith to carry אֹתוֹ בָּהֶם (* it in them).

(28) And he made אֵת the poles of acacia-wood, and overlaid אֹתָם with זָהָב (gold).

(29) And he made the holy אֵת oil of the anointing וְאֵת the incense of pure sweet spices, after the handiwork of the perfumer.

Chapter Thirty-Eight

Making The Altar

(1) And he made אֶת-מִזְבַּח (* the altar) of burnt-offering of acacia-wood: five cubits was the length thereof, and five cubits the width thereof, four-square, and three cubits the height thereof.

(2) And he made the horns thereof עַל (on) the four corners of it; the horns thereof were of one piece with it; and he overlaid אֹתוֹ נְחֹשֶׁת (* it copper).

(3) And he made אֶת-כָּל-כְּלֵי הַמִּזְבֵּחַ (* all the implements of the altar) אֶת the pots וְאֶת the shovels וְאֶת the basins אֶת the flesh-hooks וְאֶת the fire-pans כָּל-כֵּלָיו (all the implements) thereof he made of נְחֹשֶׁת (copper).

(4) And he made לַמִּזְבֵּחַ (for the altar) a grating of network of נְחֹשֶׁת (copper) under the ledge round it beneath, reaching halfway up.

(5) And he cast four rings for the four ends of the grating of הַנְּחֹשֶׁת (the copper) to be בָּתִּים (housings) for the poles.

(6) And he made אֵת the poles of acacia-wood, and overlaid אֹתָם נְחֹשֶׁת (* them copper).

(7) And he put אֵת the poles in the rings עַל (on) the sides of הַמִּזְבֵּחַ (the altar) to carry אֹתוֹ בָּהֶם (* it in them) he made אֹתוֹ hollow with planks.

(8) And he made אֵת הַכִּיּוֹר נְחֹשֶׁת (* the laver of copper) וְאֵת the base thereof of נְחֹשֶׁת (copper) of the mirrors of those stationed that did work at the door of אֹהֶל מוֹעֵד (the tent of appointment).

Making The Court

(9) And he made אֶת-הֶחָצֵר (* the court) for the side נֶגֶב תֵּימָנָה (Negev southward) the hangings of הֶחָצֵר (the court) were of fine twined linen, a hundred cubits.

Exodus ~ 38

(10) Their pillars were twenty, and their pedestals twenty, of נְחֹשֶׁת (copper) the hooks of the pillars and their connections were of כֶּסֶף (silver).

(11) And for צָפוֹן (the north) side a hundred cubits, their pillars twenty, and their pedestals twenty, of נְחֹשֶׁת (copper) the hooks of the pillars and their connections of כֶּסֶף (silver).

(12) And for יָם (sea/the west) side were hangings of fifty cubits, their pillars ten, and their pedestals ten; the hooks of the pillars and their connections of כֶּסֶף (silver).

(13) And for side of קֵדְמָה מִזְרָחָה (the east towards the sunrise) fifty cubits.

(14) The hangings for the one side of the gate were fifteen cubits; their pillars three, and their pedestals three.

(15) And so for the second side מִזֶּה וּמִזֶּה (from this and from that) by the gate of הֶחָצֵר (the court) were hangings of fifteen cubits; their pillars three, and their pedestals three.

(16) כָּל (All) the hangings of הֶחָצֵר (the court) round about were of fine twined linen.

(17) And the pedestals for the pillars were of נְחֹשֶׁת (copper) the hooks of the pillars and their connections of כֶּסֶף (silver) and the overlaying of רָאשֵׁיהֶם כֶּסֶף (their heads of silver) וְהֵם (and they) were connected with כֶּסֶף (silver) כֹּל (all) the pillars of הֶחָצֵר (the court).

(18) And the screen for the gate of הֶחָצֵר (the court) was the handiwork of embroidery תְּכֵלֶת (blue) וְאַרְגָּמָן (and purple) וְתוֹלַעַת שָׁנִי (and scarlet) וְשֵׁשׁ מָשְׁזָר (and fine twined linen); and twenty cubits was the length, and the height in the width was five cubits, answerable to the hangings of הֶחָצֵר (the court).

(19) And their pillars were four, and their pedestals four, of נְחֹשֶׁת (copper) their hooks of כֶּסֶף (silver), and the overlaying of רָאשֵׁיהֶם (their heads) and their

Level Two   שְׁמוֹת ~ לח

connections of כֶּסֶף (silver).

(20) וְכָל (And all) the pins לַמִּשְׁכָּן וְלֶחָצֵר (for the tabernacle and of the court) round about, were of נְחֹשֶׁת (copper).

Finishing The Tabernacle

(21) These are the accounts of הַמִּשְׁכָּן מִשְׁכַּן הָעֵדֻת (the tabernacle, the tabernacle of the testimony) as they were rendered עַל (on) the commandment of מֹשֶׁה through עֲבֹדַת הַלְוִיִּם (the work of the Levites) בְּיַד אִיתָמָר בֶּן אַהֲרֹן (by the hand of Ithamar, the son of Aaron) the priest.

(22) וּבְצַלְאֵל בֶּן-אוּרִי בֶן-חוּר לְמַטֵּה יְהוּדָה (And Bezalel the son of Uri, the son of Hur of the tribe of Judah) made אֵת כָּל (* all) that יהוה commanded מֹשֶׁה.

(23) וְאִתּוֹ אָהֳלִיאָב בֶּן-אֲחִיסָמָךְ לְמַטֵּה-דָן (And with * him was Aholiab, the son of Ahisamach of the tribe of Dan) a craftsman, and a skillful workman, and embroidering בַּתְּכֵלֶת (in blue) וּבָאַרְגָּמָן (and in purple) בְתוֹלַעַת הַשָּׁנִי (in scarlet) וּבַשֵּׁשׁ (and in fine linen).

(24) כָּל-הַזָּהָב (All the gold) that was used for the work בְּכֹל (in all) the work of הַקֹּדֶשׁ (the sanctuary) even the זְהַב (gold) of the offering, was twenty and nine talents, and seven hundred and thirty shekels, after the shekel of הַקֹּדֶשׁ (the sanctuary).

(25) וְכֶסֶף (And the silver) of them that were numbered of הָעֵדָה (the congregation) was a hundred talents, and a thousand seven hundred and three-score and fifteen shekels, after the shekel of הַקֹּדֶשׁ (the sanctuary):

(26) a beka for the poll, that is, half a shekel, after the shekel of הַקֹּדֶשׁ (the sanctuary) לְכֹל (for every) one that passed עַל (over) to them that are numbered מִבֶּן (from a son) of twenty years old and upward, for six hundred thousand and

three thousand and five hundred and fifty men.

(27) And the hundred talents of הַכֶּסֶף (the silver) were for casting אֵת the pedestals of הַקֹּדֶשׁ (the sanctuary) וְאֵת the pedestals of הַפָּרֹכֶת (the veil) a hundred pedestals for the hundred talents, a talent for a socket.

(28) וְאֶת the thousand seven hundred seventy and five shekels he made hooks for the pillars, and overlaid רָאשֵׁיהֶם (their heads) and he connected for אֹתָם

(29) וּנְחֹשֶׁת (And the copper) of the offering was seventy talents and two thousand and four hundred shekels.

(30) And he made אֵת the pedestals בָּהּ (in it) to the door of אֹהֶל מוֹעֵד (the tent of appointment) וְאֵת מִזְבַּח הַנְּחֹשֶׁת (and* the altar of the copper) וְאֶת the grate הַנְּחֹשֶׁת (of the copper) לוֹ (for it) וְאֵת כָּל־כְּלֵי הַמִּזְבֵּחַ (and * all the implements of the altar)

(31) וְאֶת the pedestals of הֶחָצֵר (the court) round about וְאֶת the pedestals of the gate of הֶחָצֵר (the court) וְאֶת כָּל (and * all) the pins of הַמִּשְׁכָּן (the tabernacle) וְאֶת־כָּל (and * all) the pins of הֶחָצֵר (the court) round about.

Chapter Thirty-Nine

Making The Ephod

(1) וּמִן-הַתְּכֵלֶת (And from the blue) וְהָאַרְגָּמָן (and purple) וְתוֹלַעַת הַשָּׁנִי (and scarlet) they made garments of tapestry, for ministering בַּקֹּדֶשׁ (in the holy place) and made אֶת-בִּגְדֵי הַקֹּדֶשׁ (* the holy garments) לְאַהֲרֹן as יהוה commanded אֶת-מֹשֶׁה.

(2) And he made אֶת-הָאֵפֹד זָהָב (* the ephod of gold) תְּכֵלֶת (blue) וְאַרְגָּמָן (and purple) וְתוֹלַעַת שָׁנִי (and scarlet) וְשֵׁשׁ מָשְׁזָר (and fine twined linen).

(3) And they did beat הַזָּהָב (the gold) in אֶת thin plates, and cut it in threads, to work it in הַתְּכֵלֶת (the blue) and in הָאַרְגָּמָן (the purple) and in תּוֹלַעַת הַשָּׁנִי (the scarlet) and in הַשֵּׁשׁ (the fine linen) the work of the skillful workman.

(4) They made shoulder-pieces לוֹ (for it) joined together עַל (on) the two ends was it joined together.

(5) And the skillfully woven band of אֲפֻדָּתוֹ (his ephod) that was עָלָיו (on it) was of the same piece הוּא (it) was like the handiwork זָהָב (gold) תְּכֵלֶת (blue) וְאַרְגָּמָן (and purple) וְתוֹלַעַת שָׁנִי (and scarlet) וְשֵׁשׁ מָשְׁזָר (and fine twined linen) as יהוה commanded אֶת-מֹשֶׁה.

(6) And they wrought אֶת-אַבְנֵי (* stones of) the onyx, enclosed in settings of זָהָב (gold) graven with the engravings of a signet, עַל-שְׁמוֹת בְּנֵי יִשְׂרָאֵל (on the names of the children of Israel).

(7) And he put אֹתָם עַל (* them on) the shoulder-pieces of הָאֵפֹד (the ephod) to be אַבְנֵי זִכָּרוֹן (a stone of a memorial) לִבְנֵי יִשְׂרָאֵל (for the children of Israel) as יהוה commanded אֶת-מֹשֶׁה.

Exodus ~ 39

Making The Breastplate

(8)   And he made אֶת-הַחֹשֶׁן (* the breastplate) the work of the skillful workman, like the work of אֵפֹד (an ephod) זָהָב (gold) תְּכֵלֶת (blue) וְאַרְגָּמָן (and purple) וְתוֹלַעַת שָׁנִי (and scarlet) וְשֵׁשׁ מָשְׁזָר (and fine twined linen).

(9)   It was four-square; they made אֶת-הַחֹשֶׁן (* the breastplate) double; a span was the length thereof, and a span the width thereof, being double.

(10)   And they set בוֹ (in it) four rows of אֶבֶן (stone): a row of [a red gem – perhaps a ruby], topaz, and emerald was the first row.

(11)   And the second row, [a glistening gem – perhaps a garnet], a sapphire, and [a hard gem - perhaps a diamond].

(12)   And the third row, a jacinth, an agate, and an amethyst.

(13)   And the fourth row, [a yellow gem – perhaps a chrysolite], and an onyx, and a jasper; they were enclosed in fittings of זָהָב (gold) in their settings.

(14)   וְהָאֲבָנִים עַל-שְׁמֹת בְּנֵי-יִשְׂרָאֵל (And the stones were on the names of the children of Israel) twelve עַל שְׁמֹתָם (on their names) like the engravings of a signet אִישׁ עַל-שְׁמוֹ (a man on his name) for the twelve tribes.

(15)   And they made עַל-הַחֹשֶׁן (on the breastplate) plaited chains, of wreathen work of זָהָב טָהוֹר (pure gold).

(16)   And they made two settings of זָהָב (gold) and two זָהָב (gold) rings; and put אֵת the two rings עַל (on) the two ends of הַחֹשֶׁן (the breastplate).

(17)   And they put the two wreathen chains of הַזָּהָב (the gold) עַל (on) the two rings at the ends of הַחֹשֶׁן (the breastplate).

(18)   וְאֵת two of the ends of the two wreathen chains they put עַל (on) the two settings, and put them עַל (on) the shoulder-pieces of הָאֵפֹד (the ephod) in the forepart thereof.

(19)   And they made two rings of זָהָב (gold) and put them עַל (on) the two ends

Level Two שְׁמוֹת ~ לט

of הַחֹשֶׁן (the breastplate) עַל (on) the edge thereof, which was toward the side of הָאֵפֹד (the ephod) inward.

(20) And they made two rings of זָהָב (gold) and put them עַל (on) the two shoulder-pieces of הָאֵפֹד (the ephod) underneath, in the forepart thereof, close by the coupling thereof, above the skillfully woven band of הָאֵפֹד (the ephod).

(21) And they did bind אֶת-הַחֹשֶׁן (*the breastplate) by the rings thereof to the rings of הָאֵפֹד (the ephod) with a thread of תְּכֵלֶת (blue) that it might be עַל (on) the skillfully woven band of הָאֵפֹד (the ephod) and that הַחֹשֶׁן (the breastplate) might not be loosed מֵעַל הָאֵפֹד (from against the ephod) as יהוה commanded אֶת-מֹשֶׁה.

Making The Robe

(22) And he made אֶת-מְעִיל הָאֵפֹד (* the robe of the ephod) of woven work כְּלִיל תְּכֵלֶת (all of blue)

(23) and the hole of הַמְּעִיל (the robe) in the midst thereof, as the hole of a coat of mail, with a binding round about the hole of it, that it should not be rent.

(24) And they made עַל (on) the skirts of הַמְּעִיל (the robe) pomegranates of תְּכֵלֶת (blue) וְאַרְגָּמָן (and purple) וְתוֹלַעַת שָׁנִי (and scarlet) מָשְׁזָר (being twined).

(25) And they made bells of זָהָב טָהוֹר (pure gold) and put אֵת the bells between the pomegranates עַל (on) the skirts of הַמְּעִיל (the robe) round about, between the pomegranates:

(26) a bell and a pomegranate, a bell and a pomegranate עַל (on) the skirts of הַמְּעִיל (the robe) round about, to minister in; as יהוה commanded אֶת-מֹשֶׁה.

Exodus ~ 39

The Rest Of The Garments

(27) And they made אֶת-הַכָּתְנֹת שֵׁשׁ (* the tunics of fine linen) of woven work לְאַהֲרֹן וּלְבָנָיו (for Aaron and for his sons).

(28) וְאֵת-פַּאֲרֵי הַמִּגְבָּעֹת שֵׁשׁ וְאֵת הַמִּצְנֶפֶת (And * the turban of fine linen) שֵׁשׁ (and * the goodly head-tires of fine linen) וְאֵת-מִכְנְסֵי (and * breeches of) הַבָּד (the linen) שֵׁשׁ מָשְׁזָר (of fine twined linen)

(29) וְאֶת-הָאַבְנֵט שֵׁשׁ מָשְׁזָר (And * the sash of fine twined linen) וּתְכֵלֶת וְאַרְגָּמָן וְתוֹלַעַת שָׁנִי (and blue and purple and scarlet) the handiwork of embroidering; as יהוה commanded אֶת-מֹשֶׁה

(30) And they made אֶת-צִיץ נֵזֶר-הַקֹּדֶשׁ זָהָב טָהוֹר (* the plate of the holy crown of pure gold) and wrote עָלָיו (on it) a writing, like the engravings of a signet: קֹדֶשׁ לַיהוה (HOLY TO YHVH).

(31) And they tied עָלָיו (on it) a thread of תְּכֵלֶת (blue) to fasten it עַל-הַמִּצְנֶפֶת (on the turban) above; as יהוה commanded אֶת-מֹשֶׁה

The Tabernacle Completed

(32) Thus was finished כָּל-עֲבֹדַת מִשְׁכַּן אֹהֶל מוֹעֵד (all the service of the tabernacle of the tent of appointment) and בְּנֵי יִשְׂרָאֵל (the children of Israel) did according to all that יהוה commanded אֶת-מֹשֶׁה so did they.

(33) And they brought אֶת-הַמִּשְׁכָּן אֶל-מֹשֶׁה (* the tabernacle to Moses) אֶת-הָאֹהֶל וְאֶת-כָּל-כֵּלָיו (* the tent and * all its implements) its clasps, its boards, its bars, and its pillars, and its pedestals;

(34) וְאֶת the covering of rams' skins הַמְאָדָּמִים (dyed red) וְאֶת the covering of [unknown animal] skins וְאֶת פָּרֹכֶת (and * the veil) of the screen;

(35) אֶת-אֲרוֹן הָעֵדֻת (* the ark of the testimony) וְאֶת the poles thereof וְאֶת הַכַּפֹּרֶת (and * the mercy-seat);

350

Level Two — שְׁמוֹת ~ לט

(36) וְאֵת (* all the implements of it) אֶת-כָּל-כֵּלָיו (* the table) הַשֻּׁלְחָן (and * the bread of the presence) לֶחֶם הַפָּנִים

(37) אֶת-הַמְּנֹרָה (* the candlestick) the pure one אֶת נֵרֹתֶיהָ (* lamps of it) even נֵרֹת (the lamps of) the array, וְאֶת-כָּל-כֵּלֶיהָ (and * all the implements of it) וְאֵת שֶׁמֶן (and * oil) for the light;

(38) וְאֵת שֶׁמֶן הַמִּשְׁחָה (and the golden * altar) וְאֵת מִזְבַּח הַזָּהָב (and the anointing * oil) וְאֵת קְטֹרֶת הַסַּמִּים (and * incense of the spices) וְאֵת the screen for the door of הָאֹהֶל (the tent)

(39) וְאֵת מִזְבַּח הַנְּחֹשֶׁת (the * altar of the copper) וְאֶת the grate of הַנְּחֹשֶׁת (the copper) which is לוֹ (for it) אֶת its poles וְאֶת-כָּל-כֵּלָיו (and * all its implements) אֶת-הַכִּיֹּר (* the laver) וְאֶת its base;

(40) אֵת the hangings of הֶחָצֵר (the court) אֵת its pillars וְאֵת its pedestals וְאֵת the screen for the gate of הֶחָצֵר (the court) אֵת the cords of it, and the pins of it וְאֵת כָּל-כְּלֵי עֲבֹדַת הַמִּשְׁכָּן לְאֹהֶל מוֹעֵד (and * all the implements of the service of the tabernacle of the tent of appointment),

(41) אֶת-בִּגְדֵי (* the garments) of tapestry for ministering בַּקֹּדֶשׁ (in the holy place) אֶת-בִּגְדֵי הַקֹּדֶשׁ לְאַהֲרֹן (* the holy garments for Aaron) the priest- וְאֶת בִּגְדֵי בָנָיו (and * the garments of his sons) for being priest.

(42) כְּכֹל (As all) that יהוה commanded אֶת-מֹשֶׁה so בְּנֵי יִשְׂרָאֵל (the children of Israel) did אֵת כָּל-הָעֲבֹדָה (* all the service).

(43) וַיַּרְא מֹשֶׁה (And Moses saw) אֶת-כָּל (* all) the work, and, behold, they had done אֹתָהּ as יהוה had commanded, even so had they done it. And מֹשֶׁה blessed אֹתָם

Chapter Forty

YHVH Tells How To Set Up

(1) וַיְדַבֵּר יהוה אֶל-מֹשֶׁה לֵּאמֹר *(And YHVH spoke to Moses saying):*

(2)
בְּיוֹם-הַחֹדֶשׁ הָרִאשׁוֹן בְּאֶחָד לַחֹדֶשׁ

תָּקִים אֶת-מִשְׁכַּן

אֹהֶל מוֹעֵד

On the first day of the first month

*you shall set up * the tabernacle of*

the tent of appointment.

(3)
וְשַׂמְתָּ שָׁם

אֵת אֲרוֹן הָעֵדוּת

וְסַכֹּתָ עַל-הָאָרֹן אֶת-הַפָּרֹכֶת

And you shall put there

** the ark of the testimony,*

*and you shall screen the ark with * the veil.*

(4)
וְהֵבֵאתָ אֶת-הַשֻּׁלְחָן

וְעָרַכְתָּ אֶת-עֶרְכּוֹ

*And you shall bring in * the table,*

*and set in order * its array;*

Level Two

שְׁמוֹת ~ מ

וְהֵבֵאתָ אֶת-הַמְּנֹרָה
וְהַעֲלֵיתָ אֶת-נֵרֹתֶיהָ

and you shall bring in * the candlestick,
and set up * its lamps.

(5)

וְנָתַתָּה אֶת-מִזְבַּח
הַזָּהָב לִקְטֹרֶת
לִפְנֵי אֲרוֹן הָעֵדֻת
וְשַׂמְתָּ אֶת-מָסַךְ הַפֶּתַח לַמִּשְׁכָּן

And you shall set the * altar
of gold for incense
before the ark of the testimony,
and put * the screen of the door to the tabernacle.

(6)

וְנָתַתָּה אֵת מִזְבַּח
הָעֹלָה
לִפְנֵי פֶּתַח
מִשְׁכַּן אֹהֶל-מוֹעֵד

And you shall set * the altar
of burnt-offering
before the door of
the tabernacle of the tent of appointment.

(7)

Exodus ~ 40

וְנָתַתָּ אֶת-הַכִּיֹּר

בֵּין-אֹהֶל מוֹעֵד וּבֵין הַמִּזְבֵּחַ

וְנָתַתָּ שָׁם מָיִם

And you shall set * the laver

between the tent of appointment and the altar,

and shall put water there.

(8)

וְשַׂמְתָּ אֶת-הֶחָצֵר סָבִיב

וְנָתַתָּ אֶת-מָסַךְ שַׁעַר הֶחָצֵר

And you shall set up* the court round about,

and hang up * the screen of the gate of the court.

(9)

וְלָקַחְתָּ אֶת-שֶׁמֶן הַמִּשְׁחָה

וּמָשַׁחְתָּ אֶת-הַמִּשְׁכָּן

וְאֶת-כָּל-אֲשֶׁר-בּוֹ

And you shall take the anointing * oil,

and anoint * the tabernacle,

and * all that is in it,

וְקִדַּשְׁתָּ אֹתוֹ

וְאֶת-כָּל-כֵּלָיו

וְהָיָה קֹדֶשׁ

Level Two שְׁמוֹת ~ מ

and shall hallow * it,
and * all the implements of it;
and it shall be holy.

(10)

וּמָשַׁחְתָּ אֶת־מִזְבַּח הָעֹלָה
וְאֶת־כָּל־כֵּלָיו
וְקִדַּשְׁתָּ אֶת־הַמִּזְבֵּחַ
וְהָיָה הַמִּזְבֵּחַ קֹדֶשׁ קָדָשִׁים

And you shall anoint *the altar of burnt-offering,
and * all its implements,
and sanctify * the altar;
and the altar shall be most holy.

(11)

וּמָשַׁחְתָּ אֶת־הַכִּיֹּר
וְאֶת־כַּנּוֹ וְקִדַּשְׁתָּ, אֹתוֹ

And you shall anoint * the laver
and * its base, and sanctify * it.

(12)

וְהִקְרַבְתָּ אֶת־אַהֲרֹן וְאֶת־בָּנָיו
אֶל־פֶּתַח אֹהֶל מוֹעֵד
וְרָחַצְתָּ אֹתָם בַּמָּיִם

And you shall bring * Aaron and * his sons
to the door of the tent of appointment,
and shall wash * them with water.

(13)

וְהִלְבַּשְׁתָּ אֶת־אַהֲרֹן
אֵת בִּגְדֵי הַקֹּדֶשׁ
וּמָשַׁחְתָּ אֹתוֹ
וְקִדַּשְׁתָּ אֹתוֹ
וְכִהֵן לִי

And you shall put on * Aaron
the holy * garments;
and you shall anoint * him,
and sanctify * him,
and he will serve as priest for Me.

(14)

וְאֶת־בָּנָיו תַּקְרִיב
וְהִלְבַּשְׁתָּ אֹתָם כֻּתֳּנֹת

And you shall bring * his sons,
and put tunics on * them.

(15)

וּמָשַׁחְתָּ אֹתָם
כַּאֲשֶׁר מָשַׁחְתָּ אֶת־אֲבִיהֶם
וְכִהֲנוּ לִי

And you shall anoint * them,
as you anointed * their father,
and they shall serve as priests for Me;

וְהָיְתָה לִהְיֹת לָהֶם מָשְׁחָתָם
לִכְהֻנַּת עוֹלָם
לְדֹרֹתָם

and their anointing shall be to them
for an everlasting priesthood
for their generations.

Moses Sets Up The Tabernacle

(16) Thus מֹשֶׁה did כְּכֹל *(as all)* that יהוה commanded אֹתוֹ so he did.

(17) And it was in the first month in the second year, on the first day of the month, that הַמִּשְׁכָּן *(the tabernacle)* was set up.

(18) And מֹשֶׁה set up אֶת-הַמִּשְׁכָּן *(* the tabernacle)* and laid אֵת its pedestals, and set up אֵת the boards thereof, and put in אֵת the bars thereof, and set up אֵת its pillars.

(19) And he spread אֶת-הָאֹהֶל עַל-הַמִּשְׁכָּן *(* the tent over the tabernacle)* and put אֵת the covering of הָאֹהֶל *(the tent)* above עָלָיו *(on it)* as יהוה commanded אֶת-מֹשֶׁה.

(20) And he took and gave אֶת-הָעֵדֻת אֶל-הָאָרֹן *(* the testimony to the ark)* and set אֵת the poles עַל-הָאָרֹן *(on the ark)* and put אֵת הַכַּפֹּרֶת *(* the mercy-seat)* above עַל-הָאָרֹן *(on the ark).*

(21) And he brought אֶת-הָאָרֹן אֶל-הַמִּשְׁכָּן *(* the ark to the tabernacle)* and set up אֵת פָּרֹכֶת *(* the veil)* of the screen, and screened עַל אֲרוֹן הָעֵדוּת *(over the ark of the testimony)* as יהוה commanded אֵת מֹשֶׁה.

(22) And he put אֶת-הַשֻּׁלְחָן בְּאֹהֶל מוֹעֵד *(* the table in the tent of appointment)*

Exodus ~ 40

לְפָרֹכֶת עַל (on) the side of הַמִּשְׁכָּן צָפֹנָה (the tabernacle northward) from outside (to the veil).

(23) And he set עָלָיו (on it) an array of לֶחֶם (bread) לִפְנֵי יהוה (before YHVH) as יהוה commanded אֶת-מֹשֶׁה.

(24) And he put אֶת-הַמְּנֹרָה בְּאֹהֶל מוֹעֵד (* the candlestick in the tent of appointment) opposite הַשֻּׁלְחָן (the table) עַל (on) the side of הַמִּשְׁכָּן נֶגְבָּה (the tabernacle towards the Negev/southward).

(25) And he set up הַנֵּרֹת (the lamps) לִפְנֵי יהוה (before YHVH) as יהוה commanded אֶת-מֹשֶׁה.

(26) And he put אֶת-מִזְבַּח הַזָּהָב בְּאֹהֶל מוֹעֵד (the golden * altar in the tent of appointment) לִפְנֵי הַפָּרֹכֶת (before the veil);

(27) and he burnt עָלָיו (on it) קְטֹרֶת סַמִּים (incense of spices) as יהוה commanded אֶת-מֹשֶׁה.

(28) And he put אֶת the screen of the door לַמִּשְׁכָּן (to the tabernacle).

(29) וְאֵת מִזְבַּח הָעֹלָה (And * the altar of burnt-offering) he set at the door of מִשְׁכַּן אֹהֶל-מוֹעֵד (the tabernacle of the tent of appointment) and offered עָלָיו (on it) אֶת the burnt-offering וְאֶת the meal-offering; as יהוה commanded אֶת מֹשֶׁה.

(30) And he set אֶת-הַכִּיֹּר בֵּין-אֹהֶל מוֹעֵד וּבֵין הַמִּזְבֵּחַ (* the laver between the tent of appointment and the altar) and put מַיִם (water) therein, wherewith to wash;

(31) And מֹשֶׁה וְאַהֲרֹן וּבָנָיו (Moses and Aaron and his sons) washed מִמֶּנּוּ (from it) אֶת-יְדֵיהֶם וְאֶת-רַגְלֵיהֶם (* their hands and * their feet);

(32) And they went in אֶל-אֹהֶל מוֹעֵד (to the tent of appointment) and they came near אֶל-הַמִּזְבֵּחַ (to the altar) they wash as יהוה commanded אֶת-מֹשֶׁה.

(33) And he set up אֶת-הֶחָצֵר (* the court) round about לַמִּשְׁכָּן וְלַמִּזְבֵּחַ (to the tabernacle and to the altar) and set up אֶת the screen of the gate of הֶחָצֵר (the

Level Two   שְׁמוֹת ~ מ

court). So מֹשֶׁה finished אֵת the work.

(34) Then הֶעָנָן (the cloud) covered אֶת אֹהֶל מוֹעֵד (* the tent of appointment) וּכְבוֹד יהוה (and the glory of YHVH) filled אֶת הַמִּשְׁכָּן (* the tabernacle).

(35) And מֹשֶׁה was not able to enter in אֶל-אֹהֶל מוֹעֵד (to the tent of appointment) because הֶעָנָן (the cloud) שָׁכַן עָלָיו (tabernacled on it) וּכְבוֹד יהוה (and the glory of YHVH) filled אֶת הַמִּשְׁכָּן (* the tabernacle).

(36) And whenever הֶעָנָן (the cloud) was taken up מֵעַל הַמִּשְׁכָּן (from over the tabernacle) בְּנֵי יִשְׂרָאֵל (the children of Israel) went onward, בְּכֹל (in all) their journeys.

(37) But if הֶעָנָן (the cloud) was not taken up, then they journeyed not till the day that it was taken up.

(38) For עֲנַן יהוה (the cloud of YHVH) was עַל-הַמִּשְׁכָּן (over the tabernacle) by day וְאֵשׁ (and fire) was therein by night לְעֵינֵי כָל בֵּית יִשְׂרָאֵל (in the eyes of all the house of Israel) בְּכָל (in all) their journeys.

359

Index

Below is a list of words that have been restored in the Hebrew. We have chosen to leave the Scripture index off each word because that makes the index very large. Therefore, for ease of finding the words, we have simply put the basic form of the word along with its definition.

*PLEASE NOTE *   on the last few pages of this book. There is a useful key for dissecting the words that have been restored. The Key shows the common prefixes and suffixes along with their meanings.

As in Genesis, the English translation is not the full picture of the word or a complete translation of the word, but it is rather a simplified translation.

Definitions	Hebrew
Father	אב
Stone	אבן
Sash, girdle, waistband	אבנט
To be red	אדם
Ground, land	אדמה
Tent, dwelling	אהל
Brother, relative	אח
Sister, relative	אחות
Man	איש
To, toward, unto, in	אל
Mother	אם
Maid-servant, handmaid, concubine	אמה

Level Two שְׁמוֹת

To say, speak, utter	אמר
I (first person singular)	אני
Ephod, priestly garment	אפד / אפוד
Locust	ארבה
Ark, chest	ארן / ארון
Purple	ארגמן
Land, earth	ארץ
Fire, flames	אש
Woman, wife / women, wives	נשים / אשה
Animal, cattle, beast	בהמה
House	בית
Firstborn, firstling	בכור
Son, child, member of a group	בן
Hail	ברד
Covenant, alliance, pledge, agreement	ברית
Flesh	בשר
Daughter	בת
Also, even, moreover	גם
Sojourner, temporary inhabitant	גיר / גר
To speak, declare	דבר
Word, thing, matter, business	דבר
Generation, period of time, habitation,	דר / דור
Blood	דם
Way, road, journey, manner	דרך
He, she, it, that	היא / הוא
To go, walk, come, depart	הלך

Mountain, hill	הר
Darkness, obscurity	חשך
Breastplate	חשן
Pure, clean	טהר / טהור
This, that, here, which	זה
Gold	זהב
To remember, recall, call to mind	זכר
Life, living, alive	חי
Bosom, hollow, bottom, midst	חוק / חק / חיק
Hand	יד
To bear, help to bring forth, midwife	ילד
Sea, west	ים
Boy, son, child, youth, offspring	ילד
Glory, honor, abundance	כבד / כבוד
Laver, basin, pot, pan	כיר / כיור
All, every, the whole	כול / כל
Implement, vessel, article, utensil	כלי
Gnat, louse, fastening	כן
Silver, money	כסף
Palm, hand, hollow of the hand	כף
Mercy-seat, place of atonement	כפרת
Cherub, and angelic being	כרוב
Tunic, undergarment	כתנת / כתנת
Heart, mind, will, understanding	לב
Flame, tip of weapon, point	לבה
Bread, food, grain	לחם

Level Two שְׁמוֹת

Turban, head-gear	מגבעה
Wilderness, uninhabited land	מדבר
Appointed time	מועדה / מעד / מועד
Altar	מזבח
Staff, branch, tribe	מטה / מטה
Rain	מטר
Water, of danger, violence	מים
Breeches, underwear, trousers	מכנס
King	מלך
From, out of, on account of, off, above	מני / מן
Veil	מסוה
Unleavened, without leaven	מצה
Turban of the high priest	מצנפת
Candlestick, lampstand	מנרה / מנורה
Robe, garment worn over a tunic	מעיל
Sight, appearance, vision	מראה
Dwelling place, tabernacle	משכן
Family, clan, species, kind	משפחה
South, Negev (root – to be parched)	נגב
Serpent, snake	נחש
Copper, bronze	נחשת
Foreign, alien, unfamiliar	נכרי
Young man, lad, youth, boy	נער
Young woman, damsel, female servant	נערה
Soul, self, life, person, living being	נפש
Lamp	נרה / נר / ניר

English	Hebrew
Servant, slave	עבד
Labor, service, work	עבודה / עבדה
Congregation, gathering	עדה
Testimony	עדוּת
Eye	עין
City, town, excitement, anguish	ער / עיר
Young woman, newly married, virgin, maid,	עלמה
Upon, about, on, over, to	על
People, nation	עם
Cloud	ענן
Swarm, mixture (root – braid, intermix)	ערב
To face, to turn toward or away from	פנה
Face, faces, presence, before, in front of	פנה / פנים
Veil, curtain	פרכת
North (root- to hide, treasure, store up)	צפן / צפון
Frog	צפרדע
Holiness, apartness, sacredness	קדש
Assembly, congregation, convocation	קהל
Voice, sound, noise	קל / קול
To call, cry, utter a loud sound, proclaim	קרא
East, antiquity, of old	קדמה / קדם
To see, perceive, look, observe, consider	ראה
Head, top, summit	ראש
Foot, leg	רגל
Sabbath	שבת
To twist	שזר

Level Two — שְׁמוֹת

Boil, inflamed spot, eruption	שחין
To send, send away, let go, stretch out	שלח
Table	שלחן
Peace, completeness	שלם / שלום
Name, reputation	שם
Sky, heaven, abode of the stars	שמה / שמים
To hear, listen to, obey	שמע
To keep, guard, observe	שמר
Scarlet – the insect "coccus ilicis"	שני
Fine linen, something bleached white	ששי / שש
Ark (vessel Noah built, vessel Moses was in)	תבה
Scarlet, worm – the insect "coccus ilicis"	תלעת / תולעת
Blue, violet	תכלת
Dragon, sea monster	תנים / תנין

Quick Reference Chart for Nouns

Suffixes	Main Word	Prefixes
ה of her/it	שׁם	בּ / ב in, on, with
הם / מו of them (masculine)	שׁם	ה the
הן of them (feminine)	שׁם	ו and
ו of him/it	שׁם	כּ / כ like, as
י of me, of	שׁם	ל to, for
ךָ of you (masculine singular)	שׁם	מ from
ךְ of you (feminine singular)	שׁם	
כם of you (masculine plural)	שׁם	
כן of you (feminine plural)	שׁם	
ים / ם plural ending	שׁם	
נו of us	שׁם	
ת / ות plural ending	שׁם	

Final Notes

We hope your journey has been enriched and you are blessed through the production of The Progressive Torah series! Minister 2 Others would like to hear from you. If you have comments or questions concerning our materials, or if you find errors in our projects, misspellings, or formatting issues. We work hard to provide quality materials, however, sometimes things can squeak by unnoticed. Your feedback is truly appreciated.

If you have enjoyed this production, please consider writing a review and letting others know about our materials.

Thanks!

Minister 2 Others
Minister2others.com

Like reading the stories found in the book of Genesis? Then you'll love our series Ancient Texts and the Bible! This ten volume set completely synchronizes the Bible, with the books of *Enoch, Jasher, and Jubilees;* making one harmonizing story out of the four!

Available in Easy Reader Edition and Expanded Edition!

www.ingramcontent.com/pod-product-compliance
Lightning Source LLC
Chambersburg PA
CBHW081332080526

44588CB00017B/2600